RISE OF TERRORISM AND SECESSIONISM IN EURASIA

RISE OF TERRORISM AND SECESSIONISM IN EURASIA

Edited
by

V. D. Chopra

GYAN

GYAN PUBLISHING HOUSE

NEW DELHI-110 002

on behalf of

INTERNATIONAL INSTITUTE FOR ASIA-PACIFIC STUDIES NEW DELHI

RISE OF TERRORISM AND SECESSIONISM IN EURASIA

ISBN: 81-212-0738-X

Published in 2001 in India by
Gyan Publishing House
5, Ansari Road,
New Delhi-110 002
Phone: 3282060, 3261060, Fax: 3285914.
E-mail: gyanbook@del2.vsnl.net.in
Visit Our Web Site At http:\\www.gyanbooks.com

Laser Typesetting at: Power Photocomposers, New Delhi-110 002
Printed at: Mehra Offset Printers, Delhi-110 002

Dedicated to the memory

of

P.N. Haksar

and

T.N. Kaul

Contents

विशेष कार्य अधिकारी
Officer on Special Duty

राष्ट्रपति सचिवालय,
राष्ट्रपति भवन,
नई दिल्ली–110 004
President's Secretariat,
Rashtrapati Bhavan,
New Delhi-110004.

No. F. 2-M/2000

17th April, 2000

Dear Shri Chopra,

The President of India, Shri K.R. Narayanan, is happy to know that the International Institute for Asia-Pacific Studies, New Delhi is organising a National Seminar on "Rise of Terrorism and Secessionism in the Region—Politico, Economic, Strategic and Social Implications" on 30th April and 1st May, 2000 at New Delhi.

The President extends his warm greetings and felicitations to all those associated with the Institute and wishes the Seminar all success.

With regards,

Yours sincerely,

(P.P. Kaushik)

Shri V.D. Chopra,
Vice Chairman,
International Institute
for Asia-Pacific Studies,
K-22, Sainik Farm,,
New Delhi 110 062.

सत्यमेव जयते

प्रधानमंत्री

PRIME MINISTER

Message

I am happy to learn that the International Institute for Asia-Pacific Studies is organising a two-day national seminar on "Rise of Terrorism and Secessionism in the Region—Politico, Economic, Strategic and Social Implications", on 30th April and 1st May, 2000 in New Delhi.

I am sure that the seminar will provide a platform for useful deliberations and discussions on the issue of terrorism which has emerged as a major challenge for India and the international community in the 21st century.

I extend my greetings to the participants and best wishes to the organisers.

(A.B. Vajpayee)

New Delhi
April 19, 2000

Preface

In the beginning of the 21st century, the entire Eurasian belt of our planet is witnessing a new ferment—the rise of terrorism, secessionism and ethnic conflicts. Though the form and content of this new resurgence of conflicts varies from country to country, the harsh reality is that this new development has led to a large number of inter-state and intra-state tensions. The academics, researchers and security experts are engaged in critically assessing this new development to provide intellectual inputs to the political elite. This book makes a modest attempt in that direction by outstanding Indian scholars and experts.

There are two ways of looking at this problem. One methodology is based on the experience of nation-state building in the developed nations, the United States in particular. This methodology does not fit into the ground realities of Eurasian nation states. These nation states, unlike the developed nations, are multi-ethnic, multi-cultural and multi-religious. They have also not witnessed transformation of their religious philosophies, as for instance Christianity has done. Above all, these nation states have multi-structural economy and are struggling to come out of tribal, clan and caste loyalties. In this sense, these nation states are coming out of their old grooves with a view to come to grips with the challenges facing them in a period of industrialization, modernization and technical revolution. It is within the womb of this transition that these divisive and fissiparous tendencies have surfaced themselves. Therefore, the Western assessment to trace them to religious fundamentalism appears to be lopsided.

In recent years, a new phrase, the 'rise of fundamentalism' has entered the currency of journalistic jargon and academic discourse, though the term 'fundamentalism' has not yet acquired a precise definition. *The Concise Oxford Dictionary* defines 'fundamentalism' as "maintenance, in opposition to modernism, of traditional orthodox beliefs such as the inerrancy of scriptures and literal acceptance of the creeds as fundamentals of protestant Christianity", whereas 'fundamental' is explained as "of the groundwork, going to the root of matter, serving as base or foundation, essential, primary, original, from which others are derived". But this does not lead us much to present day's understanding. In fact, this phrase seems to have come in usage in the recent decades and it originated in the United States. It has now acquired a definite content. 'Fundamentalist' is a group of theologically conservative protestant churches that arose in the United States in the 1920s. Derived from a group of dissenters who called themselves 'fundamentalists', these churches have claimed to defend the standards of orthodox Christianity against the Liberals or Moderates; i.e., those protestants who incorporated biblical criticism into their theologies and attempted to make the church relevant to the social dilemma of the era. It is also relevant in this context that Reinhold Niebuhr was one of the most influential American theologians of the 20th century. His special contribution was his stress on the issues on the borderline between theology and social ethics. His criticism of the prevailing theological liberalism of the 1920s significantly changed the intellectual climate within the protestant churches in the United States, and his enormous contribution in political thought, both inside and outside the church made him the "greatest living political philosopher of America". This is no place to go into the details of fundamentalist, revivalist movements in Eurasia but, one thing is certain that a blind veneration for the various religious philosophies did exist in the long history of this region.

Therefore, religious philosophies are being misinterpreted to disorientate people by rousing their passions. This has to be candidly admitted. However, this should not be equated with 'civilizational conflicts' as some American scholars are doing. The crux of the problem is that rise of terrorism and secessionism have deeper roots than what appears on the surface. It has both internal and external factors. This is what precisely stands out in this book.

I am grateful to the various scholars who have contributed their papers to this book. But for their active participation and deep interest in this exercise, it would not have been possible to bring out this book. I must also compliment the senior members of the staff of the Gyan Publishing House for their cooperation.

V.D. Chopra

October, 2000
New Delhi

List of Contributors

1. **V.D. Chopra** : Vice Chairman, International Institute for Asia-Pacific Studies, New Delhi and a well known author.
2. **Prof. K.R. Singh** : Former Professor, School of International Studies, Jawaharlal Nehru University, New Delhi.
3. **Prof. B. K. Shrivastava** : Former Professor, Centre for American Studies, Jawaharlal Nehru University, New Delhi and an outstanding expert on the United States.
4. **Mr. Ashwini Kumar** : Former Director General, Border Security Force of India.
5. **Prof. Rakesh Gupta** : Professor, Centre for Political Studies, School of International Studies, Jawaharlal Nehru University, New Delhi.
6. **Dr. A.K. Merchant** : Director, Baha'i Office of External Affairs and Trustee, National Spiritual Assembly of the Baha'i of India, New Delhi.
7. **Maj. Gen. Afsir Karim (Retd.)** : Security expert and Editor, *Aakrosh*, Quarterly, New Delhi.
8. **Prof. Kalim Bahadur** : Professor, School of International Studies, Jawaharlal Nehru University, New Delhi, and an expert on Pakistan.
9. **Prof. Shri Prakash** : Director, Academy of Third World Studies, Jamia Millia Islamia, New Delhi.
10. **Brig. Chandra B. Khanduri** : Security expert and an author on military matters.
11. **Prof. K. Warikoo** : Professor, School of International Studies, Jawaharlal Nehru University, New Delhi.

12. **Dr. G.M. Shah** : Lecturer, Academy of Third World Studies, Jamia Millia Islamia, New Delhi.

13. **Mr. Satya Pal Dang** : Freedom fighter, former Minister of Punjab, and an author.

14. **Prof. Devendra Kaushik** : Former Professor, Centre for Russian and East European Studies, Jawaharlal Nehru University, New Delhi and Chairman, Maulana Abul Kalam Azad Institute of Asian Studies, Calcutta.

15. **Dr. Jagdish P. Sharma** : Specialist on West Asian and North African affairs, Department of African Studies, University of Delhi, New Delhi.

16. **Brig. Vinod Anand** : Senior Fellow, Institute for Defence Studies and Analysis, New Delhi.

17. **Prof. Ravi M. Bakaya** : Former Professor, Jawaharlal Nehru University, New Delhi.

18. **Dr. O.N. Mehrotra** : Senior Fellow, Institute for Defence Studies and Analysis, New Delhi and an expert on Russia, East European and Central European Countries.

19. **Dr. Udai Bhanu Singh** : Research Fellow, Institute for Defence Studies and Analysis, New Delhi and an expert on South East Asia.

20. **Dr. K.N. Ramachandran** : Former Senior Fellow, Institute for Defence Studies and Analysis, New Delhi and an expert on China.

21. **Prof. V. Suryanarayan** : Former Professor, University of Madras, Chennai, author and an expert on Sri Lanka.

22. **Dr. Parmanand** : Reader in Political Science, University of Delhi, visiting Professor at Tribhuvan University, Kathmandu (Nepal) and Hon. Director, South Asian Studies Foundation, New Delhi.

23. **Dr. Kshitij Prabha** : Associate Fellow, Institute for Defence Studies and Analysis, New Delhi.

Introduction

Terrorism, secessionism and ethnic conflicts, particularly in multi-cultural, multi-religious and multi-ethnic societies have assumed a new dimension, both in their sweep and intensity in the beginning of the 21st century. The international community including the United Nations can no longer ignore this new development in the post-Cold War period. Use of violence, individual violence and organized violence to achieve certain political objectives is not a new phenomena in the human history. It is relevant for instance to mention that after the end of the second world war in 1945 till 1984, there were more than 150 instances of major inter and intra-state violence; 140 of them took place in the developing world. Thus, while the industrialized countries spend well over 80 per cent of the world's military expenditure and produce 95 per cent of weapons, most of the violence was witnessed in the developing world. But there is no paradox really. In two-thirds of the conflicts, the developed nations intervened directly or indirectly. Many of them were anti-colonial wars, only about a fifth of them being inter-state wars, a number of them caused by religious, tribal and secessionist factors. This facts are being recapitulated to make out how the current wave of terrorism is qualitatively different from the anti-colonial wars. After the process of decolonisation was completed, through the liberation struggles, use of violence by individuals and a group of individuals has undergone a qualitative change.

Turbulence and violence at the time when nation states are being formed is not unusual. Nation state as a concept emerged only in the 16th century, and we have four centuries of history of evolution of nation states, mostly in Europe and for the last one and a half century in the Western hemisphere as well. That period of history was marked by extraordinary violence, such as the 30 years war, Napoleonic wars, the Balkan wars, the first and second world wars, the American civil war, the decimation of the Red Indian population, the French revolution, the Bolshevik revolution, etc. Countries are today known for their commitment to peace—such as Sweden and Switzerland—had their full share of violence. Religious intolerance, genocide, ethnic conflicts and oppression marked this period. The development of science and technology, industrialization, spread of education and a spirit of secularism over a period of a century, and finally two horrible wars within a span of two successive generations, have stabilized the industrialized world.

There is yet another aspect which is relevant in any study of rise of terrorism and secessionism. During the colonial period, the foreign rulers in the colonies and semi-colonies under their domination followed a calculated policy of 'divide and rule' with a view to disorientate the nation-state consciousness of the people through economic and political instruments. Anyone with some knowledge about India's recent history would agree with this conclusion. But what is of immediate relevance is that the 'religious factor'—Hindu Muslim conflict in India and the 'Islamic factor' in the Muslim dominated countries—has been increasingly used by the Western powers since the second half of 1970s, though such a generalization may appear to be too sweeping. This was the period when the cold war was at its peak. In the 70s the process of decolonization entered a new phase and the people of Africa and Asia began to assert their independence and sovereignty, and a new trend developed among the liberal democrats and radicals in a number of these countries. They advocated that doctrinal rhetoric about the role of religion in shaping human consciousness should be avoided at all costs. In fact, in some of the African, Latin American and West Asian countries, a new concept of 'liberation theology' and 'liberation church' were also evolved. The Nasserites, the Arab Ba'ath Socialist Party of Syria and Iraq, the Palestinian Liberation Organization in varying degrees began to interpret Islam as a sum total of the fundamental Islamic and social revolutionary principles and doctrines aimed at ameliorating social conditions of the masses as a brotherhood of believers, their equality and collectivization of means of production and distribution. This was the period when the Arab countries embarked on the path of nationalization of their oil wealth. Thus, the religious philosophies began to be given two diverse interpretations—modern and conservative. In this context the Western and American scholars and their philosophers did not have merely academic interests in the religious and revivalist movements.

It is relevant to mention here that the Muslim countries of the Middle East and North Africa at that time provided as much as 55 per cent of the oil for the capitalist world, exporting as much as 75 per cent of their oil production. Only from the second half of the 1970s did Washington begin to show special interest in Islam, and this, to no small measure, was caused by the unprecedented energy crisis of 1973-1974. From then onwards all events in these regions have been the focus of Washington's attention. Another important factor was that these Muslim countries had built up huge financial reserves, which enabled their ruling elite to exert far greater influence on the economy of the entire world. The USA also took into account the growing political and economic weightage of the Muslim oil-producing countries in the Non Aligned Movement, among the developing countries and in international organizations.

In the beginning of the 21st century, oil wealth of the Central Asian Republics has assumed a new importance and therefore rise of terrorism and religious fundamentalism in this region can not be delinked from this factor.

In January 1979, Zbigniew Brezinski, the Assistant to the US President for National Security Affairs, even instructed the relevant departments to arrange for an intensive study of Islam and its political role in the world and prepare a detailed report on the situation in a number of Muslim countries and the relevant religious movements in them. Thus, at the turn of the 1970s and 1980s the problems in Islam came to figure prominently in the activities of the US and other Western countries. In India, the rise of Hindu revivalism also entered a new phase in this period.

Historically speaking, it is during the Cold War period that revivalist movement gained ascendancy. This is proof enough that to disintegrate the Soviet Union, revivalist movements were used as an important instrument. It is a strange coincidence that during the Cold War period, the revivalist movements in India as well as in some of the Muslim countries became powerful. The demand for Khalistan and the secessionist movements in Jammu and Kashmir and in some other parts of India gained momentum in this period. The assassination of Indira Gandhi should also be seen in this context.

It is true that the West European liberal democratic circles, including influential political leaders, have expressed concern over these religious revivalist movements. In the United States two conflicting assessments are being voiced about this trend, though there is a powerful section which advocates "third party" interventions in regional conflicts, including religious conflicts.

Yet one thing is certain—such movements are receiving encouragements, help and assistance from abroad. Algeria, Egypt and Tunisia are facing violent threats from militant Islamists. Some of the leaders of these countries are convinced that certain Muslim countries —Iran and Sudan directly, and Afghanistan and Pakistan indirectly— have been fanning the fires of militancy and extremism. In the recent developments in Chechnya too the same forces are operating. The foreign hand in Jammu and Kashmir is too well known and needs no recapitulation. The Russian Federation, like India is multi-religious, multi-ethnic and multi- cultural. It has 16 autonomous republics, mainly populated by non-Russians, totaling 22 million people and another five autonomous regions, again populated by non-Russians. About one million Russians live outside Russia, while the Muslim population in Russia is 18 million. Thus, Russia like India is facing a serious challenge to its unity and integrity. This brings into focus how religious revivalism has become the single biggest destabilizing factor in the nation-state building process in the very big and most populated countries of the world. No new international order in the post-Cold War era can be brought into being without taking into account this factor. Western and American models cannot be mechanically transplanted in these countries and the question of human rights should not be seen in isolation.

In the 80s of the last century, Pakistan became a "frontline" state and spring-board of organizing terrorism in Afghanistan by training, financing and equipping the Mujahidins (i.e., Islamic holy warriors). It was liberally financed and supplied sophisticated arms by the United States, other Western countries and conservative regimes like Saudi Arabia. This process continued even after the withdrawal of the Soviet troops. This is how the Taliban became the most important factor in the internal situation of Afghanistan. After the disintegration of the Soviet Union, Pakistan and Afghanistan have become a launching pad for organizing terrorism and secessionism in whole of Eurasia as has been underlined in the various papers in this book. The situation has become so dangerous that even the American ruling elite has begun to feel its pinch.

The most dangerous outcome of rise of terrorism and secessionism in Eurasia is that now a nexus has developed between the terrorists, drug mafia, illegal arms suppliers and criminals. That too under the cover of what is called "religious revivalism".

Narcotic smuggling has become a prime source of financing for civil wars already under way—or rapidly brewing—in southern Europe and the eastern Mediterranean, according to a report of March 1999. Another report, by the Paris based 'Observatoire Geopolitique des Dorgues' or Geopolitical Observatory of Drugs, identifies belligerents in the former Yugoslav republics and Turkey as key players in the region's accelerating drugs-for-arms traffic. Albanian nationalists' in ethnically tense Macedonia and the Serbian province of Kosovo have built a vast heroin network leading from the opium fields of Pakistan to black market arms dealers in Switzerland, which transport up to $2 billion worth of the drug annually into the heart of Europe, the report says. More than 500 Kosovo or Macedonian Albanians are in prison in Switzerland for drug or arms trafficking offences, and more than 1,000 others are under indictment. The arms are reportedly stockpiled in Kosovo for eventual use against the Serbian government in Belgrade, which imposed a violent crackdown on Albanian autonomy advocates in the province six years ago. ['Separatists Supporting Themselves with Traffic in Narcotics', *San Francisco Chronicle,* 10/6/1994]

An intelligence report which was prepared by Germany's Federal Criminal Agency concluded "Ethnic Albanians are now the most prominent group in the distribution of heroin in Western consumer countries". Europol, which is based in The Hague, is preparing a report for European interior and justice ministers on a connection between the Kosovo Liberation Army and Albanian drug gangs. Police in the Czech Republic recently tracked down a Kosovo Albanian drug dealer named Doboshi who had escaped from a Norwegian prison where he was serving 12 years for heroin trading. A raid on Doboshi's apartment turned up documents linking him with arms purchases for the KLA. ('Drugs Money Linked to the Kosovo Rebels', *The London Times*, 24/3/1999).

"A group of Kosovo Albanians smuggling arms back to their troubled province were among 100 people arrested in a massive, countrywide anti-drug operation in Italy, police here said Tuesday. All the 100—90 of whom were arrested in Italy, the rest in other European countries—face charges related to international drug trafficking. Anti-Mafia prosecutors in Milan, who conducted the operation with paramilitary police units, identified eight criminal structures active on an international scale. One hundred kilos (220 pounds) of heroin and cocaine was seized in the bust across several Italian regions. Investigators said the groups used Milan as a base, with cafes, restaurants, garages and other firms acting as fronts. The Kosovar Albanian gang allegedly used drug money to buy the weapons in Italy, which were then sent to Kosovo. Another separatist group of Egyptians with links to Calabrian and Albanian gangs were arrested on suspicions of laundering money through Switzerland for use by fundamentalists in Egypt." ('Major Italian Drug Bust Breaks Kosovo Arms Trafficking', Agence France-Presse, 9/6/1998).

"Socially organized in extended families bound together in clan alliances, Kosovar Albanians dominate the Albanian mafia in the southern Balkans. Other than Kosovo, the Albanian mafia is also active in northern Albania and western Macedonia. In this context, the so-called 'Balkan Medellin' is made up of a number of geographically connected border towns. ...If left unchecked, this growing Albanian narco-terrorism could lead to a Colombian syndrome in the southern Balkans, or the emergence of a situation in which the Albanian mafia becomes powerful enough to control one or more states in the region. In practical terms, this will involve either Albania or Macedonia, or both. Politically, this is now being done by channeling growing foreign exchange (forex) profits from narco-terrorism into local governments and political parties. In Albania, the ruling Democratic Party (DP) led by President Sali Berisha is now widely suspected of tacitly tolerating and even directly profiting from drug-trafficking for wider politico-economic reasons, namely the financing of secessionist political parties and other groupings in Kosovo and Macedonia." ('The Balkan Medellin', Jane's 1/3/1995; Albanian then- president Berisha lost power in 1997 and is now a known KLA patron in northern Albania).

The following reports note the presence of foreign Mujahidin in the Kosovo war, some of them *jihad* veterans from Bosnia, Chechnya, and Afghanistan. Some of the reports specifically cite assets of Iran or Osama bin-Laden, or both, in support of the KLA. To some, "Mujahidin" do not necessarily mean "terrorists." But since the foreign fighters have not been considerate enough to provide an organizational chart detailing the exact relationship among the various groups, the reported presence of foreign fighters together with known terrorists in the KLA's stronghold at least raises serious questions about the implications for the Clinton Administration's increasingly close ties to the KLA.

"Serbian officials say Mujahidin have formed groups that remained behind in Bosnia. Groups from Saudi Arabia, Yemen, and Chechnya are also involved in Albanian guerrilla operations. A document found on the body of Alija Rabic, an Albanian UCK member killed in a border crossing incident July, 1998 indicated he was guiding a 50 man group from Albania into Kosovo. The group included one Yemeni and 16 Saudis, six of whom bore passports with Macedonian Albanian names. Other UCK rebels killed crossing the Albanian frontier have carried Bosnian Muslim Federation papers." ('Unhealthy Climate in Kosovo as Guerrillas Gear Up for a Summer Confrontation', Jane's International Defense Review, 1/2/1999).

"Diplomats in the region say Bosnia was the first bastion of Islamic power. The autonomous Yugoslav region of Kosovo promises to be the second. During the current rebellion against the Yugoslav army, the ethnic Albanians in the province, most of whom are Moslem, have been provided with financial and military support from Islamic countries. They are being bolstered by hundreds of Iranian fighters, or Mujahidin, who infiltrate from nearby Albania and call themselves the KLA. US defense officials say the support includes that of Bin Laden accused of masterminding the bombings of the US embassies in Nairobi and Dar es Salaam. A Defense Department statement on August 20 said, 'Bin Laden's Al Qa'ida organization supports Moslem fighters in both Bosnia and Kosovo.' ...The KLA strength was not the southern Kosovo region, which over the centuries turned from a majority of Serbs to ethnic Albanians. The KLA, however, was strong in neighboring Albania, which today has virtually no central government. The crisis in Albania led Iran to quickly move in to fill the vacuum. Iranian Revolutionary Guards began to train KLA members. Selected groups of Albanians were sent to Iran to study that country's version of militant Islam. So far, Yugoslav officials and Western diplomats agree that millions of dollars have been funneled through Bosnia and Albania to buy arms for the KLA. The money is raised from both Islamic governments and from Islamic communities in Western Europe, particularly Germany. Iran has been active in helping out the Kosovo rebels, Ephraim Kam, deputy director of Tel Aviv University's Jaffe Center for Strategic Studies, said, 'Iran sees Kosovo and Albania as containing Moslem communities that require help and Teheran is willing to do it. But much of the training of the KLA remains based in Bosnia.' Intelligence sources say mercenaries and volunteers for the separatist movement have been recruited and paid handsome salaries. ...The trainers and fighters in the KLA include many of the Iranians who fought in Bosnia in the early 1990s. Intelligence sources place their number at 7,000, many of whom have married Bosnian women. There are also Afghans, Algerians, Chechens and Egyptians." ('Kosovo Seen as New Islamic Bastion', *Jerusalem Post,* 14/9/1998).

These facts speak for themselves and throw light on rise of terrorism and secessionism in a large number of countries particularly in the Balkans. There is sufficient evidence to prove that both in Pakistan and Afghanistan, the linkages between terrorists, drug mafia and dealers in illicit arms trade are as strong as elsewhere.

This mass of facts conclusively proves that it would be naive to equate or identify terrorists with any religion or religious preaching. They are product of a new phenomenon that is drugs and illegal arms trade. In this sense, rise of terrorism has deeper ramifications than what appears on the surface. In this book an attempt has been made to focus attention on this aspect with a view to awaken the international community to the dangerous potentialities of this new development. Though the weapon of violence is used to achieve certain political objectives, the crucial questions are; who is using this instrument and what are the social and political implications of this for the international community as a whole.

In his paper in this book Prof K.R. Singh has underlined that "the fast growing tentacles of the new phenomenon of non-state actors operating from what can be called *res nulis* and indulging in illegal trafficking in drugs and arms and fired by the *jehadi* mindset is a far more serious threat to national and international stability than mere national or transnational terrorism. It is time that international community directs its attention to restoring effective state control over these areas so as to prevent these irresponsible non-state actors not only from creating and enlarging but also getting entrenched into a parallel global system that aims at destroying the very foundations of the existing world order."

Prof B.K. Shrivastava in his paper entitled 'The United States and International Terrorism in South Asia' has analyzed the various facets of the American policy on terrorism. According to him "though South Asia is currently the worst affect region, the United States views terrorism in its wider global perspective. It is alarmed by the rise of Islamic militancy in Pakistan and Apghanistan. " However, in his opinion " American policy in South Asia swings between hope and frustration. Its vital security interest deters it from declaring it as a terrorist state."

Prof. Rakesh Gupta in his paper entitled 'Towards a Political Economy of Intra State Conflicts' focuses on the increasing incidence of intra state conflicts since 1945, but especially since 1989, as products of the project of modernity of globalization. With reference to India, it looks at the intra state wars in the mould of terrorist framework within the paradigm of modernity and globalization.

Mr. Ashwini Kumar, a leading security expert in his paper on 'Latest Trends in Terrorism' argues that "mass-destructive terror, is now the greatest threat terrorism poses. A terrorist use of a nuclear yield device is the most devastating type of terrorism and a radiological attack is the most likely variety of non-conventional terrorism. It is a danger that cannot be ignored; since it is not the current proliferation problem, but rather the current psycho-dynamics of terrorist groups combined with the nature of terrorism in the last decade that makes the threat so potent. It will not recede in the foreseeable future."

In his paper Dr. A.K. Merchant has summed up 'A Baha'i Viewpoint on Rise of Terrorism and Secessionism in South Asia' and has underlined the significance of a profound change in human consciousness.

Maj. Gen. Afsir Karim (Retd.) in his paper on 'Terrorism and National Security Concerns' has advocated that both long term and short term policies should be evolved to meet the new challenges. He has suggested among other steps that along with initiating diplomatic and political measures, "military measures" should be taken to destroy Pakistan's covert political and military infrastructure, which threatens India.

Prof. Kalim Bahadur in his paper on 'Pakistan and Afghanistan as sources of Terrorism in the Region', after detailed analysis has come to the conclusion that "some of the terrorist camps are now being used by Osama Bin Laden, for training his bands of terrorists to carry on attacks against United States agencies. The Afghan Mujahidin had been running the flourishing drug trade even then the Western agencies had turned a Nelson's eye to that. The United States had not realized the social and political implications of the emergence of the Taliban on the Afghan scene."

In his paper Prof. Shri Prakash on 'Transformation of Pakistan and Afghanistan as Spring-boards of Cross Country Terrorism in the Region', after giving concrete evidence to prove this, he has emphasized that India would remain a secular country. It has the largest number of Muslims after Indonesia of which only four per cent live in Kashmir. All negotiations on Kashmir problem have to be based on this historic fact.

Brig. Chandra B. Khanduri (Retd.) after analyzing how Pakistan is organizing a proxy-war in Jammu and Kashmir in his paper, that has warned that if all the indicators are taken into account, it becomes clear that Pakistan "perhaps has provided adequate cause for turning", proxy war into a mission. In his opinion, it is probable that this proxy war might inevitably turn "into a regular war."

Prof. K. Warikoo in his paper has made an analysis of the nature and character of Islamist extremism and terrorism in Kashmir. On the basis of this study he has suggested specific measures to meet this challenge including affective legislative and criminal proceedings against the terrorists. He has further suggested that they should be dealt with a firm hand. Trans-border and international terrorism should be curbed including following a policy of hot pursuit. Media should play positive role and above all the international community should be mobilized in the fight against terrorism.

As against the above mentioned paper on rise of terrorism and secessionism in Jammu and Kashmir, Dr. G.M. Shah examined the problem from another angle. The running thread of his analysis is that dialogue with various formations should be started to find a solution of this problem. He has analyzed that the rise of terrorism and secessionism are rooted in the history of state.

In his paper entitled 'Cross-border terrorism in Punjab', Mr. Satya Pal Dang, an outstanding political personality of the state has made an objective analysis of genesis of terrorism and secessionism in Punjab. He has highlighted how threat of terrorism and secessionism still looms large in the state. He has pointed out "the danger of terrorism re-emerging in Punjab, though in a different way, remains. Efforts to revive it continue to be made by the ruling circles in Pakistan as well."

After making analysis of terrorism and secessionism in India the book is devoted to the study of this problem in other countries of Eurasia. Experts on these countries have contributed valuable papers. These Papers are: —

(a) Islamist Factor and Fundamentalist Threat in Central Asia.
Prof. Devendra Kaushik

(b) Rise of Islamic Extremism in West Asia and North Africa.
Dr. Jagdish P. Sharma

(c) Pakistan and Taliban Role in Chechnya Conflict.
Brig. Vinod Anand

(d) Chechnya : Background and Prospects
Prof. Ravi M. Bakaya

(e) The Yugoslav Tragedy
Dr. O.N. Mehrotra

(f) Nature and Genesis of Terrorism and Ethnic Conflicts in Indonesia
Dr. Udai Bhanu Singh

(g) Ethnic Issues and Insurgency in Xinjiang
Dr. K.N. Ramachandran

(h) Ethnic Cauldron in Sri Lanka
Prof. V. Suryanarayan

(i) Maoist Terrorism in Nepal: Growth, Spread and Prospects
Prof. Parmanand

(j) Narco-Terrorism, The Case of the Golden Crescent
Dr. Kshitij Prabha

This study is first of its kind on the available literature on terrorism, secessionism and ethnic conflicts. In the sense that it makes a critical and objective analysis of this development. What is of farreaching importance is that this book is the product of an intellectual exercise by scholars, academics and strategic experts who have specialized in their research work on the various countries of Eurasia. This book has another merit. The various papers included in the book are based on concrete evidence and do not suffer from any ideological overtones. The book therefore is a rich contribution to the thought structures on the contemporary politics, above all, on the rise of terrorism and secessionism, which threaten regional and international stability on a scale, which has no parallel in the recent human history. The inevitable conclusion of this book is that if multi-cultural, multi-ethnic and multi-religious societies of Eurasia go in flames by this turbulence, it will have its own fall out on the international stability and peace. This is the moral of this book.

V. D. Chopra

CHAPTER 1

Terrorism and the Erosion of State Power

K.R. Singh

Terrorism, whether national or transnational, aims, among other things, at eroding not only the state power but also the state system *per se*, with a view to attaining the desired objectives. These objectives are often rationalized on ethnic, religious, ideological and even political grounds or by a combination of these variables. Though terrorism might often target innocent civilians, the primary focus of attack is the existing state system because only a weak and degraded state system can offer an appropriate environment to the forces that resort to terrorism to dictate terms not only to the legitimate government but also to the people in a given area. Thus, eroding state power becomes the primary objective of terrorist groups or those agencies that sponsor, support and protect them, so as to use them *vis-a-vis* their targets. This aspect of terrorism needs a more in-depth analysis if we have to counter the long-term and fundamental threat it poses.

Since the established state system is the norm of the present world order, terrorism needs to be seen as a conflict between those who believe in the concept of an established and therefore, an accountable world order, and those who work towards its destruction. Conflicts are unavoidable. Therefore, mechanism is provided to contain them and even to resolve them. Such conflicts are generally between two or more states. Internationally accepted norms exist for conducting conflicts, leading even to war, as well as mechanism for de-escalation conducive for restoration of peace. Under these circumstances, the accountability of the parties concerned is reasonably assured. Covenant of the League of Nations, Charter of the United Nations Organization as well as several international agreements like the Geneva Protocol, etc., define these norms.

In the post-World War II era traditional means of resolving conflicts have come under increasing pressure due to the new roles assigned to non-state actors. It began with the question of decolonization. Wherever smooth transition of power from the imperial authority to the colonized people was impeded, national liberation movement increasingly took recourse to the threat or even to the use of force. Fortunately, most of them had acquired international legitimacy and though non state actors *per se,* they could be classified as potential state actors. These non-state actors were primarily interested in transfer of power from the imperial government to the nationalist government and not in destroying the state system itself. Hence, a negotiated settlement was possible and often led to effective decolonization. Consequently, *de facto* state actor—the national liberation movement—acquired a *de jure* status. The *Front de Libération Nationale* (FLN) of Algeria and the Palestine Liberation Organization (PLO) in Palestine represent that trend.

However, for various reasons several other non-state actors also began to operate during that period. These had a very narrow and restricted ethnic, religious or ideological base. While the Multinational Companies (MNCs) and Non-Government Organizations (NGOs), which are also non-state actors, normally do not resort to the use of violence, several others do. Most of them are splinter or extremist groups. These non-state actors began to resort to what can be termed as indiscriminate acts of terrorism as instruments of their political and ideological propaganda as well as of intimidation.

Because of their extremist policies, they were unacceptable to the state actors who saw in them a threat to the very foundation of the state structure and therefore, of state security. Consequently, the established state system itself became the primary target of these radical or extremist non-state actors whether they defined their role in terms of ethnic, religious or ideological radicalism.

While some of these non-state actors restrict their activities within a given state boundary many of them tend to extend their activities to other states. Obviously, the framework of negotiations in the case of non-state actors that restrict their operations within the state will be different and will not normally include foreign elements. For example, the framework of negotiations with the People's War Group (PWG) in India or certain extremist groups in the North-East will fall under that category.

By contrast, there are non-state actors that have very pronounced transnational linkages. In this context, it is necessary to differentiate between those non-state actors that have only support bases abroad and those actors that operate as surrogates of foreign powers and are created, protected and supported by one or more state actors with the object of destabilizing another state with which it has antagonistic relations. Kurdish groups of Iraq were offered support and sanctuary in Iran and were used by the Shah of Iran against the Baathi regime in Iraq till 1975 when, under the terms of the Iraq-Iran agreement, Iran withdrew its support. Iraqi Kurds have been used by the West against the Baathi regime since 1991. Other examples are the alleged use of the Hezbullah in South Lebanon by Syria and of the Taliban by Pakistan.

Very often, these non-state actors that were fashioned as a tool began to acquire an autonomous identity of their own by generating their own socio-economic and military base. While several experts have highlighted the nexus between these groups and illegal traffic in drugs and arms, there are reasons to believe that their support base could also consist of what can be called legitimate business like banking, shipping, etc., as well as donations from their supporters.

This is especially true in the case of organizations drawing support based upon ethnic and religious loyalties. In some events, these non-state actors can even acquire sufficient autonomous power base that enables them to influence domestic and foreign policies even of the state that had sponsored them or the state from where they operate. The capability of the Hezbullah to influence the politics of Lebanon, of the Taliban in Pakistan and of the Liberation Tamil Tiger Elaem (LTTE) in India, particularly in Tamil Nadu, can no longer be denied.

The net result of these developments, especially during the last two decades is that these non-state actors which are not responsible to any given national or international order, have started playing an increasing role in eroding not only the state system *per se* but also the very fundamentals of international relations based upon recognized state system.

Another point that needs to be stressed in this context is that these non-state actors, whether they are targetting their activities within a given state or beyond it, can act best from areas where state power has been grossly degraded. Thus, irrespective of their national or transnational base, these non-state actors have a vested interest in eroding the state power in a specific area so as to penetrate and control it and logically to expand that zone under their control. This is true of the PWG, the LTTE and the Taliban.

Such a development poses a totally new set of challenges for those who wish to work for a negotiated settlement. Unlike conflicts between legitimate state actors, there is no responsible and legitimate authority with which one can conduct fruitful negotiations. As noted earlier, in some selected cases, the non-state actors that were earlier branded as terrorists, were granted legitimacy so that political negotiation could be initiated. The PLO and the LTTE are such examples. Such a transformation is possible only when these non-state actors enjoy a wide degree of autonomy in decision-making.

But, if these non-state actors are dependent variables, i.e., if they are created and sustained by others to serve as their surrogates, they are no better than 'front' organizations and hence cannot qualify as legitimate parties in the context of a negotiated settlement. In fact, such states that offer covert support to these non-state actors, do not wish them to emerge as *de facto* state actors lest they lose their leverage over them. Consequently, these non-state actors are preserved more as mercenaries who are expected to act only on the prompting of their pay masters.

Since the last two or three decades if not more, one is witnessing a conscious policy to create conditions in several areas whereby the established state power and state system are systematically eroded and the vacuum thus created is filled by the non-state actors. The process started with the creation of so-called 'Fateh land' in South Lebanon after the PLO was forced to evacuate Jordan following the 'Black September' events in 1970. The Hezbullah subsequently replaced the PLO there. The most damaging case was the destruction of the state of Afghanistan since the eighties and the absence of any single credible and legitimate authority there. Its impact is felt even in the neighbouring Tajikistan and Pakhtoonistan. Most of these events can be traced back to the short-sighted and ill conceived policies of the Western countries. The same group is also working hard to create a political vacuum in north Iraq, through their support to the Kurds and in Chechnya by supporting the group that is trying to secede from Russia. Geopolitically these are very sensitive zones. Not only are they adjacent to each other but they are capable of establishing the global energy requirements if left unchecked.

This new phenomenon, though linked to so-called transnational terrorism, poses a far more serious threat. Deliberate efforts to create what can be termed *res nulis* areas where there is no recognized legitimate authority—is not only meant to provide a sanctuary for transnational terrorism but is also destined to pose a far more serious threat since those who are working towards it are consciously or unconsciously trying to undermine the very foundation of contemporary national and international state system. Also, these are the areas that are the breeding ground of mercenaries legitimized under the banner of fundamentalism, financed and sustained by illegal trafficking in drugs and arms.

The fast growing tentacles of the new phenomenon of non-state actors operating and indulging in illegal trafficking in drugs and arms, fired by the *jehadi* mindset is a far more serious threat to national and international stability than mere national or transnational terrorism. It is time that international community directs its attention to restoring effective state control over these areas so as to prevent these irresponsible non-state actors not only from creating and enlarging but also getting entrenched into a parallel global system that aims at destroying the very foundations of the existing world order.

CHAPTER 2

The United States and International Terrorism in South Asia

B.K. Shrivastava

Terrorism has been defined as the 'use of violence or the threat of violence to create a climate of fear in a given population.' The terrorist organizations that perpetrate acts of violence are almost always small in size as compared to the population and institutions they oppose. They command much greater power and influence than warranted by their size through publicity and fear, which their acts generate.[1] Terrorist acts go back at least to the first century AD when Zealots, a Jewish religious sect, fought against the Romans who ruled the present day Israel. In the latter half of the twentieth century terrorist acts multiplied several fold. The terrorist groups in this era were largely moved by ideological and ethnic considerations. Technological advances in transportation, communication, microelectronics and explosives greatly facilitated the wider use of terrorist violence for the achievement of political goals.[2]

American citizens were the victims of many terrorist acts because of the opposition to its policies in many parts of the world. But a majority of these acts took place in the Middle East because of United States' support for Israel. The radical Palestinian groups and their sympathizers committed a very large number of terrorist acts against the US. In 1983, US embassy in Beirut, Lebanon was bombed by a Shíite Muslim and US marines barracks in Beirut were attacked in which nearly 300 people were killed. When Pan Am Flight 103 blew up in mid air, 259 passengers were killed which included 189 American citizens. In 1996, a truck bomb exploded outside an apartment building in Dehran in Saudi Arabia, which housed US military personnel. Nineteen Americans were killed in the blast. On August 7, 1998, trucks loaded with explosives rammed through

American embassies in Dar-es-Salaam in Tanzania and Nairobi in Kenya resulting in large number of deaths including Americans. Over 300 people were killed as a result of the blast including 12 Americans and a thousand more were wounded.

The US had very early adopted the policy of no negotiations with hostage takers and hijackers of Americans. It believed that any sort of negotiation would only encourage more hostage taking and hijacking. This policy had a corollary: pursuing the perpetrators of the crime against American citizens and bringing them to justice, if possible in the United States.

It was left for the administration to characterize a group or an organization or a state as terrorist. For years the United States called the PLO as a terrorist organization and American diplomats were forbidden to have any contact with the PLO officials even at the social level. In 1988, the PLO formally renounced terrorism as a policy. It was only after that the United States agreed to have contacts with the PLO. The US policy on terrorism has changed and has been brought in line with changed ground realities and perception of its own national interest.

After 1979, when the Soviet Union's armed forces marched into Afghanistan, the United States supported the Mujahideens in their war against the government in Kabul and the Soviet forces. The Mujahideens were seen as freedom fighters rather than as terrorist outfits. It financed, trained and supplied them with sophisticated weapons. When the war in Afghanistan ended in 1988, it offered to buy back the Stinger missiles it had supplied to these Mujahideens. Only a small number of these were retrieved, the bulk remaining in Afghanistan. The facilities which were then created for training of the Mujahideens are now being used by Osama Bin Laden. Only the destinations of the Mujahideens are different. Pakistan served as the frontline state in US war against the Soviet Union in Afghanistan.

Even before the insurgency began in Kashmir in 1989, terrorist acts had started in Punjab in the wake of Operation Blue Star and anti-Sikh riots after the assassination of Indira Gandhi. The harsh policy of suppression of terrorist violence pursued by the Indian government was projected and highlighted in the US Congress as human rights violations. Although the George Bush Administration consistently maintained that the Punjab was an integral part of India, it did not recognize the secessionist movement. However, it was a well established fact that many of the militant Sikh organizations had their bases in Pakistan and received all possible assistance but the United States did nothing about it except condemning India's record on human rights.

The Cold War ended and the insurgency in Kashmir took a turn for the worse. Though there was no direct link between the two, the ethnic upsurge and the resultant break-up of the Soviet Union boosted the morale of all ethnic secessionists throughout the world. The Bush Administration's attention was riveted to the developments that were taking place in the Soviet Union and Eastern Europe. *The World Transformed* written by George Bush and his National Security Advisor Brent Scocroft[3] devoted a major part of the book to these developments. A few chapters are on the Gulf War with which the President became preoccupied from mid-1990 to almost the end of his term. South Asia hardly gets any mention in this book. The world was transformed because the Soviet Union, the erstwhile antagonist of the United States, was cooperating with the United States.

As the insurgency in Kashmir began to gain momentum in the early 1990s, Pakistan saw a window of opportunity opening up. It threw its support behind the militancy, claiming all the time that it was only extending moral and political support and was not involved in any way in cross-border terrorism. The Indian security forces battling the militants under difficult circumstances sometimes violated the human rights of the Kashmiris, Pakistan took full advantage of this in internationalizing the Kashmir issue. The concern of the international community with human rights violations had increased and the issue could not be ignored. Thus, the issue of Kashmir, international terrorism and human rights violations were interlinked. The cross-border terrorism could not be discussed in isolation. The Bush Administration's emphasis was on human rights violations and it asked the Government of India to punish those guilty of such acts. It consistently maintained that the Kashmir problem could be solved only through bilateral negotiations between India and Pakistan.[4]

The American policy changed gears with the coming in of the Clinton Administration in 1993. It reviewed the existing policy and changed it by placing more emphasis on the insurgency in Kashmir. John Malot, the then Acting Director of the South Asian Bureau in the State

Department in his testimony before the House Foreign Affairs Subcommittee in April 1993, described South Asia "as a place of political turmoil, insurgency and warned of national, ethnic and religious tension." The primary interest of the United States was to prevent a war in the subcontinent that could lead to a nuclear exchange. Malot also acknowledged that there was outside support for the militants in Kashmir.[5] A few days later on a visit to India, Malot repeated his assertions. Pakistan felt terribly let down because it was being accused of supporting terrorism in Kashmir. In his remarks to foreign correspondents, Pakistan's then Prime Minister Balakh Sher—Mazari showed his bitterness when he remarked "When Arabs were trained in Pakistan and were going to Afghanistan, they were heroes. Now when they are going to Kashmir they were being called terrorists."[6]

While India contended that, but for the support militancy received from across the border in Kashmir, it would have collapsed, the United States regarded the insurgency to be largely indigenous. The Asia Pacific Subcommittee of the House of Representatives said so in its report submitted to its own Committee on Foreign Affairs. It predicted "continued bloodshed to be the most likely scenario as neither the militants nor the Government of India was going to tire easily." The report went on to criticize India severely for its human rights violations in Kashmir. To balance its criticism it also assailed militants for their atrocities against civilians, particularly against the Pundits[7]. The report by calling militancy in Kashmir largely indigenous exonerated Pakistan.

In contrast to the Asia Pacific Subcommittee's report, the Research Committee of the House of Representatives provided solid evidence of the complicity of Pakistan in the terrorist activities in Kashmir. It stated that altogether 20,000 young Kashmiri had been trained and armed by Pakistan and then pushed into Kashmir. The State Department's own annual report on 'The Pattern of Global Terrorism' had stated that there were credible reports in 1992 of official Pakistani support for Kashmiri militants who undertook acts of terrorism in the Indian controlled Kashmir.[8] In January 1993, President Clinton wrote to Nawaz Sharif, then Pakistan's Prime Minister that if it continued to back militants in Punjab and Kashmir, the United States would declare it as a state sponsoring terrorism.[9] John Malot while visiting Pakistan in May 1993, stated that the US was informally watching Pakistan to decide whether it should be added to the list of states sponsoring terrorism.[10] But on July 14, the Clinton Administration decided not to cite Pakistan as a state sponsoring terrorism. The United States did not want to complicate things for the new caretaker government that was to assume office in a few days time especially when Moeen Qureshi, regarded by many as America's own man, being brought from Washington to head the government.

The US was not interested in pushing Pakistan over the brink by declaring it a terrorist state nor did it desire to give it a clean chit. Secretary of State Warren Christopher in an *aide-memoire* handed over to Pakistan declared that Washington would not hesitate to declare Pakistan a terrorist state "without notice if positive trends do not continue or there was resurgence of ISI inland or offshore activities." The *aide-memoire* warned that a review would be made by December and "it is essential that your government's support for the militants must end or face the consequences." American govenrment based its action not on the basis of reports received from the Indian sources but on credible independent information from other sources.[11]

After Robin Raphel, Assistant Secretary of State and the Director of the Bureau of South Asia assumed charge the American policy began to swing towards Pakistan. She contended that the United States indeed received credible reports on Pakistan's support for the terrorist activities in Kashmir but as a result of the pressure exerted by the United States in the last few years "there seems to be a lot less of that going now." She went on to add that "whatever outside support, there is a strong indigenous element to the insurgency. I can also argue that it is self sustaining." She sent the ball thundering to India's court. She advised India to "look at the underlying cause of insurgency and these are not linked to outside assistance."[12]

Throughout her tenure Raphel showed great sympathy for the insurgency and soft pedalled Pakistan's support for cross-border terrorism. She did not acknowledge that the nature of insurgency had changed, that it was masterminded from across the border and that the veterans of the Afghan war from Muslim countries were being pushed into Kashmir and were in control of the movement. In March 1994, the Administration had decided not to declare Pakistan as a terrorist state . She gave a clean chit to Pakistan government. "It looks to us," she said, "that Pakistan has closed off the tap. There is a problem of private organizations in

Pakistan supporting the Kashmiri groups, and they have agreed to close off that tap also."[13] But, there was no let up in cross-border terrorism. She took all assertions by Pakistan at its face value and questioned the veracity of the statements by India. Pakistan repeated these very arguments time and again.

As the first term of the Clinton Administration neared its end the threat of international terrorism appeared to be moving towards the centre of its concern. American officials frequently referred to it as serious threat to American security. On April 26, 1996 National Security Advisor Anthony Lake in his address to the Flecher School of law and diplomacy said: "a host of modern threats from terrorism to the weapons of mass destruction ignore national borders and undermine our security."[14] President Clinton in July 1996, referred to the fact that thirteen Arab countries for the first time had condemned terrorism in Israel as well as every other country in the Middle East. He added that "there are still those who desperately want the fighting to continue to preserve their own position, to serve their own priorities that terrorism is still alive and well there."[15]

It was attack on the two American embassies in Tanzania and Kenya, which was the defining moment for the American policy on international terrorism in South Asia. The American intelligence traced these attacks to a terrorist group, Al Qaid, which is led by Osama Bin Laden, a Saudi Arabian millionaire who had established his headquarters in Afghanistan. The US announced an award of 5 million dollars to the person who would give information leading to his arrest. His name was placed at the top of 'Most Wanted'. Earlier also attacks on American citizens had taken place in the Middle East. Some of these had spilled over into Europe but their source was in the Middle East. The bomb explosion at the World Trade Centre in New York by a terrorist outfit led by a blind Egyptian cleric and the attacks on the two embassies in eastern Africa showed the growing reach of fundamentalist Muslim terrorist organizations which were against the United States.

On August 20, exactly a week after the bodies of 12 Americans killed in East Africa were received, the United States launched missile attacks against the facilities of Osama Bin Laden in Khost, Afghanistan and on a chemical factory in Sudan, in which Osama was alleged to have some financial stakes. The factory, according to the Americans was producing a substance used in preparation of nerve gas. The charge was subsequently denied by the government of Sudan.

American Secretary of Defence William Cohen briefing the media on the missile attacks elaborated US policy:

The United States and the rest of the international community of civilized nations have made it clear time and again that violence, bloodshed and murderous acts by international terrorists will not be tolerated .... Our message is clear. There will be no sanctuary for terrorists and no limits to our resolve to defend American citizens and our interests, our ideals of democracy and law against these cowardly attacks ... Those who attack our people will find no safe place, no refuge, from the long arm of justice ... We are engaged in a difficult confrontation with the forces of international terrorism, the unique nature of terrorist threat, the lack of regard for international law, and the willingness to specifically target innocent civilians; transnational operations that defy traditional means of influence.[16]

While briefing the media on the missile attacks Secretary Cohen was addressing a wider audience outside. He wanted to assure Americans that the Administration was doing its best to prevent such attacks from further taking place. General Shelton in his remarks emphasized that the objective of the missile attacks was not to target Osama Bin Laden but to destroy his facilities and to disrupt his plans for further attacks.[17] Secretary of State Albright told the reporters on the same day: "Today the United States is asking every nation to stand publicly against those who perpetrate, finance, and otherwise support terrorism. We are asking governments to join us in taking necessary action to deter and defeat terrorism." These remarks were relevant in the context of South Asian cross-border terrorism. Samuel Berger, the National Security Advisor, pointed out that three months before the attacks on the two embassies, Osama had issued a *fatwa* against the United States indicating that they had targeted the United States for the attacks.[18] In his Oval Office remarks, President Clinton quoted Osama as stating "We do not differentiate between those dressed in military uniform and civilians. They are all targets." Besides placing emphasis on attacks on the civilians, the President warned the Americans that the missile attacks were neither the beginning nor the end of the struggle against international terrorism. It was going to be a long and arduous battle against terrorism.[19] In its battle against international terrorism the United States was looking for cooperation from other nations.

The nuclear explosions by India and Pakistan in May 1998, led the United States to believe that South Asia had become even a more dangerous place than before. If the Kashmir problem, the root cause of the tension between India and Pakistan, was not resolved it could become the flash point of a nuclear war in the region. Prime Minister Vajpayee's Lahore visit in February 1999, was therefore viewed as a step in the right direction as it could lead to meaningful negotiations between the two countries. The Kargil conflict, initiated by Pakistan, was seen as reversing the movement towards resolution of the problem. Pakistan was considered as solely responsible for the conflict and was severely criticized. Its assumption that if the conflict broke out, the international community, more particularly the United States would intervene proved to be illusory. Its contention that the Line of Control (LoC) was not clearly marked and that Pakistan's army was not involved was rejected. Faced with the humilitating prospect of being driven away from the positions it had occupied across the LoC, Nawaz Sharif rushed to the United States. He had a meeting with Clinton on July 4. The President persuaded him to withdraw behind the LoC. Both Nawaz Sharif and the army tried to blame each other for initiating the conflict. Later, President Clinton admitted that by forcing him to withdraw behind the LoC, he had contributed to the weakening of Nawaz Sharif's position. It was against the background of mounting tension between the army and the Prime Minister and the prospect of the army's take over of the government that the United States issued the warning that the overthrow of a democratically elected regime would not be acceptable to it.

The warning turned out to be ineffective and on October 12, 1999, the army overthrew the Government of Nawaz Sharif. Army's Chief of Staff, General Pervaiz Musharraf declared emergency in Pakistan and himself to be the Chief Executive Officer. After assuming office, General Musharraf gave several statements in which he tried to draw a line between *jihad* and international terrorism. According to him those who were fighting in Kashmir were freedom fighters and not terrorists.

There was no let up in American effort to bring Osama Bin Laden to justice either in the United States or any other country. On the one hand it closed 19 of its embassies on the ground of security, it also strengthened security of other embassies and American establishments abroad and on the other, asked the Taliban to hand over Osama Bin Laden to it or at least to expel him from Afghanistan. When the Taliban refused to accede to the American demand, President Clinton signed an executive order on July 5, imposing financial sanctions on the Taliban controlled Afghanistan. The US stated that it had received credible reports in June, that the outfit of Osama Bin Laden planned further attacks on US diplomatic missions similar to those carried out in 1988. According to a report published in the *Financial Times* on July 7, the US trade with the Taliban controlled Afghanistan was a meagre $25 million. It was unlikely to cause too much worry to the Taliban.[20]

The United States brought the issue before the UN Security Council which unanimously adopted resolution 1267 (1999) on October 15. The resolution drafted by US officials gave Taliban thirty days time to hand over Bin Laden otherwise the assets of Ariane, the national carrier of Afghanistan, were to be frozen and a flight ban on all its routes was to be imposed. On October 23, Taliban's Minister of Culture and Information, Amir Khan Motaqi announced that Taliban was willing to hold talks with the United States on the issue. However, he also insisted that Taliban wanted to resolve the issue taking US concern into consideration but the solution had to be within the framework of Islamic law and Afghan culture. Later, it was clarified that Bin Laden was a guest and therefore neither could be arrested nor could he be asked to leave. He could depart on his own.[21] The US could not agree to such a proposal. On November 14, the UN Security Council imposed limited sanctions against Afghanistan for its refusal to hand over Osama Bin Laden. Angry Afghans attacked several UN compounds in Kabul after the UN sanctions were imposed. In Pakistan two days before that on November 12, six rockets were fired at US embassy and UN buildings in Islamabad. Frustrated by the inability of the investigation to come up with information on the perpetrators of the crime, the United States issued public notice announcing award for those providing information leading to arrest of the culprits.[22]

On December 24, an Indian Airlines plane on its flight from Kathmandu to New Delhi was hijacked over the Indian air space with 158 passengers and crew aboard. The hijacked plane finally landed in Kandhar in Afghanistan. The hijackers demanded the release of Maulana

Masood Azhar, the ideologue of Harkat-ul Mujahideen (formerly known as Harkat-ul-Ansar) who had been in the Indian custody since 1992. The terrorist organization has made several attempts to get Azhar out of the Indian jail by perpetrating terrorist activities in India. Of the other two terrorists, Mustaq Ahmad Zaegar, was the co-founder of another outfit named al Ummar Mujahideen and the other was Ahmad Uma Sayeed Shaikh, a Pakistan born UK citizen who had been held since 1994, for kidnapping four Western tourists. The police had succeeded in rescuing the tourists and arresting Shaikh. In 1995, a terrorist organization calling itself Al Faran had abducted six Western tourists. One of the six escaped, one was murdered and there was no information regarding the other four. The Al Faran presumably also killed them. One American citizen was among these four. After this incident the United States had declared the Harkat-ul-Mujahideen to be a terrorist organization. The ultimate objective of these attempts was to get Azhar out of India. The Government of India had refused to negotiate the release of the abducted tourists in exchange for the terrorist whose release was being demanded. But it could not withstand the pressure generated by the relatives of the passengers of the hijacked plane and agreed to release the three terrorists. The three released terrorists travelled in the same plane, which took India's Foreign Minister Jaswant Singh to Kandhar. The sordid drama ended on December 31.

After his release Azhar surfaced in Pakistan, moved freely and delivered inflammatory speeches against India and the United States. One of the demands the United States made on General Musharraf was to ask him to curb the activities of the militants. On February 15, 2000 General Musharraf announced the plan for de-weaponization. Under it a ban was imposed on public display of guns. New licensing of the guns was also stopped. Reportedly Azhar was asked by the government not to give provocative speeches. In the United States doubts were expressed whether these small measures could effectively control or even reduce international terrorism. "...skeptics wonder how the anti-gun plan will work if the government continues to support religious militants. Heavily armed radical Islamic groups use Pakistan as a staging ground for attacks against the Indian controlled area of Kashmir. Musharraf himself calls the Kashmiri militants "freedom fighters" and their cause is extremely popular within the army... Analysts say that if the government places gun restrictions on the militants there could be serious political consequences for Musharraf—including a rift within the military," wrote *Newsweek*.[23] The General on the one hand wanted to appear reasonable and conciliatory to the United States and on the other hand keep the militants happy by conveying to them that he supported their *jihad* in Kashmir against India. His remarks that the centre of *jihad* has shifted from Afghanistan to Kashmir should be seen as a sop to the militants. The former Prime Minister Nawaz Sharif's wife Kulsoom said that she did not know when the *jihad* was declared. If she knew she would like to send her two sons to fight in it.[24] The United States on the other hand was concerned with the tremendous growth of militancy in Pakistan, especially its penetration of the army. The upbeat militants in Pakistan were in no mood to restrain themselves or to differentiate between what they termed as three major enemies of Islam: India, Israel and the United States.

President Clinton's official visit to South Asia took a long-time in materializing. After the army overthrew democratically elected government of Nawaz Sharif, the matter of including Pakistan in the itinerary of the President became the subject of an intense debate. Those opposing inclusion of Pakistan argued that the visit would send a wrong signal to the rest of the world, which will consider it as an endorsement of the army's coup. They pointed out that under similar circumstances President Carter had bypassed Pakistan in 1977. Congressman Frank Pallone, the co-chairman of the India Caucus, expressed the sentiment of those who were opposed to the President going to Pakistan. He rejected Pakistan's claim that the militants crossing the LoC and going to Kashmir were fighting a war of liberation. He termed it as "a violent terrorist campaign pure and simple." He pointed out that Musharraf had publicly pleaded support for the terrorist groups fighting in Jammu and Kashmir, the same groups that committed atrocities against Pandits. Speaking in the House of Representatives, Pallone said "the US must send an unequivocal message that this continued provocation in Kashmir by the Pakistani military regime is unacceptable. At a minimum, the President should not visit Pakistan during his trip to South Asia. The State Department should declare Pakistan a terrorist state and make it clear that there will be no further contact with the Pakistani government until it stops the provocative actions in Kashmir and take steps to restore democracy'.[25]

Those who supported inclusion of Pakistan pointed to important American interests in the country and argued in favour of remaining engaged. When Secretary of State Madeleine Albright went to the Capitol Hill to back up Foreign Affairs budget, three Senators spoke in favour of the inclusion of Pakistan in the itinerary. Senator Joseph Biden (D., Del.) conceded that within a few weeks the Kashmir problem could not be solved. But Musharraf could at least issue some statements on terrorism and restoration of democracy. The Senator wanted to know what issues Karl Inderfurth, Assistant Secretary of State, raised with Musharraf. Albright assured Biden that the United States had several conversations with Musharraf on all these issues and sought his cooperation in dealing with terrorism. Albright informed Senator Dodd that on the terrorist front there had been cooperation at some level "but not as much as we would like" Senator Sam Brownback (R., Ks), the Chairman of the Asia Pacific Subcommittee, agreed with Dodd that the President should go to Pakistan. We must remain engaged with Pakistan. "If you don't go to Pakistan... we move Pakistan further away from us." Albright conceded that "we need to view the area as one and deal with it in a more proactive manner." She paid a complement to the Government of India by saying "India has a strong government that is dealing with a lot of issues that have been of concern to us."[26]

After consultations with the aides and long discussions, the Administration worked out a compromise between the two contradictory positions. The President would stop for five hours on his return trip and would have a meeting with the Pakistan's Chief Executive and would address the people of Pakistan directly on television.

After the stunning and humiliating withdrawal behind the LoC in Kargil, the terrorist outfits intensified their activities in Jammu and Kashmir. They began to send suicide squads which attacked the headquarters of the Indian security forces. They were eventually killed but they inflicted heavy casualties on the Indian forces as well. Besides they continued to plant explosives in crowded places, which resulted in the death of innocent civilians. For these terrorist organizations like Harkat-ul-Mujahideen, Lashkar-a-Toiba and *Al Bader*, the border between Pakistan and Afghanistan simply did not exist. In face of intensified cross-border terrorism the Government of India declared that it would not agree to talk with Pakistan on Kashmir till it stopped its support to cross-border terrorist activities.

Before President Clinton's visit to South Asia, a Task Force headed by Richard Haas of the Brookings Institution and comprising of former US Ambassadors and academics specializing on South Asia submitted a report to the President. The report advised that he should let the leaders of Pakistan know that the United States would have no option except to declare it as a state sponsoring terrorism if they do not act more decisively against the threat of international terrorism. "You should voice strong criticism of their provocative posture towards the Kashmir insurgency, making it clear that they and their country would not be better off if Pakistan foments a war with India over Kashmir or anything else," the members said. They also stated that "there is a widely held view in Pakistan that if it can provoke enough of a crisis, the Unied States will be forced to step in and resolve the Kashmir matter in some manner that Pakistan would view as preferable to status quo." The President was advised to disabuse the leadership of the idea. The long-term goal of the United States should be "to persuade Pakistan on more responsible behaviour in the realm of terrorism.[27]

In her speech before the Asia Society a few days before the visit, Ms. Albright enumerated United States interest in Pakistan. Among others, she mentioned fighting terrorism. "The terrorist camps next door in Afghanistan directly threaten American lives. Because of Pakistan's influence with its neighbour, this matter will be high on the President's agenda. General Musharraf has offered to go to Afghanistan himself to discuss our concern about terrorism. We hope to hear from him more about it. And we want to see steps to address the effects of terror on Pakistan's neighbours, notably India."[28]

In an interview to *Newsweek* before the beginning of the visit, General Musharraf presented Pakistan's perspective. He said: "Every Muslim here is talking of *jihad* against India in Kashmir because Kashmir is not India. It is disputed territory." He asserted "I give full assurance that no group in Pakistan's soil is involved in terrorism" and insisted that Harkat-ul-Mujahideen, identified by the United States as a terrorist organization, was not a terrorist organization.[29] Harkat-ul-Mujahideen's leader Fazal-ur-Rehman Khalil also insisted like Musharraf: "We are not terrorists. We are mujahideens (holy warriors). Mujahideens fight only in Kashmir. It is a great injustice to us that America has declared us a terrorist organization." He added for good measure "terrorist acts against the civilians is against Islam. We don't believe in killing innocent civilians." Clearly defining the goal of the organization, he said that it was "To wrest from Hindu majority India its part of Kashmir, which is dominated by Muslims and merge it with Islamic Pakistan. If that takes a holy war with India, so be it."[30] Pakistan was soon to discover that its understanding of international terrorism was entirely at variance with the rest of the world.

Pakistan is one of the three countries, which recognize the Taliban regime in Afghanistan. The other two are Saudi Arabia and UAE. After Osama Bin Laden was given shelter by the Taliban, the Saudi Arabia withdrew its representatives. Osama Bin Laden was also a fugitive from Saudi Arabia. He was opposed to the pro-American policy being pursued by its ruling family. Pakistan had provided every possible assistance to the Taliban in its struggle for power against the Government of Burhanudin Rabbani and therefore had considerable influence over it.

On the night of March 20, the terrorists came to Chatti Singhpura, a Sikh village in Kashmir and killed 36 Sikhs in cold blood. Whatever motive the perpetrators of the crime might have, they brought the problem of cross-border terrorism into focus. In his speech to the Indian Parliament, President Clinton referred to this problem. He said: Americans understand the pain and the agony you went through during the Indian Airlines hijacking "... We grieve with you for the Sikhs who were killed in Kashmir and our heart goes to their families." He promised to work with India "a system of justice, to strengthen our cooperation against terror" and added "we must never relax our vigilance or allow the perpetrators to intimidate us into retreating from our democratic ideals."[31]

The massacre at Chatti Singhpura was timed to have an impact on Clinton's visit. India pointed its finger at the terrorist groups operating out of Pakistan. The police blamed it on Harkat-ul-Mujahideen and Laskar-e-Toiba. The charge was denied by these militant groups. Some people charged that the Indian security forces perpetrated it. The police was under pressure to arrest the perpetrators of the crime. They claimed to have five terrorists holed out in a building to be responsible for the assassinations. These were supposed to have been killed in the encounter. But the local people claimed that those killed were not terrorists but five people who had suddenly disappeared. Due to public pressure, the bodies of the 'terrorists' were exhumed and it was found that indeed they were not terrorists but the local people who were missing. The Indian security forces blotted their own record as they came under the cloud of suspicion. Thereafter a FIR was registered and an inquiry was begun to find out those responsible for the crime. On April 12, in Atlanta, Georgia, President Clinton said: "I am sure they were murdered because I was there. Those people lost their lives because I went to India and to Pakistan, "The people who don't want their turmoil to be eased, used my trip there as a pretext to highlight the difficulties and somebody, we don't know who killed 36 perfectly innocent people, who I might add had never been targeted in all the conflicts in Kashmir."[32] President Clinton did not point his finger at Pakistan but left others to draw their own conclusion as to who was responsible for the massacre at Chatti Singhpura.

A day earlier in an interview with the ABC, President Bill Clinton said that he was "troubled by the fact that there is so much violence. A lot of it is obviously propagated beyond the borders of Kashmir and I don't think the LoC is adequately respected." When the interviewer, Peter Jennings asked him: "and what would you tell those Kashmiris, or Pakistanis, who believe they are fighting to free the Muslim Kashmiris from Indian control?" He responded by saying: "I don't think there can be a military solution to Kashmir...I think that the best chance the Pakistanis have, if they want to have a positive impact on what they believe the legitimate concern of the people who live in that part of Kashmir that is in India, is through a dialogue, not through acts of violence and supporting acts of violence." In outlining American policy, he again reiterated his advice, "do not promote violence by third parties in Kashmir." While delineating the American policy, he said, that one important aspect of the policy was to oppose violence by the third parties. "But the most I do right now is to oppose violence, particularly violence by third parties within Kashmir and support the LoC," he affirmed. Equally important, if not more was his statement that, "we think that an ethnically diverse country like India cannot exist any more. I do not agree with that." Pakistan could not claim to integrate Kashmir simply because it was a Muslim majority area.

He did not charge the Government of Pakistan with supporting third parties perpetrating acts of violence. The nearest he came to it was when he said that he believed that "there are elements within Pakistan government that have supported those who have engaged in violence."[33]

Pakistan has been used to being treated on par with India by the United States. After the dates of the President's visit to South Asia were announced, Pakistan launched a campaign for being included in the itinerary of the visit. It went to the extent of saying that if it would be excluded it will result in destabilizing South Asia. It succeeded in getting five hours stop over. While in India, President Clinton was repeatedly asked what message he would convey to Pakistan. He responded by saying that his message would be same as told to India that the LoC must be respected, that it cannot be changed by force and negotiation was the only way to solve the tangled Kashmir issue. The United States cannot be dragged into the conflict he added. US National Security Advisor Sandy Berger indicated in Jaipur that the President would talk tough. President Clinton had one and a half hour meeting with General Musharraf. The impression gained from the briefings given by the senior American officials was that "cross-border terrorism did not figure as prominently or concretely in the talks as New Delhi might have hoped." He sought Pakistan's help in getting Osama Bin Laden handed over to the United States and tracing Don Hutchins, whom Al Faran had kidnapped several years ago.[34] In his television address to the people of Pakistan he was more forthright. He told them that Pakistan should desist from trying to redraw the border with blood and made a plea to intensify efforts to curb those who inflict terror." He said: "International sympathy, support and intervention cannot be won by provoking a bigger bloodier conflict. No matter how great the grievance, it is wrong to support attacks on civilians across the LoC." But Pakistan made no new offer to the President. People in Pakistan were greatly disappointed. Imran Khan, former cricketer turned politician, said that President Clinton's visit was sheer humiliation for the people of Pakistan and it would have been much better if he had not visited the country at all."[35]

In a press conference after President Clinton left Pakistan on March 25, General Musharraf repeatedly stressed that Pakistan was not involved in sending militants across the LoC. When a Western reporter ironically asked whether hundreds of militants in Muzaffarabad were attending a summer camp, he conceded that "some people were infiltrating but not with "our knowledge". On the issue of curbing cross border terrorism the General asked India to stop its atrocities in Kashmir, only then Pakistan would use its influence to moderate the activities of these groups.

He asserted that it was made clear (to the United States) that unilateral action on the issue by Pakistan was not possible."[36] This linkage was henceforth to be emphasized by all Pakistan officials. On Osama Bin Laden and training of terrorists in Afghanistan the rulers of Pakistan dispalyed reasonableness, offering to persuade Taliban though with a caveat. They were not sure whether they would succeed. After all, Afghanistan was an independent country. Minister of Interior Moinuddin Haider told the press that during his visit to the United States the FBI officials raised the Osama issue and he told them to hold direct talks with the Afghan government. However, he also said that he would raise the issue of terrorism and training of terrorists when his counterpart from Afghanistan visited Pakistan.[37]

The terrorist groups in Pakistan were angry with President Clinton. The cadres of Lashkar-e-Toiba bitterly remarked to the correspondent of the *Washington Post* that Clinton did not utter a word on "terrorism in uniform by Indian forces in Kashmir". To wage *jihad* was their "divinely ordained duty." The Post reported that President Clinton's speech had reinforced the determination of Harkat-ul-Mujahideen, Lashkar-e-Toiba and Hizbul Mujahideen. Prof. Hafiz Sayeed, founder of Markaz-al Dawa, a wing of the Lashkar was reported as saying "even if the government puts pressure on our Mujahideens, they will not give up Kashmir until the Indian troops leave Kashmir. Musharraf cannot stop it. It is not in his control." Other militant leaders voiced similar views. Syed Salahuddin, supreme commander of the Hizbul Mujahideen said, "We did not start our struggle on the advice of President Clinton and the US government. If somebody thinks that we will end it on their beckoning, it would be a fallacy."[38] After proclaiming himself the Chief Executive Officer Musharraf himself had given statements supporting *jihad* by the terrorist groups. He could not suddenly resile from his position.[39]

The United States was satisfied with the results of President Clinton's South Asia visit. It was beyond all expectations. An official described it as a 'perfect ten'. The Administration, however, felt the need to dispel the impression that either it had given up its non-proliferation agenda in South Asia or had tilted towards India and away from Pakistan. In an article, Madeleine Albright described India as the centerpiece of President's South Asia trip. Then she went on to state, "He delivered a strong message in this regard to both the capitals. He called for both the governments to respect the LoC that divides Kashmir, exercise restraint with respect to violence and to resume their dialogue." The impression in India on the contrary was that it was Pakistan that had crossed the LoC during the Kargil conflict and was promoting cross-border terrorism and therefore the message as only for Pakistan except the last part relating to dialogue. Albright also wrote that "in addition, the President stressed that the people of Kashmir must have a way to have their concerns and grievances addressed."[40]

Soon after the President Clinton's visit, the Indian government released the leaders of the All Party Hurriyat Conference (APHC) from the prison and expressed its willingness to enter into dialogue with them for the resolution of the Kashmir problem. This was a marked shift from its earlier position. The leaders of the APHC believed that they were released because of international pressure, more particularly of the United States.[41] Thomas Pickering Under Secretary of State for Political Affairs, in a press conference in India in May; considered the release to be an important step "as it opened the possibility of opening conversation with them." He hoped that "India would consider talking with others from Kashmir as well who might as well be able to contribute to a process of resolving the conflict and particularly beginning to understand and find ways to deal with the wishes of the people of Kashmir themselves". He assured that when he would go to Pakistan "I will have to confirm that the US too understand this situation and is prepared to make its own positive contribution."[42] Though Pickering did not specify what that contribution could be, it could well be restraining the militants.

The military regime as well for the people in Pakistan were greatly disappointed with President Clinton's visit. The regime realized its growing isolation from the international community on the issue of cross border terrorism in Kashmir. The Kargil misadventure and the high drama of hijacking of the Indian plane ensured that. Afghanistan and Pakistan were seen as the centre from which international terrorism was radiating not only in Kashmir but to far-off places like Bosnia, Chechnya and Central Asian republics. The world capitals were talking about terrorism and not about UN resolutions on Kashmir. India's diplomatic initiative to get an international convention on international terrorism was receiving support from a large number of countries.

The Pakistani military regime therefore decided to present itself as reasonable and conciliatory on the issue of cross-border terrorism. It assured the United States that it would, take steps to control the militant groups operating from Pakistan. It asked Masood Azhar, the militant leader for whose release the Indian plane was hijacked and was currently living in Pakistan, to tone down his rhetoric against the United States. For years, the Pakistani leadership had patronized militant organizations and encouraged them to carry out terrorist acts in Kashmir. They were lauded as freedom fighters and *Jihadis*. These fundamentalists Islamic groups had gained tremendous clout. They had even infiltrated the armed forces. The military regime found it difficult to challenge them. Pakistan, therefore spoke in two different voices. Foreign Minister Abdul Sattar told the *Telegraph* (London) that the government would take action against the militants crossing over into Kashmir. Sattar outlining his programme of action, stated that he would first identify *madarsas* where weapons training were given and then stop it. Then he would ask the Afghans to stop giving Pakistanis training in guerrilla warfare, ban the public display of arms and begin the programme of acquiring the millions of illegally held arms.[43] This was for the first time that a senior Pakistani official had spoken about the government's intention to stop the *jihadis* from crossing the LoC. Earlier, on March 26, General Musharraf had expressed his helplessness in stopping the *jihadis*. Striking a different note Pakistan's Minister of Interior Lt. General Moinudeen Haider told the FBI officials in Washington that the government could not ban Lashkar-e-Toiba and Harkat-ul-Mujahideen.[44] The Harkat-ul-Mujahideen had been declared as a terrorist organization by the United States. The ambivalence about *jihad* continues even now. The *New York Times* Magazine quoted General Musharraf as saying that "there is no question that terrorism and *jihad* are absolutely different. You in the west are allergic to *jihad* but it is a tolerant concept."[45]

In an interview with the *Times of India* in Cartegna on April 8, Sattar again brought up the issue of reciprocal action by India. He said that if there was militant violence there was equally reprehensible killing by the Indian security forces. He asked India to look at the Kashmir situation afresh and if India did that, Pakistan would be in a better position to advise moderation to militants. The linkages were first articulated by Musharraf on March 26. Pakistan, he had then said, "would find it easier to control militant groups operating from its soil if India also did its bit about the situation in Kashmir... It has to be a two-way street".[46]

In May, the US State Department brought out is Annual Report on Global Terrorism. It noted that the locus of terrorism against the American citizens had shifted from the Middle East to South Asia. There was lack of progress in the talks with the Taliban on terrorism and handing over of Osama Bin Laden or ending his asylum status. The report asked Pakistan to end support for harbouring and training terrorists and close the *madarsas* that served as conduit for terrorists. The report noted that the official Pakistani support for Kashmiri militant groups like Harkat-ul-Mujahideen, and said, "Kashmiri extremist groups continued to operate in Pakistan, raising funds and recruiting new cadre..." However, the report also recorded that Pakistan denied providing military training or material."[47]

While releasing the report the Secretary of State expressed the determination of the United States to carry out its campaign against terrorism with vigour. It wanted to work with countries that want to make progress "not by pointing finger but by linking arms."[48]

In the first week of June, an advisory panel appointed by the US Congress released its 64 page report on international terrorism. It recommended that Pakistan and Greece be declared as states "not cooperating fully against terrorism" under a statute Congress passed four years ago. The report stated that Pakistan has cooperated with counter terrorism but not consistently. It provided safe haven, transit and moral, political and diplomatic support to several groups engaged in terrorism. The nations not cooperating fully are barred from purchasing arms. This is a lower category than the state sponsoring terrorism. Surprisingly, Afghanistan is the only country in the category of states not cooperating fully.[49] The United States still cherishes the hope that Pakistan would come round and cooperate with the United States in counter terrorism.

There is no respite for India from cross-border terrorism. On the contrary it has increased significantly not only in numbers but in the use of sophisticated weapons as well. Though South Asia is currently the worst affected region, the United States views terrorism in its wider global perspective. It is alarmed by the rise of Islamic militancy in Pakistan and Afghanistan. Islamic militants trained in Pakistan were responsible for the blast in New York World Trade Center. Osama and his group, Al Qaida, organized their murderous assault from their hide outs in

Afghanistan and was also responsible for the blast in American embassies in East Africa. More attacks against American citizens have taken place in Pakistan than in some of the states which have been designated as states sponsoring terrorism. The United States still seeks the cooperation of the Government of Pakistan in curbing terrorism which is radiating from Afghanistan and Pakistan. Whether Pakistan would be able to do it or even curb the activities of the terrorists operating from its own territory is doubtful. The military regime could not even make minor procedural changes in the blasphemy law because of the opposition of the fundamentalist groups. In June, Moinuddin Haider declared in Washington that the Pakistani government was slowly going to curb the networks of militants not because of American pressure but it was in the country's own interest. Pakistan, he said "should become a progressive, modern and tolerant state". An unnamed official expressed doubts whether Pakistan would really go ahead and curb the militant network. Another high official believed the Administration felt that Islamabad's action reflected higher level of effort than seen recently.[50] But is it really enough and would it bring about the expected result. American policy on terrorism in South Asia swings between hope and frustration. Its vital security interest deters it from declaring Pakistan as a terrorist state. One wonders as to what would be the American position if Osama Bin Laden problem is solved one way or the other. Though India is getting support for its position, such as the adoption of an international convention on international terrorism, from many countries, ultimately it has to rely on its own capacity to curb cross-border terrorism. The sure way of doing it is to end the alienation of the people of Kashmir.

REFERENCES

1. CD Encarta 1998 Encyclopedia
2. *Ibid.*
3. George Bush and Brent Scow croft, *A World Transformed,* New York Alfred a. Knopf, 1998.
4. For a more detailed discussion see B.K. Shrivastava, "Kashmir Dispute and the Clinton Administration" in V.D. Chopra and M. Rasgotra (eds.), *Genesis of Regional Conflicts,* New Delhi : Gyan Publishing House, 1995, pp. 11-36.

5. John Malot's testimony before the subcommittee on Asia Pacific of the House Committee on Foreign Affairs on April, 20, 1993. Computer print out of the document.
6. *Times of India*, New Delhi, May 19, 1993.
7. Aziz Hanifa in *The Hindustan Times*, 7 June, 1991.
8. *Ibid.*, April 30 and July 31, 1993.
9. *Times of India*, May 1, 1993. J7
10. *Ibid.*, May 17, 1993.
11. Vinod Sharma, "US Warning to Pak, *The Hindustan Times*, July 18,1993.
12. Ms. Raphel's press briefing was on October 28, 1993, USIS, Foreign Center Briefings Washington, DC.
13. *The Hindustan Times*, March 12, 1993.
14. Official Text, New Delhi, USIS, 1996.
15. Speech on July 23, 1996, in San Francisco at the National Conference DNC Gala.
16. "Cohen, Shelton on Anti Terrorist Strikes," August 21. Wireless File, New Delhi: USIS, 1998.
17. *Ibid.*
18. "Briefings by Albright and Berger on Terrorist Sites" August 22, Wireless file, New Delhi: USIS, 1998.
19. "Clinton's Oval Office Remarks on Anti-Terrorist attacks" August 21, Official Text, New Delhi: USIS, 1998.
20. Kessings Record of World Events, Vol. 45, 'No. 7/8, July, 1998, p. 43064.
21. *Ibid.*, Vol. 45, No. 10, October 1999, p. 43212.
22. *The Hindu*, March 17, 2000.
23. *Newsweek*, quoted in *The Hindu*, March 17, 2000.
24. *The Hindu,* April 20, 2000.
25. *Ibid.*, February 10, 2000.
26. The debate on the inclusion of Pakistan continued till the President's itinerary was finally announced. Many more congressmen joined the debate, *The Hindu* during February and early March, frequently published their statements. .
27. Sridhar Krisnaswami, "Don't Corner India on N-Issue," *ibid.*, March 15, 2000.

28. "Albright's Remarks to Asia Society on President's S. Asia trip," March 14, Official Text, New Delhi: Public Relations Office of US embassy, 2000, Hereafter this source is cited as Official Text.
29. *The Hindu*, 13, 2000.
30. Kathy Gannon, "Mujahideen's Holy Cry Take Kashmir From India, *The Times of India*, March, 28, 2000.
31. President Clinton's address to Indian Parliament," March 23, 2000, Official Text.
32. *Times of India*, April 16, 2000.
33. "Clinton's Interview with ABC World News in New Delhi," March 23, 2000, Official Text.
34. Siddharth Vardrajan, "Restore Democracy," Respect Line of Control Clinton Tells Pakistan," *Times of India*, March 26, 2000.
35. *Times of India*, April 3, 2000.
36. Amit Baruah, "Hard Choice Before Pak People," *The Hindu*, March 26, 2000.
37. *Ibid.*, April 14, 2000.
38. Quoted in "First Person" *Times of India*, April 3, 2000.
40. Madeleine Albright's article was published in Diario Las Americas, Miami, Fla. On April 2, 2000, reprinted in Official Text April 5, 2000.
41. See the interview of Abdul Ghani Bhatt, leader of Muslim United Front which became part of the Hurriyat conference, by Vidya Subramaniam. Subramaniam asked "Was your release ordered under American pressure?" Bhatt replied: "Absolutely. This is why this wonder has happened." Earlier Omar Farooq had expressed similar views. *Times of India*, June 24, 2000.
42. Transcript of the press conference of Under Secretary of State For Political Affairs Thomas K. Pickering in New Delhi on May 25, 2000. Official Text, May 30, 2000.
43. *Times of India*, April 7, 2000.
44. *Ibid.*
45. Cited in *The Hindu*, June 26, 2000.
46. *The Times of India*, April 10, 2000.
47. "Patterns of Global Terrorism 1999, South Asia Overview." Official Text, May 2, 2000.
48. "Albright Says International Cooperation Needed to Combat Terrorism." Official Text, May 2, 2000.

49. The National Commission on Terrorism was appointed by the United States Congress in 1998 after the bombing of the American embassies in East Africa. It was headed by L. Paul Bremmer, 3d, who had served as American ambassador at large for counter terrorism. The commission submitted its report after six months of investigation. It made several suggestions for reorganization of the counter terrorism activities which was costing the United States a hefty sum of $10 billion dollars annually. *International Herald Tribune*, June 5 and 12, 2000. Also see Executive Summary: National Commission on Terrorism, Official Text, June 6, 2000.
50. *International Herald Tribune*, June 12, 2000.

CHAPTER 3

Towards a Political Economy of Intra State Conflicts

Rakesh Gupta

This paper focuses on the increasing incidence of Intra State Conflicts since 1945, especially since 1989, as products of the project: Modernity and Globalization. With reference to India it looks at the intra state wars in the mould of terrorist framework within the paradigm of modernity and globalization. The first part of the paper refers to the escalating incidence of intra state wars and their conceptualizations on the basis of death rates and the process of wars. The second part brings forth the argument that it is the current capitalist globalization that creates its own faultlines that coincide with internal fissures to produce the new turbulence and terrorist politics.

There is evidence to show that intra state conflicts have marked the post-Second World War international community. The escalation of intra state conflicts especially after the 1989 phase of the end of the Cold War and the decline of the USSR in 1991 shows that intra state conflicts are mostly post-modern in that they are non-Westphalen. The new characteristics of the contemporary wars are the following.

(1) The neo-realist paradigm posited anarchy externally and hierarchy internally. Now there is increasing evidence that the external anarchy is being replaced by order in the NATO countries and the internal hierarchy is being replaced by anarchy. This is most evidenced in the decline of the internal governing structures in face of internal wars. In some cases parallel authorities seem to be emerging and having sway.

(2) The fights are not between states. There are more than two parties to it internally.

(3) One of them is a regular force of the State—military, para-military and police.

(4) Contemporary wars are on issues of territoriality, scarce natural resources, for primordial, instrumental and constructivist use of ethnicity.

The constructivist theory suggests that ethnic constructs may be from within the webs of social interactions. As social interactions change the conceptions of ethnicity also evolve. Federal arrangements in Yugoslavia led to the growth of Yugoslav identity. Failure of federalism may force the same individuals to return to their more particular ethnic roots. In case of India we notice that the category of the secular Indian, made people identify themselves with Indian nationalism. With the rising attack on political nationalism from a religious and communal perspective, cultural nationalism is becoming the basis of identity of an individual and groups. To take an example, at the time of Indian independence, when Assam was asserting its linguistic identity there was no sub-regional linguistic demand for Bodo language to be recognised. But once the Assamese language was granted and the Indian nationalism was faced with the agitation in Assam in the context of immigration, the Bodos raised the issue of their language identity. This has led to inter-ethnic conflict and war.

(5) Conflict resolution is through military means, which has led to the introduction of the electoral process as in Punjab and Jammu and Kashmir in India. Apart from this, 28 wars ended during in post-World War phase in military victory. In 42 out of 61 cases it was the defending side that could repulse aggression.

(6) These wars are protracted that lasted for more than twenty years, e.g. Angola, Philippines, in Kurdistan, in Columbia and the longest lasting was in Myanmar starting in 1948 and the shortest was between Peru and Ecuador. In India the intra state conflict with reference to Nagaland is a continual one since the 1950s.

(7) Many of them are conducted with foreign intervention—both overt and covert.

(8) The anti-regime fighters are not regulars. They are mercenaries, women, children, and civilians.

(9) In some cases they are doctors, dentists, ancient holy men, farmers, professors and workers.

(10) The methods of warfare are gang wars, genocide, repression, ethnic cleansing, communal violence, assassinations, contamination, bomb blasts, hijackings, visits abroad to commit acts of terror and

accordingly select targets. In some cases the danger of use of weapons of mass destruction has been hinted.

Intra state wars are defined on two bases: quantitative and qualitative. The quantitative basis relates to the death casualties. Those wars that have less than 1000 death casualties are regarded as minor wars. Those wars in which there are 1000 deaths or more in their history but less in one year are intermediate and are major wars. The second and the third are in 1998. Most affected regions have been Asia and Africa. Out of 13 wars, nine are in Africa. During 1989-99 there were 108 conflicts in 73 locations and out of these 36 were active in 1998; 5 new ones broke out in 1998 and 7 were listed in 1997. Intra state conflicts escalated from 43 in 1989 to 92 in 1998. Those that had foreign intervention escalated from one in 1989 to 9 in 1998 in the total of 108 conflicts.

The qualitative dimension relates to the process of war. The Study group of the Hamburg University suggests that a war is a violent mass conflict, fulfilling the following three characteristics.

(a) Two or more armed forces are involved in fighting, where at least one of them is a regular-armed force of the government in power.
(b) Both sides have a centrally directed organisation of battles even if this means only organized defense or strategically planned attacks.
(c) The armed operations show a certain degree of continuity and are not simply spontaneous, occasional confrontations. The involved actors are acting according to a recognizable strategy.

A different process is highlighted in another study. Three questions are involved in this as well.

(a) Does the activity involve lethal force by a political entity for a political end?
(b) Does the activity involve the reciprocal use of lethal force against the cohesion of the employment of the targeted political entity?
(c) Does this activity involve the reciprocal use of lethal force by both sides employed in accordance with the principles of combat? These three involve the new face of wars in the context of post-nuclear war scenario.

From the perspective of Indian experience we notice that intra state conflicts involve (a) training of combatants in arms of the home country in the neighbouring country; (b) Existence of trained foreign mercenaries; (c) Financed by arms-drugs covert trade across borders with foreign planned actions to engage military forces or blast military buildings and civilian targets. The post-Kargil winter offensive showed the newness of the strategy in that the attacks and blasts were against military targets.

The three variants of war focus on the characteristics of the war process in intra state conflicts. The Hamburg school notes that the number of wars peaked in 1992 at 45. Secondly that 129 out of 196 wars during the period are intra state wars. Only 46 are classical inter state wars. The remaining cases are mixed, showing components of the two. Anti-regime wars and other intra state wars waged for secession or autonomy of regions have been the most frequent types of war in the last few decades.

In India there are no gang wars except in Bihar. There are no genocide campaigns as in Rwanda and no wars of decolonization in contrast to the ones in some Third World countries. It has anti-regime, ethno religious and intere-thnic wars. These have internal and external linkages. They are influenced by transnational autonomous movement of arms and drugs.

The writings in India have certain common features. Common to all these writings is a nuanced appraisal of the external linkages of this politics and its roots in bad governance. Invariably all of them have blamed the political class, or segments of it, the operation of the political process especially the politics of vote banks. There is a view that terrorism is high voltage party politics, which has found its expression in comments on the activities of the RSS, Akali Party, Congress party, National Conference, Naxalism and regional parties. The party system in India has shifted from one dominant party to coalition party governments at the Centre and to multi-party system through two-party system in the states. Terrorism begins after 1967, but especially after 1971. These two decades are related to the emergence of the coalition governments in the States, the crisis of the Congress government in the Centre and the victory of India against Pakistan, respectively. The political process was threatened to be disrupted by the demographic changes that were recognised both by the political parties in Assam and the then Chief Election Commissioner, S.L. Shakdher in 1978. It was prognosticated that by 1991 "...the state would have to reckon with the foreign nationals who may probably constitute a sizeable percentage, if not a majority of the population of state." And after the end of the Assam agitation the growth of ULFA and its rise, shows the growth of the politician-bureaucrat-contractor-smuggler nexus especially in the important routes of illegal cross-border trade including drug trade. There is the growth of an alternative personality as a result of this gang up, this is that of the warlord terrorist creamy layer.

They also perform government functions, namely, protection to life and property and provision of justice to local communities. They are described as criminal entrepreneurs and in their group life they represent the process and operations of organized crime. This elite has symbiotic relations to the market. The public distribution assets come to the open market to be sold in black. A major chunk of the rural development fund goes to them. As a result these centres become centres of employment and give salaries that are much higher than given to the police officers. All this leads to decline of government's capacity to perform certain roles, i.e., protect lives, enforce ordinary laws, reward and punish, collect taxes, carry out functions of financial management, to enforce discipline among state employees and to evoke a fear of sanctions.

This insightful analysis has parallels with analysis of other intra state conflicts, i.e., with the intra state wars' economy and war lordism. Wars have become in Columbia and Afghanistan, in Liberia and Myanmar avenues of livelihood. They have become a system of social production, which on the one hand is costly for the population but profitable for the minority. In this, war and trade are not mutually exclusive. The economy becomes a means of warfare. In the post-modern phase of intra state wars the actors in regional wars are more and more compelled to secure their material reproduction beyond inspired political support. With collapse of states, wars are essential resource gathering exercise. For this purpose new warlords emerge with or without external links. The warlord is the political and military leader and has become an entrepreneur whose activities are grounded in military power and the use of force. This is also true of Cambodia and Sri Lanka.

This internal situation coalesced with the external factor: Pakistan's ISI, China, Myanmar and Bangladesh. The transnational character of the terrorist menace as well as its all-India linkages in terms of the Pakistan factor, gun running, hawala, the role of the LTTE and the geographical reach of this spread of network to Europe is well-known. The analyses show that the trends in the spread of the network are not only foreign state centred as also they have assumed autonomous networks at the back of sovereign states. Every Indian commentator has referred to the transnational character of the terrorist and other intra state conflicts.

It is not adequate to say that the religious fanaticism is the factor, with or without the external linkage to fuel terrorism. Study of motivations can be helpful in understanding the cause of terrorism. The issue of motivations may lead one to look at Freudian analysis but it need not mutilate against the structural analysis. The former indicates the latter too in telling us about the setting as well as the motivating factors. The casual chain that leads to the commission of acts of terror is complex. There is consensus on the decision to go for terrorist act. It is influenced like any other political decision by psychological considerations and internal bargaining, as well as reasoned or strategic reactions to opportunities and constraints, perceived in the light of organisation's goals. It appears religion has not been the motivating factor for the terrorists. It could be good things of life, like making quick gains and having status symbols. This has been clear by the life led by Paresh Barua of ULFA. The girl who became a human bomb killing Rajiv Gandhi spent the last few days of her life by happily eating chicken biryani and watching movies. This also is true of certain terrorist leaders of Punjab, i.e., its creamy layer. There is no denying the fact that religion is used for mobilization purposes to cause the crisis of legitimacy especially by the rightwing forces. To look for sources of conflict in religions is like climbing a wrong wall. The dominant ideological practice of Hindu communalism is not very different from other cultural nationalism if no aim is do strike terror in the hearts of the audience.

The entire gamut of analyses indicates the crisis of functioning of Indian democracy with reference to political class, bureaucrats and business. Here decision making, policy formulation and its implementation are defined as a knee jerk response in terms of treating the phenomenon of terrorism as either a law and order problem or as problems of development funds. One leads to policing as policy option while the other leads to throwing money at the problem with the hope that this will solve the problem. However, this does not happen. Rather it leads to corruption and growth of criminal entrepreneurs or warlords. Corruption is a psychological-cum-structural problem which has direct links with the economy. Corruption is by and large official. Its beginning is with bribing the government to gain legitimate business. The symbiotic relationship is expressed as 'criminogenic asymmetries'. The existence of illegal markets furnish opportunities for illicit profit, reduce transparency, prevent accountability and weaken social controls. It allows for the flow of funds into covert activities. In the 1980s, we notice the Iran-contra Scandal in the USA. In the l980s in India, we notice the hawala transactions and their links with Bombay blasts and Kashmir conflict.

II

The post-Second World War globalization has crumbled and with it the liberal, socialist and national liberation agenda. The crisis of liberalism is clear in all the three if one looks at each of them as variants of the liberal paradigm. Even if one does not read the Marxist paradigm in this manner, one has to recognise that the three intellectual trends have now at the empirical level given way to the neo-liberal agenda to contain the newer tensions generated by larger groups of people coming on the global stage. The two hundred years of history of global transformation is marked by break-up of the world around new axis. These are in relation to macro and micro regions. The NAFTA and the European Union with a common currency live with micro regions that want to go beyond the confines of the state boundaries for purposes of integration. The macro-regions are political economic frameworks for capital accumulation and for organizing inter-regional competition for investment and shares of the world market. They also allow for development through internal struggles of different forms of capitalism. Macro-regionalism is one facet of globalization, one aspect of how a globalizing world is being restructured. The political and cultural implications of the new cultural movements have emerged around issues of feminism, environment and peace led by new social groups belonging to better sections of the society. At the political level a new restructuring might involve not local governance but integrated one, e.g., as in Switzerland. It has also meant massive and permanent unemployment within USA, Europe, Japan, further joined by erstwhile eastern bloc European countries. The welfare agenda of the state is eroded and neo-liberal agenda is being fostered and foistered. A typical case of what is happening in the new Europe is the instability of new states and the meltdown is Russia that began in the Russian Federation. The meltdown in Russia has meant spiraling of crime in which contract killings are followed by suicide. It has meant deconstruction of the Russian federal state into regional business and political elite that is dealing with Europe independently. The growth of an all-Russian elite stymieing state-building is the new reality that Russian President Putin faces. In the earlier East European polities a new managerial capitalism is developing.

The Third World is divided among three categories. These are the emerging countries (Korea, Taiwan, Singapore, along with China), marginalised countries of Latin America and India whose industrial capacities are not being utilized owing to lack of regional integration and whose growth rates become modest combined with huge inequalities. The African, Arab and the Islamic world are excluded ones in the international division of labour. In the last category are the swelling and pauperised people owing to their respective processes of modernization in the hitherto globalization process. Growth is non-existent even though some of them are extremely oil rich dollar countries. They are not active agents in the world system.

There is a need to distinguish between active and marginalized peripheries. China and India belong to the other category of active peripheries. These two are now at different stages of state capitalism with attendant problems of relative and absolute deprivation. Both have large chunks of society behind them especially China. Both have their inequalities, which in some cases transform into criminogenic asymmetries. Others who are at other levels of activism are countries in South-East Asia, and some Latin American countries. They have their own national projects that confront the global project. The marginalized peripheries have specific problems that do not let any light of existence come upon them. For example, in Africa which is the centre of major intra state conflicts, the story is one of failure. Along with the failure of socialism, there is the still larger and much more failure of whatever, in Africa, has been introduced as capitalism; the failure, that is to say, to solve by the methods or systems of capitalism, any great social or economic problem of indigenous African development. There is hopeless bankruptcy and by 2025, Africa will be a continental slum. Starvation is the naked truth. Petty crime, gang warfare, lineage solidarity among those not yet severely divorced from their rural origins, and a host of ingenious escape routes from starvation are witnessed. Civil society is fast vanishing. In certain states, capitalism has not even created the conditions of primitive accumulation, as in Zaire. In Rwanda, despite development funds, Hutu-Tutsi, genocide occurred because of the model of modernization that was followed.

The processes of globalization has created a global society which is a fractured one. It is divided by fractures of many kinds of income, wealth and class; of knowledge and power; of gender, lifestyle and culture; and of course of nation, race and ethnicity. The obstacles to social integration (of the kind classically understood by sociologists) are so many that even a comprehensive description and analysis would actually be very different. The advanced West is getting integrated but the Third World is disintegrating along faultlines created by the processes of modernity and globalization. Both globalizing and localizing forces together are responsible for weakening the state: its sovereignty made hollow by supra-state institutions, its authority being challenged by subnational minorities. Localization implies rise of ethnic identities and of communalisms and nationalisms not foreseen 40 years ago. All this seems to be related, in the sense that globalizing force triggers the localizing ethnic phenomena. The dissent in both the advanced West and deaccelerating Third World has a single source decentring of the individual and atomizing communities.

This has led to mixing of religion and politics. In case of Punjab, for example, religion and allegiance to the national state had achieved a strange linguistic diversity. This is true with other conflicts in India as well as in Sri Lanka, where the hostility of the Hindus and the Buddhists has been central to the conflict and intra state wars. Added to these are the cultural conflicts in the North-East and the religious conflict in Kashmir. Implicit in these wars of identity and integrity is a great language game. The post-modernist panorama about shifting language games is being staged in India. Take some examples of it: (a) nationalism was accepted as political; now it is acquiring a cultural connotation as Hindutva. (b) Patriotism was regarded as commitment to the modern nation state of India; now it is commitment to Hindu values. (c) Secularism meant no state religion, now it means commitment to Saffron enclosures. (d) Communalism meant earlier Hindu-Muslim riots; then it meant appeasing the Muslims. Similarly no-body believed under the new Constitution that the principle of national self-determination could be applied to India. Now this is disputed. Self-determination is now the focus of autonomy, sub-state nationalism though one is not sure if there is a linguistic agreement on the use of these words. There are different language games being played in the political forum e.g., the struggle between the state and the insurgents/militants communalists and terrorists with reference to the commitment to the Constitution. The shifting rules of these games create discord despite various accords signed for internal peace. This may well be a post-modern condition here since these language games also are related to the rejection of the dominant paradigm of development and ecological management. This post-modern condition is the other of the modern nation state. The Meta-narrative is caught in dissensus of political language games of discord in which consensus has to be arrived at incrementally by asserting the original elan of the Constitution. The management of the liberal agenda has to be dovetailed by such considerations if deconstruction has to be avoided. Today, the political man in India is caught in the nodal points of parallel language games that the current political discourse entails. If atomization of communities involves decentering of the individual around such political language games, then myopia of state policy and decentering of the individual psyche will be the gun-powder of new intra state conflicts.

CHAPTER 4

Latest Trends in Terrorism

Ashwini Kumar

This paper is not meant to be very comprehensive in its enumeration of various new trends in terrorism today in the world, but, it does touch on certain aspects as have been recently observed in terroristies activities globally—Japan, USA, Russia, Middle East, Afghanistan, Pakistan, India, Sri Lanka, IRA, ETA, etc. The main aspect of the new trend in terrorism is the recent erasure from the minds of the assassins and perpetrators, the inhibition which kept them back to destroy life and property with impunity, by the use of Weapons of Mass Destruction. The other aspect is a trend which shows that even as the number of terrorist acts are decreasing globally, their lethality is multiplying rapidly. A lot more innocent people are being killed than ever before. The third aspect which is very significant is the economy practiced in self-losses by terrorists who commit these heinous acts.

And lastly and perhaps the most significant factor is the growth of religious fundamentalism which makes it possible for the other three aspects to succeed. The singleton or two-somes who commit these horrific crimes today are deeply motivated religious zealots, who have been transformed into martyrs for a cause. An inordinate amount of fascination and horror has been generated by the suicide missions of Hizbullah, Hamas, LTTE and foreign mercenaries in Kashmir. I have studied deeply some of the suicide missions, and found their description very exaggerated, although their acts were daring and unique in character.

In 1986 one of the Ayatollahs, Mohammed Hussein decreed in his treatise, on, "Islam and Violence," "We don't see ourselves as terrorists, because we don't believe in terrorism.... We don't see resisting the occupier as a terrorist action. We see ourselves as Mujahideens who fight a Holy War (*jihad*) for the people. Faith, whether religious or political is all. To the individual terrorist, or supporter of terrorism a murder can be an expression of defence of freedom; a car bomb which kills civilians can be a blow struck in a war of liberation; a kidnapping and a murder can be a step towards justice." The intensity of conviction that justifies one mans justice at any price almost inevitably means that the freedom or justice of others will be ignored. Radicalism of social aims of the various terrorist groups in South Asia has gone far beyond the narrow nationalist or social aims of the previous groups.

Terrorism today has become accessible to anyone with a grievance, an agenda, a purpose or any idiosyncratic combination of three elements. The "Una-bomber" in America dispatched home made bombs so graphically described on websites on the internet, or the Arm Shirinkyo Cult in Japan, or the Oklahoma bomber, or hijacking of countless airliners and destroying them in the air, with awesome and lethal destruction of life and property are all of the same family. As the judge remarked in his judgement on the World Trade Centre bombing, that if the cyanide capsules had got released as they were meant to, the toxic effect of sodium cyanide would have killed thousands of New Yorkers. By comparison, there is no evidence that the secular terrorists of the past, like Carlos, Abu Nidal or Abu Abbas, ever contemplated the complete destruction of high rise buildings and the attendant massacre of hundreds of innocent lives.

In Kashmir recently there have been lethal attacks on Sikh habitations, and 'suicide' bombing on at least nine headquarters of the army and police, to demoralize rank and file by devastating their sanctum sanctorums. The growth of religious terrorism and its advent in recent times as a driving force behind the increasing lethality of international terrorism shatters some of the basic assumptions about terrorism and the violence they commit. The repeated attacks by terrorists on high profile political leaders in South Asia by suicide bombers raises serious questions about the continued relevance of much of the conventional wisdom on terrorism, particularly as it pertains to the potential future use of Weapons of Mass Destruction (WMD). In the past, most analyses of the possibility of mass indiscriminate killing involving chemical, biological, radiological or nuclear terrorism tended to discount it. It was argued that terrorists were ignorant of the intricacies of either developing or dispersing such weapons, attacks in suburbia Moscow by Chechens proved it otherwise. We had thought that terrorists wanted more people watching than dead, and we fondly believed that they had little interest in killing wantonly and indiscriminately. Bombay, Moscow, Chechnya, East Africa have disproved these fallacies. Incidents like the nerve gas attack on the Tokyo subway, the World Trade Centre in New York, Oklahoma City and the Bombay Stock Exchange destruction and U.S. Embassy bombings in East Africa have highlighted our dangerously anachronistic view. In sum, the compelling new motives notably those associated with religious terrorism, coupled with increasing access to critical information and key components, notably involving Weapons of Mass Destruction leading to enhanced terrorist activities, portends a demonic, sanguine and destructive period of violence ahead than we have seen before. It is only by keeping focused on this scenario that we can effectively tackle the security hazards and hurdles ahead.

To what extent will the stigma attached to the use of biological and chemical weapons influence terrorist groups ? It would be unrealistic to comprehend this at a time when many governments: are themselves undertaking major efforts to acquire such weapons. Governments know fully well that they have more to fear from using such weapons or merely threatening to do so.

Even if nationalistic passions and religious fanaticism should abate there is not much ground for optimism because the idea of a holy war that is a sacred duty and permits use of the most infernal weapons, causing unlimited bloodshed could also serve non-religious interests. Are the killers in Kashmir, or Algeria not pious Muslims, for according to Islam, women and children should not be killed or mutilated, even in the course of *jihad* ? In fact, leading historians believe that the Islamic conquest in the past was motivated more by secular than religious reasons.

Sadly we must realize that the terrorist may appear on the fringes of nearly any extremist movement. Even if radicals could become more moderate, there will be for the foreseeable future individuals firmly convinced of the words of Goethe's Mephistopheles, "all that comes into being is worthy of destruction." Neither madness nor fanaticism will vanish. Let us not forget that after the defeat of Iraq in the nineties, by U.N. forces, Islamist theorists and terrorists met in Cairo, and came to the conclusion that because of advancement in technology it was not possible to fight the West, which was far superior in it, and the only way to combat it, was by terrorism and assassination. All that one can hope is that the damage should be limited and the punishment to the transgressors will be even more devastating and deterrent than their atrocities.

When they met at a tavern, novelist Dostoevsky's character Ivan Karamazov, tells his brother Alyosha, that the happiness of all mankind, is not worth the tears of a tortured child.

New Trends

Suicide attacks have been carried as long as wars have been fought. There has been a certain mystique surrounding the killings by Japanese Kamikaze, and other acts perpetrated by Irish terrorism, Arab attacks in Israel, attacks on military headquarters in Kashmir, assassins of Prime Ministers in India, Israel and Sri Lanka. Chances of escape, were remote and it appears as if the assassins had a fascination for death. In Japanese cultural tradition suicide plays an essential role. The Kamikaze missions are well known. Beant Singh the murderer of Indira Gandhi considered himself as a martyr. Trucks full of explosives which were detonated have been driven into American installations in the Middle East and East Africa by dare-devils. Today it is difficult to think of terrorist movements that have not engaged in such missions. They have often been "veiled' by secret organizations, because the Quran frowns on such killings. Its mainly the radical Islamist groups which are behind these 'suicide' attacks, whether in East Africa, Turkey, Armenia, Lebanon, Israel, and Egypt. Sri Lanka is an exception.

The first real non-conventional terrorist event, the Sarin gas used by the Aum Shirinkyo Cult in March 1995, for the attack in the Tokyo sub-way, has broken the taboo in the use of the Weapons of Mass Destruction and this is a very significant event and precedent in the history of Modern Terrorism.

In 1984, a non-lethal but a disturbingly portentous incident occurred in the US (Town Dallas in Oregon). Followers of Bhagvan Rajneesh, poisoned the local reservoir and contaminated local restaurants and bars with Salmonella bacteria, in hope of debilitating the local population. The intention was to influence and rig municipal elections that were due, in the cults favour. The plot failed but the bacterial poison was dispersed.

The release of deadly nerve gas in the Tokyo underground in March 1995, confirmed this fear, and forms a historical watershed in terrorist tactics and weaponry. Previously most terrorists had shown aversion to the esoteric and exotic Weapons of Mass Destruction. They did not want to depart from the conservative methods of operation. The Aum Shirinkyo (supreme truth) represents a new kind of threat in terrorism, by a mass religious movement, motivated by a mystical, almost transcendental divinely inspired imperative. The group was founded by Shoko Asahara —partially blind, owner of a yoga school with a rather blemished record for petty infringements of law. He had messianic inclinations and gave out that he had been sent by God to lead an army. A crank historian acquaintance convinced him, that Armageddon would come before the end of the 20th century and no one would survive it, except a "small merciful, godly race". Asahara dreamt that he was the leader of this 'small merciful army'. With a beginning of just ten followers he began his cult, and very soon built it into a 2,00,000 force. This philosophy was a strange mixture of Buddhism and Hinduism, and attracted a youthful host of frustrated, alienated Japanese youth, still nursing the wounds of defeat in a nuclear holocaust. And the leader of the race was the Japanese—Asahara himself.

By the end of 1987 Aum had 150 member centres with branches all over Japan; and with additional member centres in other countries.

From the start Asahara preached about the inevitability of an impending apocalypse, stressing the unique messianic mission—they called him the saviour of the 20th century. Emphasis was given on Shiva the Hindu God of destruction and subsequent regeneration. The laboratory where the chemicals for Sarin gas were manufactured had a 15 foot image of Shiva. Even the French 16th century astrologer Nostradamus was quoted for the coming apocalypse. The only way to avert the tragedy was to establish an Aum set-up all over Japan and the world. The U.S. was considered the main enemy, and it was announced that Japan would be soon destroyed by an atomic attack—a nuclear desert would be created. A paranoia expectation was declared amongst the cult; and there were more than 10,000 Japanese militia men, who were cult followers when the party was banned.

The Aum also embarked on a programme to acquire an array of conventional and non-conventional arms. Scientists were recruited from a number of countries, including two Russian nuclear scientist. The cults assets of one billion dollars were admittedly used to get the best technicians from all over the world. Tank, helicopter, and fighter planes parts were collected and purchased. A M-117 helicopter was recovered by the police when their headquarters were raided.

Aums intentions included development of chemical and biochemical weapons. When the police raided their headquarters in 1985, they found a huge array of chemical and biological warfare agents. It had also an unrequited nuclear programme. To this end the Aum group had purchased 5,00,000 acre sheep farm in a remote part of Western Australia. Here they had hoped to mine uranium to ship back to its laboratories in Japan, enrich it with the help of its scientists and convert it to weapon grade. The massive explosion that occurred near Aum's Australian holdings on the 28th May 1993, and which lit the whole sky, has still remained unworked but was obviously related to their nuclear research.

"With the use of Sarin Gas we will eliminate major cities in the world" Asahara had declared. On March 1995 when they attacked the Tokyo streets, it was much earlier than what they had planned. They struck early because it was rumored by their informants inside the government, that police raids were imminent. Actually it was a surprise move and I know it as a fact that the police were itself surprised.

The world does not know even now that Aum had struck in 1990 with biological germs near Tokyo. The attack miscarried. At Matsumoto near Nagano they had tried to kill judges who were trying their cases with gas, and nearly succeeded. To this day the Japanese police never disclosed that this was connected with the Aum Cult.

It is obvious that every day brings to light a new adversary to the established order. These new entities are sometime so ethereal that a complete picture of them will never be known.

We are it seems on the fringes of new discoveries of clandestine terrorism. One cannot predict the effect that this pivotal symbolic watershed where WMD's have actually been used, will have on the course of future terrorism. Will there be further attempts to implement the Armageddon by the apocalypse use of weapons of mass destruction ? The pattern used by religious inspired terrorism over the past few years alone suggests the potential for still more and even greater acts of violence that cannot be prudently discounted.

With the collapse of the Soviet Bloc and Eastern Europe in the early 1990s it was assumed that the international system was on the threshold of an era of peace and stability. However, the initial euphoria that was evoked by the collapse of the authoritarian regimes of Central and Eastern

Europe was replaced by a growing sense of unease and the clashes over economic, ethnic, territorial, religious and political issues were created as a result of the lifting of the totalitarian lid that had previously kept the tensions capped. From the perspective of global terrorism such realities have been reflected by the dramatic increase in the incidence of this type of violence. In the nineties worldwide domestic and international levels of terrorism were higher than 70's and 80's.

The information technology has greatly enhanced the ability of the groups to spread terror and thus achieve the desired emotional response that made this particular mode of violence a psychologically effective weapon. Modern media networks have provided terrorists with readymade communication channels that allow them to frankly and effectively spread the messages of death, destruction and mayhem, to watching and listening audiences both at home and abroad. The transformed world networks have provided an effective publicity platform for even the most far flung and isolated terrorist groups. This is from Blacks in South Africa to Palestinians in West Asia and from Catholics in Northern Ireland, to Basques in Spain and Kurds in Turkey. The reporting and televising of spectacular terrorist incidents has almost certainly a contagious effect on other disaffected groups. There is overwhelming evidence to suggest that various types of media portrayals are immediately followed by 'copy cat' commissions.

Islamic Fundamentalism

Two main factors have driven the focus of militant Islamic fundamentalism. First, is the external aid that extremist organizations here received from Iran and Sudan. Since coming to power both the Tehran and Khartoum forum, fundamentalist regimes have taken a big leap beyond other Islamic revolutionaries. Iran and Sudan are thought to have established strong financial and operational links with numerous Islamic groups in West Asia and Africa such as HAMAS in the Israeli occupied territories, GAMA'S EL-Islamia in Egypt, Muhammads Army in Jordan and the NAHADA movement in Tunisia and Islamic Salvation fronts in Algeria. It is estimated that Iran supplies almost 30 million dollars worth of training, cash and arms to these other extremist Muslim groups around the world.

Religious Terrorism

Religious Terrorism-a New Trend

It is worth noting that nationalism and ethnicism remains the main motivation for domestic terrorism. In 1995, 42 per cent of the known active international terrorist groups had a predominantly religious component of motivation. These figures exclude organizations, such as the IRA, ETA or Armenian groups, that clearly have a religious element but whose main impetus is nationalist. The upsurge in religious terrorism, especially from 1988, can in part be attributed to the widespread belief that a group's respective religion lies at a vital historical point. This stems from increased globalization, and the perceived erosion of traditional values, along with widespread economic and political upheaval and inequality, leading to heightened feelings of fragility, instability and uncertainty about the future. Terrorists feel the need to preserve their religious identity, but also believe that there is the opportunity to fundamentally alter their future. Religion has become an instrument for political action in the eyes of clerical leaders. The more activist ideologues increase their support, strengthen the group and act as a legitimating force for the use of violence through their theological justifications for terrorism.

In 1968, none of the 11 identifiable active terrorist groups could be classed as religious. The importance of religion in enhancing the likelihood of violence being employed by some groups is that it has the ability to inspire total loyalty and commitment, and as has been seen in the case of secular terrorism, such an uncompromisingly holistic attitude is a prime factor in the utilization of force as a valid means. The intensity of feeling that religion engenders also mitigates against ready resolutions to religious disputes and encourages more violent solutions that might otherwise have been the case.

Martyrdom is important for the likelihood of new nuclear and chemical/biological terrorism in two respects. Firstly, it shows that there are individuals who might be willing to sacrifice themselves to ensure that a nuclear attack was executed effectively. Given the potential affect of such an attack, if the terrorist had to have the chance to escape, it would require more time than is the case with a conventional attack, increasing the possibility that the device might be discovered in the meantime. Secondly, it is clear that martyrdom is solely the province of extremely motivated suicidebent terrorist individuals willing to sacrifice themselves for such an attack. They could also come from a much wider secular background.

The Tokyo attack was unusual not because it was an attempt to kill hundreds of people, although, in this century fewer than a dozen incidents have resulted in over 100 deaths, but rather because of the method chosen. Tokyo was by far the most serious sub-state actor to use non-conventional weaponry. However, most terrorist groups do not want to cause mass killings; and conventional means remain sufficient to achieve their objectives. There is the added disincentive for using high level non-conventional weapons in that the results are highly unpredictable, and radiological, chemical or biological effects continue to occur over a long time, denying the immediacy that many terrorists seek and providing a residue of counter-productive publicity long after the event. However, this should not be overstated as a reason against terrorist use of WMD because this element of uncertainty exists, to some extent, with any weapon and where the objective is to maximize casualities, while concept of uncertainty is largely meaningless.

It is worth considering chemical and biological weapons as alternatives to nuclear devices. Both have the potential to cause a range of effects, varying from mass-murder to incapacitating a small portion of the population. The Aum cult undoubtedly sought to cause as many fatalities as possible, but was betrayed in its objective by the poor quality of the Sarin gas the dispersal device that they employed. However, prior to Aum's assault, even if they had the opportunity and the resources to launch such an attack, terrorists have abstained from doing so. The ramifications of Aum's attack on future uses to nuclear, chemical or biological weapons by terrorists is far from clear.

The factors that mitigate against most terrorists, and especially those with left-wing or nationalist-separatist motivations, resorting to nuclear weapons apply equally to both biological and chemical weapons. Aum represented a new type of terrorist group, being both apocalyptic and, in part criminal, since they sought to extort money from both members and non-members to promote the activities of the organization. However, even groups such as Aum are not certain to resort to these weapons again. Possibly, the cult represented a unique combination of factors, motivated by revenge, apocalyptic desires and material greed. It would be unwise, to preclude the possibility that they were not unique and may represent the pattern of future attempts to produce mass-destructive terrorism. Many terrorist groups mimic other groups' actions, so the fact that one chemical attack has occurred would significantly increase the likelihood of another such incident.

Both chemical and biological weapons would have some appeal for a terrorist group intent on a non-conventional attack because compared to a nuclear weapon, chemical and biological weapons have the potential to be cheap and are lethal in small quantities, easing the problems of production, concealment, transportation and delivery. A biological weapon attack would almost certainly be undetectable, both because it is odourless, colourless, and tasteless and because its effects would not be manifest for hours or even days, depending on the agent used. Therefore, the likelihood would be that if the attack was conducted covertly, its perpetrators would have ample time to make their escape, increasing the possibility that they might 'get away with it'. In addition due to the possibility of protesting and in spite of the various uncertainties, they are still likely to be more reliable than a nuclear weapon. Furthermore, the lead time between 'desiring and acquiring' a useful capability is much shorter for chemical weapons than for their nuclear equivalent. Shoko Asahara ordered his cult to develop chemical weapons in 1993, only slightly over a year before the Tokyo attack. Thus, the most immediate terrorist threat is from a chemical or biological weapons attack.

This does not preclude the possibility that terrorists might covertly acquire their capability from a states' stockpile. In addition to states such as Iraq, Syria, Libya, and North Korea, all of which possess such a supply, Russia alone has as per its own admission, 40,000 metric tons of chemical-warfare agents. These are stored at seven declared sites, at least four of which have recently been found to have lax security, closely replicating the situation at a number of storage sites for nuclear material. Terrorists' other option would be to manufacture the chemical or biological weapons themselves. Although this would not be an easy process, depending on the agents being manufactured, neither would it be an impossible one particularly for groups that like Aum had sufficient financial and technical resources.

Aum had faced in particular the difficulty in finding an effective means of delivery for their chemical weapons. This problem is especially acute due to the highly hazardous nature of the agents. This risk could be minimized by using 'binary' chemical weapons since they are easier to produce, transport and use. This means that two precursor chemicals are stored separately and then mixed to form the agent immediately before use. There are methods to achieve this mixing process automatically or by remote-control but for Aum, these proved technologically too difficult and unreliable. The most likely possibility is an extremely hazardous procedure and one that partly defeats the purpose of separating the chemicals initially.

The increased availability of fissile material has probably had relatively little impact on the likelihood of a terrorist nuclear bomb: it would still be difficult and expensive to build, hence the credibility of all but a cult group using such a device remains low. Aum may have investigated the possibility of building a nuclear bomb. But they were still a long way from achieving it, and consequently chose a more straightforward method of creating terror. However, fissile material availability has made the feasibility and thus the credibility of a threat or hoax involving radiological terrorism a much more real possibility, one that will have to be taken seriously and would give considerable leverage to any group using such a threat. This may mean that the arguments against any secular sub-state actor to use non-conventional means are lessened. Religious terrorism is undoubtedly on the increase, but for the above reasons the attack in Moscow and possibly the threat to New York, is the most likely model for nuclear terrorism in the near future. Aum set a precedent being the first terrorist attempt as an act of mass destruction using non-conventional means, it breaks a taboo and has psychological import. Others will ask whether such tactics should be adopted by them. It is now more likely that at least some will say yes. According to some writers, 'We have definitely crossed a threshold. This is the cutting edge of hi-tech terrorism for the year 2000 and beyond. It is a nightmarish scenario that people have quietly talked about for years, coming true'.

However, even when the utility of terrorism, as an instrument with which to achieve strategic objectives has declined, many groups remain committed to the military option. Faced with the failure of their campaign, terrorist groups face series of unpalatable choices, all of which may ultimately risk the destruction of the group. Since terrorist organizations defined themselves in terms of their ability to pursue twin-track strategies, their solution to the threat of extinction is likely to be further violence. In such circumstances, it is not unreasonable to suggest that an escalation of violence is the most plausible outcome. Such an assertion is supported by examples such as the IRA's campaign, particularly in the 1970s, or of the Tamil Tigers recently. In the latter example, as Sri Lankan Government forces compelled a Tamil retreat, the violence of Tiger attacks in Colombo increased, culminating in devastating bombings.

As a group declines, it may be tempted to attempt a 'spectacular' showdown such as the Tamil bombings, to achieve publicity and thus to reassert its cause and attract the much-needed support from potential sympathizers, impressed with the group's capability and commitment to its objectives. While the need for publicity is by no means universal, it is a common motivation for many organizations. It emphasizes their power and importance, to reinforce, the psycho-dynamics of terrorism that make such groups attractive to their members in the first instance. This need to set themselves apart, means that terrorists must either resort to new tactics or adopt new level of violence. The series of hijacking of airlines in 1968 by the PFLP was an example of the former, and any act of mass-destructive terrorism would be an example of both.

Terrorism in general is becoming increasingly lethal: in 1995, 29 per cent of incidents resulted in at least one fatality, the highest percentage since 1965. During the 1980s, the number of terrorist incidents rose by roughly 30 per cent compared to the 1970s; fatalities rose by 100 per cent in the same period. Religious terrorism accounts for a disproportionate amount of this. There are a number of reasons for this. In the case of religious terrorism, violence is perceived to be part of an all-encompassing struggle between good and evil. The stakes involved legitimize the means used by religious terrorists to defend their faith and even justify acts of self-sacrifice in that protection. Although such religious violence is aimed at preserving purity within that religion, it is also directed against external sources of corruption which threaten to erode that purity. It is entirely possible that in order to protect their faith from such an influence, adherents might resort to extreme levels of violence, especially given the totalistic nature of many religious beliefs.

There can be no doubt that the attraction of using nuclear weapons has had some impact on the tactical decisions of would-be terrorists. The RAF talked about using a nuclear bomb because they perceived it to be the 'ultimate thing'. However, while there are concrete examples of radiological terrorism, such as the three men accused of using radioactive material against Republican Party officials and the chief investigator for Brookhaven in New York, or the Russian Mafia's use of gamma rays emitting pellets for an assassination, Moscow business using gamma rays emitting pellets, there are a few clear-cut cases, apart from Aum, of terrorists trying to construct a nuclear-yield weapon. Instead, most examples of non-conventional attempts to cause mass casualities have involved chemical or biological weapons, as Aum ultimately used, or the alleged plot by the World Trade Centre bombers to use sodium cyanide simultaneously with a conventional bomb, so as to kill any survivors of the explosion. This suggests that chemical and biological weapons are readily accessible than nuclear-yield weapons for mass-destructive terrorism. Although both chemical and biological weapons share the problem, with nuclear-yield weapons of having an uncertain effect, they have the advantage of being cheaper to produce and may be lethal in small quantities, easing the production process. Furthermore, although, this process is not simple particularly in 'weaponising' the agent, chemical and biological weapons could be produced more rapidly and require less specialist equipment and expertise than a nuclear weapon would necessitate. Consequently, a chemical or biological weapon is a more likely method than a nuclear yield device for terrorists to achieve an attack in which mass causalities are the primary objective. However, where the objective is to set the group apart from others and to guarantee that the group continues to be noticed, acknowledged as an important entity, radiological terrorism, combining the coercive advantage of being 'nuclear', with ease of production and access to raw materials may be the most likely form of non-conventional terrorism.

The collapse of the Soviet Union has undoubtedly made the opportunities for nuclear terrorism significantly greater but even if these increased, chances for micro-proliferation had not existed, the threat of nuclear terrorism would still be significantly greater than it was fifteen years ago.

The key point is that terrorism is growing in its lethality. How individual groups achieve that is partly an instrumental decision based on the objectives of the group, and partly a matter of opportunism. Mass-destructive terror, is now the greatest threat terrorism posesses. A terrorist use of a nuclear-yield device is the most devastating type of terrorism conceivable and a radiological attack is the most likely variety of non-conventional terrorism. It is a danger that cannot be ignored; since it is not the current proliferation problem but rather the current psycho-dynamics of terrorist groups combined with the nature of terrorism in the last decade that makes the threat so potent. It will not recede in the foreseeable future.

CHAPTER 5

Rise of Terrorism and Secessionism in the 21st Century: Conflicting Perceptions

V.D. Chopra

In the beginning of the 21st century, it has become abundantly clear that secessionism and terrorism have assumed a dangerous proportion. A large number of countries are facing this menace which threatens their integrity and stability. In this sense it will not be incorrect to say that in the beginning of the present century, this ominous development will be the biggest challenge to the international community. Though terrorism did manifest itself in various forms in the twentieth century, the nature and content of both secessionism and terrorism have undergone a basic change.

In a period of globalization of economy and polity and when the concept of one world based on equality and social justice has begun to emerge, secessionism and terrorism have raised their ugly heads to reverse this process. It will therefore, be incorrect to trace this trend only to Islamic fundamentalism. It has different variants — Islamic, Jewish, Hindutva and ethnic. This point needs to be emphasized because the Western scholars and political elite look at this problem mereiy in terms of Muslim fundamentalism.

The rise of secessionism and terrorism particularly in multi-cultural, multi- religious and multi-ethnic societies has deeper roots than what appears on the surface. That explains why the Western world has a narrow view about this danger and therefore in actual practice takes a partisan stand. Let us examine these aspects.

At the moment there are three hot spots of secessionism and terrorism, namely India, Yugoslavia and Russian Republic. As far as India is concerned, cross-border terrorism carried out by Pakistan particularly by ISI, has been going on for nearly two decades in Jammu and Kashmir, Punjab and North-East region. There is clear evidence that this threat to India's stability and integrity has assumed a new dimension, particularly after the military coup in Pakistan. This is confirmed by a series of developments in Jammu and Kashmir in the post-Kargil period. Attacks on the security forces have been intensified. Mass killings of religious minorities, both Hindus and Sikhs in Jammu and Kashmir have a clear motivation. The objective is to drive out religious minorities from this state under the fake slogan of *'jihad'*.

In the initial stages, the ruling elite or the developed nations, the United States in particular, took a position of equidistance between India and Pakistan. However, in the recent period there has been a shift in the stand of the developed nations. Nonetheless the harsh reality is that the developed nations are hesitant to declare Pakistan and Afghanistan, the two main springboards of organized terrorism as terrorist states. The stand of the developed nations and the half-hearted measures and verbal denunciation will not help the international community in identifying and curbing terrorism. This double-talk is not confined only to cross-border terrorism being organized in India by Pakistan and Afghanistan. It is reflected in the policies of the developed nations on the events in the Balkans and Russian Republic.

In Kosovo, the site of what was suspected to be the country's largest mass grave. To date, however, the International War Crimes Tribunal at The Hague has had to admit that its investigation of the site has turned up with no evidence of bodies or of any wrongdoing by the Serbs. This shows how the ethnic conflicts in Kosovo was blown out of proportion to pave the way for an intervention by the NATO.

Back in June 1999, in the full heat of the Balkan summer, some NATO officials and local residents claimed that the deep shafts, the vats and the hydrochloric acid tanks of the Trepca mining complex where gold, silver, lead and zinc are extracted were used as disposal site to hide the bodies of ethnic Albanians killed by Serbian forces. But this claim has turned out to be half-truth. It was alleged that as many as 1,000 bodies a day had been burnt in the mine in two months.

"There are Kosovar witnesses and still photos of these trucks," an anonymous American official was quoted as saying in *Koha Ditore*, the Kosovo Albanian daily, giving the report the imprint of authenticity.

The idea that the Serbs were using Trepca to hide the evidence of mass killings quickly caught on in Western newspapers. "Trepca—the name will live alongside those of Belson, Auschwitz and Treblinka," said *The Mirror.* Another report in *The New York Times* said residents on the edge of the mine reported an "unusual, pungent, bittersweet smell, which they assumed to be burning bodies." However; the subsequent evidence proves that this was far from reality.

Trepca is near the town of Kosovska Mitrovica, in the sector of Kosovo assigned to the French forces. It was one of the first places to be searched by NATO peacekeeping troops after the war ended. And the French troops who entered the mines were certainly suspicious of Serb activities. They informed The Hague Tribunal (ICTY) that they had uncovered piles of Albanians' clothing, shoes, family photographs and identity documents when they searched the smelting area and mine shafts. The French also found that the vats had been cleaned before the Serb troops stationed in the complex had left, suggesting they had destroyed the evidence of their crimes.

Trepca was clearly earmarked to be one of the keys to documenting mass killings of ethnic Albanians by Serbs in Kosovo and the mine was immediately made a priority investigation site for the ICTY's forensic scientists, who began arriving in Kosovo in droves in June, 1999 on the heels of the NATO victory. Their mission was to conduct a war crimes investigation unprecedented in military history.

The finding by the tribunal that there are no bodies at Trepca and the fact that another infamous mass grave site at Ljubenic, near Pec, which was widely publicized as containing 350 bodies and which turned out to hold only fire, are now being presented as evidence that the number of civilian ethnic Albanians killed by the Serbs is much lower than NATO had originally claimed.

One analysis by Stratfor, a private analytical group that looked at reports from the FBI and other police agencies sent to Kosovo to exhume bodies, suggests that the final death toll might be in the hundreds, not thousands. And the estimate of a Spanish forensic surgeon, Emilio Perez Pujol, who had just returned home, disillusioned after investigating war crimes in Kosovo, is that as few as 2,500 civilians were killed. He said: "I calculate that the final figure of dead in Kosovo will be 2,500 at the most. This includes lots of strange deaths that cannot be blamed on anyone in particular."

In an outspoken interview, Pujol complained he had been sent to head a large investigation team attached to the ICTY consisting of pathologists and police specialists, to work in the north of the country. But he found that what was publicized as a search for mass grave was "a semantic pirouette by the war propaganda machines, because we did not find one—not one mass grave."

Pujol said his team had material for 2,000 autopsies and had expected to be in Kosovo for two-and-a-half months. But in mid-September, after digging up 97 bodies in a cemetery, which showed "no signs of mutilation or torture, but rather death from shrapnel or bullets," he decided to go home. This speaks for itself and needs no comments.

These cold facts have raised a controversy in the United States and Britain. The central question being asked is why the scale of deaths was exaggerated.

Moscow's military operation against secessionist forces in Chechnya has raised a new controversy in the West. Russian political leadership has accused the United States of trying to undermine the integrity of the country. It has not left at that. It feels that by indirectly giving moral support to the secessionist forces, attempts are being made to oust Russia from the Caucasus.

Addressing a meeting on November 12, 1999, Defence Minister Marshal Igor-Sergeyev said that the US and NATO were seeking to "weaken Russia's international positions and oust it from strategically important regions, above all, the Caspian, Trans-Caucasus and Central Asia."

In fact, Kremlin has bluntly underlined that by morally supporting forces, Washington is striving to "establish its full control" over the region. This view of US policy is being linked by Moscow to a new concept of the United States, which empowers the NATO to conduct combat operations throughout the world where it feels human rights are being trampled upon. This endangers the sovereignty, inviolability of frontiers and national interests of other states.

The moral of the situation is that this double-talk about the secessionist and terrorist forces conceals more than what it reveals. The Indian political leadership should draw appropriate lessons from this tendency.

There is no doubt that in the recent past the Western stand on cross-border terrorism being organized by Pakistan and Afghanistan in India has undergone a shift. Nonetheless, this is also a fact of life that the developed nations were critical about the role of Indian security forces in Jammu and Kashmir. The bogey of violation of human rights in this state was blown up in the various international organizations. There is something more to it than meets the eye. During the civil war in Afghanistan moral and material support was given to the insurgents and terrorists by the CIA. Billions of dollars were poured into the country even after the withdrawal of Soviet troops. In this sense, terrorism was promoted and these very terrorists are now active in a number of other countries and thus have now become a major factor in destabilizing those countries including India.

II

The threat of terrorism and secessionism has already assumed a Eurasian dimension, if one pieces together, recent developments in India, Russia, China, Egypt, Algeria, Turkey and other countries.

The first attempt to create an effective international mechanism for combating terrorism was made in March 1996, during the meeting of the leaders of 27 states in the Egyptian city of Charm-al-Chaykh. The participants in the meeting, among who were Boris Yeltsin and Bill Clinton, reached an agreement on joining efforts to cut short financial and other forms of support for terrorist groups and counter all forms of terrorism. But this half-hearted step did not go far enough. Now organized terrorism has assumed a new character.

This problem was also discussed in detail during the meeting of the G-8 heads of state and government in the French city of Lyons in June 1996. The summit participants unanimously came to the conclusion that international terrorism had become "an absolute priority" for the world community.

This assessment was quite justified. Over the past two decades, as a result of terrorist acts, many leaders, including Egyptian President, Anwar, Sadat; Swedish Prime Minister, Olof Palme; Israeli Prime Minister, Yitzhak Rabin, Indian Prime Ministers, Indira Gandhi and Rajiv Gandhi were assassinated. Attempt on the life of Sri Lankan President Chandrika Kumaratunga was made during the presidential elections recently.

Modern terrorism has already transcended state borders and is turning into a destructive force, threatening the stability of a whole number of planet regions.

No doubt, religious and ethnic conflicts are becoming a most serious threat. Its proponents have nothing to do with true religious teachings, but are, in actual fact, using religion and ethnicity to carry out their political ventures. No wonder that in the overwhelming majority or multi-religious and multi-ethnic states, this has become a serious problem. This extremism has a narrow social base as has been confirmed by presidential election in Egypt.

The threat to launch a '*jihad*' on India, must be taken seriously in this context. The debacle at Kargil has added to the frustration and humiliation of the army, political establishment and fundamentalist clergy in Pakistan and there is a deep sense of resentment and thirst for revenge in various sections of the state structure. What the Indian political elite has to understand is that Osama Bin Laden, Hekmatyar and Taliban were all the original creations of the US and indeed, Islamic fundamentalism was nurtured by the US during the anti-Soviet war in Afghanistan. The Inter-Services Intelligence acquired most of its skills from the CIA. Now the terrorists Pakistan have become an autonomous factor. In fact, sooner or later, perhaps sooner than later, they and the military establishment may threaten the stability of Pakistan itself.

Let us look at the developments in Russia in this context.

Russian leader, Vladimir Putin in the last week of September 1999, expressed the determination of his people to put an end to leniency towards terrorists. He said that Chechens are anxious to get rid of international terrorists like other Russian people. He did not leave at that. He underlined that, terrorism in this part of the Russian Republic is promoted, nursed, both morally and materially by external forces.

State-sponsored terrorism in the post-Cold war period has become a threat for the global stability. It is being used to subvert other nation states. Aggressive separatism and extremism which resort to terrorist methods, mass murders and persecution of people on religious and ethnic affiliation—these alarming events worry even those countries today which ten years ago were convinced that they would not face these misfortunes.

In the complex international situation of today, it is only the United Nations which can take firm measures against the growing trend of terrorism, on the basis of consensus among all the nations, big and small.

Russia's proposal to hold a special UN session on this subject needs to be seriously taken. India, China and Russia, which are not only the biggest nations of the world but also are multi-religious, multi-ethnic and multi-cultural societies have a vital interest in liquidation of this growing menace.

It is relevant to mention here that leaders of China, Russia, Kyrgyzstan, Kazakhstan and Tejikistan have all decided to make joint efforts to fight against separatism, religious extremism and international crimes in the region.

In the last week of August 1999, Chinese President Jiang Zemin said that these five countries should continue the fight against destablizing factors to regional security such as religious extremism, national separatism, international terrorism and other international criminal activities in the region.

This brings out clearly that a new political awareness in the international community has begun to grow.

III

At the beginning of the 21 Century, it is heartening to note that our planet has begun to witness a worldwide movement against terrorism, including the state-sponsored terrorism. This stands as a complete contrast to the situation obtaining during the Cold War period, when terrorism was sponsored and promoted, both overtly and covertly. The developments in Afghanistan graphically illustrate this point.

The situation now has radically changed. Transcending state, ideological and political barriers, all nation-states including the theocratic states and their people are coming to realize that terrorism has become the single biggest factor which is destabilizing both international and regional stability. The stand of the United Nations Security Council at the end of the 1999, confirms this conclusion.

Germany and the European Union (EU) have backed India's call for global efforts to tackle the menace of international terrorism. Taking a serious note of international terrorist Osama Bin Laden's threat, India and the United States have agreed to coordinate their efforts to combat terrorism, especially emanating from Taliban controlled area of Afghanistan.

China is worried about the dubious role of Pakistan in supporting cross-border terrorism. China does not want to be seen on the wrong side of the fence on the question of terrorism in the context of developing cooperation among three major powers of the world—the United States, Russia and India. Finally, the countries of ASEAN too are deeply worried about rise of terrorism.

If all these developments are pieced together, it becomes clear that the entire world is moving towards evolving a concrete plan to eliminate terrorism and pave the way for creating a non-violent world order. However, it will be simplistic to come to the conclusion that the international community, particularly the ruling elites of the developed countries are evolving a clear policy to face this challenge. There are obvious reasons for this, both geo-political and geo-economic. The developed nations, the United States in particular are heavily dependent on the oil resources of the Gulf countries and Central Asia. This geo-economic factor inhibits them to evolve a clear policy against terrorism and secessionism. The situation is further compounded by the fact that American model of the new world order and their concept of liberalization comes into conflict with the interests of the poverty-stricken people of the developing and underdeveloped countries. That being the position, if one undertakes to investigate into of the menace of terrorism and secessionism, it is easy to identify its soft top surface in terms of liberal democracy. However, beneath this soft top surface is the hard base of terrorism and secessionism and that base is rooted in economic poverty, social and cultural backwardness. It is this hard base which serves as the recruiting ground for all hues of extremism including terrorism and secessionism. This is the crux of the problem.

CHAPTER 6

Rise of Terrorism and Secessionism in South Asia—A Bahá'í Viewpoint

A.K. Merchant

Terrorism, so often sponsored by nations and magnified by the media, plants seeds of fear throughout the world. And fear can imprison free men and women more surely than the stoutest walls.

Rushworth M. Kidder

Present-day humanity has reached the strange position where, although people in every country cry out for peace, it has come to think that it is impossible to achieve because selfishness and aggression will always be part of human nature. We need to move on from this kind of thinking and realize that prejudice, war and unfair treatment of others have been part of humankind's growing up process, we can see that we should now progress to a period of greater maturity where we can put this childish behaviour behind us.

A number of causes for terrorism can be identified. In some ways, selfish, uncaring behaviour on the parts of groups of people, mirror the adolescent stage of individuals, where personal concerns or grievances become out of proportion. "The human race....has passed through evolutionary stages.... of infancy and childhood....and is now in its turbulent adolescence approaching its long-awaited coming of age." Part of the background to current waves of terrorism is the lack of a proper balance between the liberty of the individual and the needs of society as a whole. The rights of an individual to act as she wishes can never be absolute. The cause that the terrorists espouse is driven by a sense of injustice, as when a nation does not have independence in the family of nations, or where a minority feels that its rights are ignored. Much of modern terrorism is connected to the struggle for separate territory within given national boundaries resulting in clashes between two cultures, religions, ideological groups, *inter alia.* For instance, even if the problems between India and Pakistan were resolved, the world would still' have to deal with terrorist groups and separatist forces in the Middle East, Sri Lanka, Ireland, Latin and South America, Puerto Rico and parts of Africa, to name just some of the hot spots. The world must ensure that no situations of political injustice continue thereby removing the terrorist's motivation, justification and support. The terrorist as an excuse for his actions also frequently uses religion, despite the fact that every religion forbids murder and demands that all individuals love each other. The golden rule found in each religion is that we should treat others as we wish to be treated. The moral codes of true religion have lost their impact. The cancerous paradigm of materialism has extinguished the spiritual power of traditional religions and led to, according to the Baha'i teachings, "the perversion of human nature, the degradation of human conduct, [that] reveal themselves, under such circumstance in their worst and most revolting aspects. Human character is debased.... the voice of human conscience is stilled the sense of decency and shame is obscured."

Whilst there may be more than one description of 'terrorism' Webster's New World Dictionary states as follows: "ter'ror-ism: n. [Fr. Terrorisme] the act of terrorizing; use of force or threats to demoralize, intimidate, and subjugate, esp. used as a political weapon or policy the demoralization and intimidation produced in this way." The US Department of Justice, 1984 described it as: "violent criminal conduct apparently intended: (a) to intimidate or coerce a civilian population; (b) to influence the conduct of a government by intimidation or coercion; or (c) to affect the conduct of a government by assassination or kidnapping." Terrorism's central weapon is fear itself. It consists of an attempt by the weak to gain dominion over the strong. And since its ultimate target is not the victim but the public at large, terrorists seek access to channels of communication. As previously stated terrorism stems from some of the baser elements of human nature—hatred, revenge, and territoriality. Yet, it often comes in the guise of religious or political movements, a just attempt to gain a homeland or a remedy for past injustices.

The history of post-independent India is replete with repeated occurrences of prolonged and ongoing battle with terrorism that has spread its deadly tentacles in many states all over the country. The terms used to describe those who indulge in these nefarious activities are militants, extremists, insurgents, naxalites, anti-nationals, mercenaries and terrorists. In Jammu and Kashmir alone there are more than two dozen outfits, of which some of the well-known are: Al-Jehad Forum, Muslim Jambaz Force, Al-Mustafa Liberation Force, Al-Umer Mujahideen, Harkat-ul-Ansar (a banned outfit). Harkat ul-Jehad-i-Islami, Hizbul Mujahideen, Ikhwan-ul-Muslimeen, Tulba-Islami-Students, Jammu Kashmir Liberation Front (JKLF), Jammu Kashmir National Liberation Army, Lashkar-i-Toiba, Kashmir Jehad Force, Arkaj-i-ad-Dawa-ul-Arshad. Elsewhere, in India we hear of the United Liberation Force of Assam (ULFA), the (PGW), the Bodo militants, etc.

Today's terrorists are armed with the most sophisticated weapons, and capable of destroying targets with a high degree of success, effective manipulation of news media, use of home video equipment to make tapes for release to commercial networks. Many of the Indian terrorists groups are openly backed by the rogue Inter Services Intelligence (ISI) of Pakistan which supplies state-of-art weapons and explosives. ISI has supplied pen-shaped pistols, cigarette bombs that are laced with deadly explosives, solor energy powered land mines, anti-aircraft guns, shoulder fired Stinger Missiles, AK-47s and AK-56s.

In his five-part paper entitled "Unmasking Terrorism" by Rushworth M. Kidder, published in *The Christian Science Monitor*, June 21-27, 1986, the author offers a penetrating analysis subtitled "The Terrorist Mentality": "Is there, then, a Terrorist mindset? From dozens of interviews over four months with long-time students of terrorist ideology and psychology, certain common characteristics begin to emerge. Not surprisingly, given the typical age of the terrorist, these characteristics are also often attributed to adolescence: (a) Oversimplification of issues. Terrorists often reduce complex issues to black-and-white. Dr. Franco Ferracuti points to the intensely intellectualized, inward looking, and politically naive theorizing of many groups. The terrorist, he says, "no longer tests his ideas against reality by [engaging in] dialogue with people with different views." Instead, he lives out "a fantasy war," convinced that he has broad support from numerous like-minded followers.

(b) Frustration. Pent-up concerns about an individual's inability to change society figure strongly in this mindset. Italian historian and journalist Giorgio Bocca notes: "They have no patience, these terrorists. They are totally absorbed in their cause. One of the slogans of one of these movements [I studied] was 'We want it all and we want it now.'" (c) Self-righteousness. "They believe in [their] total rectitude," notes Prof. Paul Wilkinson, who adds that "intolerance, dogmaticism, authoritarianism, and a ruthless treatment of their own people who deviate from their own views are common to their mentality." (d) Utopianism. Many terrorists seem to feel that a near-perfect future lies just around the corner, once the present order is destroyed. This utopianism, coupled with frustration at the slow pace of social change, often leads to political extremism on both the left and the right. "Unless you catch this utopian aspect," notes Prof. Ferracuti, "its difficult to understand the mind-set." (e) Social isolation. Terrorists, says Dr. Jerrold M. Post, are often "people who really are lonely." Terrorists groups use religious or political ideals to interest potential recruits. But those taking up political violence often share traits that are less religious or political than mental and emotional. For many of them, Dr. Post says, the terrorist group is "the first family they have ever had." (f) Assertion of their own existence. Terrorist actions are often laden with symbolic overtones, involving the choice of captives, locations, weapons and timing. They are frequently meant to send messages—and the message, quite often, is simply "I exist! Pay attention to me!" French criminologist Jacques Leaute calls terrorism "a communication system" in which frustrated people are "trying to express through violence their own message." (g) Willingness to kill. Perhaps the most startling characteristic, however, is the cold-bloodedness of some terrorist murders. Students of terrorism relate this characteristic to a harsh oversimplification that allows killers to see victims simply as objects—a habit of mind observed among Nazi killers during the massacre of Jews in World War II. Researchers have noticed, however, that captors who hold hostages for protracted periods tend to develop a kind of bond with them that makes cold-blooded murder less likely. Much of the so-called suicide bombing is not carried out by fanatics who believe they are dying for a cause. Interviews with would be suicide terrorists who were captured alive indicate they were often tricked into believing they could escape before the bomb exploded or were blackmailed into accepting the task on threat of harm to their families."

Thus, with the collapse of the nation-state there is a proliferation of factionalism and such a situation can only be overcome through the creation of a world government that would be responsible for ensuring the territorial integrity of each sovereign state. To establish such a world authority we need to rethink the role of the existing United Nations Organization which to my mind has lost its mandate of preserving peace throughout the world. The globalization process demands the holding of a world conference at which the international frontiers should be permanently determined and the levels of national armaments reduced. Every nation, big or small, would be assured of its safety and every minority within each country would have its rights guaranteed. Terrorists use different states around the world as places of refuge from justice, and a number of countries harbour, supply, finance and train and sponsor terrorist groups for their own ends. Until some sort of world law is established, terrorism can never be completely eliminated. "The law must reign and not the individual; thus will the world become a place of beauty and true brotherhood will be realized."

Only a new world system of governance structured on an international rather than a national level, to deal with the urgent global problems of terrorism and secessionism, deteriorating environment, spread of poverty, HIV/AIDS, to name a just a few of the global crises, can provide the much needed panacea. Global problems have been mounting in magnitude and danger, yet there seems to be little progress in the creation of the political will or the institutional mechanisms for dealing with them. The series of United Nations convened conferences during the decade of 1990s, has certainly generated tremendous awareness and some cooperation among member nations. In the words of a United Nations executive: "We cling to concepts of national sovereignty which are outmoded and ineffective....and to a world of nation-states no longer able to deal with some of the principal issues that determine the future security and well-being of their people." Most existing international institutions lack a cutting edge and the means of enforcement. Some governments are happy to frustrate progress. They do not want to see global institutions with real powers and can point to their many defects, including lack of accountability. The power of inertia remains strong. The short-term always looms larger than the long-term.

A new world-view based on the ideal of world citizenship and the concept—prosperity of humankind can replace the narrower and more violent goals of the terrorists. The creation of a world super state would lead to the establishment of a world parliament, legislature, executive, police force and other allied agencies accompanied by worldwide laws to be upheld and enforced by all the federated members of the world commonwealth. There is no danger in a rational level of patriotism, but what needs to be developed is a love of humanity as a whole. With this ideal as a goal, replacing the fierce nationalism that is used to justify acts of terror, a sense of world citizenship can be developed. Loving all the peoples of the world should include a love of one's own country. "The well-being of mankind, its peace and security, are unattainable unless and until its unity is firmly established." "The earth is but one country and mankind its citizens." Bahá' u'lláh proclaimed over a century ago.

All the human sciences—anthropology, physiology and psychology-agree that there is only one human species, although we differ endlessly in lesser ways. "Fighting, and the employment of force, even for the right cause, will not bring about good results. The oppressed who have right on their side must not take that right by force; the evil would continue. Hearts must be changed."

In such a world as envisaged above there would be strict regulations on the carrying of arms by individual citizens. The aid agency Oxfam has estimated the global trade in small arms between 1990 and 1995, at $22 billion. Traditional arms control methods—treaties and inspection rules—can work against costly and hard-to-hide tanks and nuclear missiles. But light weapons, the mainstay of terrorist groups, are cheap, portable and easily hidden.

Progress towards a new society demands that we move away from the world-view founded on the mechanics of a clock and the interactions of billiard balls to the acceptance of an organic change in the very structure of present-day society accompanied by an equally profound change in human consciousness. This is within the power of all who share this planet as their common homeland, Bahá'is believe. "To build a new world is no easy task. The road is stony and filled with obstacles, but the journey is infinitely rewarding."

REFERENCES

1. *The Promise of World Peace* by the Universal House of Justice, New Delhi: Bahá'í Publishing Trust of India, 1986.
2. "Unmasking Terrorism" by Rushworth M. Kidder, *Christian Science Monitor,* Special Report, June 21-27, 1986, USA.
3. *World Development Forum*—A Fortnightly Report. of Facts, Trends and Opinion in International Development, Vol. 5, No. 13, July 15, 1987.
4. "Freedom from Terrorism" by the Spiritual Assembly of the Baha'ís of Warwick, 1998, reprinted by the National Spiritual Assembly of the Bahá'ís of India, 1999.
5. "Dealers in Death" by Nina Planck. London, *Time—The Weekly Newsmagazine,* October 19, 1998, Vol. 152. No. 15.
6. "Terrorists outfits target Delhi with innovative devices" by Pramod K. Singh, *Neighbourhood—Flash,* South Delhi, Vol. 2. No. 15, March 5-11, 2000.

CHAPTER 7

Terrorism and National Security Concerns

Maj. Gen. Afsir Karim (Retd.)

Terrorism is a kind of war which is waged from secret hideouts by prowling marauders. Infiltration, stealth and surprise are their weapons. Assassinations, killing of innocent people, exhausting the security forces instead of confronting them is a part of their tactics. On another level, they use subversion to retard economic progress, create unrest through religious and ethnic conflicts. It is important to understand the kind of threat a country faces under such circumstances. A covert politico-military offensive can be dangerous for the security and integrity of any country. During the last two decades, this kind of threat has been faced by many countries in South Asia. State-sponsored terrorism and religious extremists are the two forces which have been unleashed to weaken and destabilise secular countries in South Asia. Besides terrorism, illegal narcotic trafficking, smuggling of arms and explosives, subversion of the secular ethos, socio-cultural cohesion is also a part of this war. Democracy and secular traditions invariably are the main targets of attack. State-sponsored terrorism with the aim of destabilising a country uses ethnic violence, religious strife, general unrest and chaos to destroy economic, social and political infrastructure of a country.

The main difference between terrorism and other forms of violence is that terrorism employs inordinate force repeatedly against unarmed civilians to erode the political will of the targeted entity to resist. Political terrorism aims to make a targeted entity politically and economically unstable, and undermine the morale of the people by spreading despondency and panic. At an abstract level, terrorism therefore meets the basic criteria of a war.[1]

According to Barry Buzan the three main components of state are:

(a) Physical : the people and territory of a state.

(b) Institutional: the infrastructure and the constitution of the state.

(c) Metaphysical: the concept or idea of the state as it is acknowledged and accepted by the people.

The above vital components of a sovereign state come under simultaneous attack if the sponsors succeed in demolishing or subverting these elements it can no longer function as a sovereign entity.[2]

In the initial phases democratic institutions and vital organs of the state are the targets of attack and subversion. Gradually, the levels of discontent and alienation is sought to be raised to an extent that violence is institutionalized and becomes a part of the system. The common grievances of the people are highlighted through a well-planned strategy and presented in a manner which would invoke widespread violence. Raising of anti-government sentiments is a critical step in the mobilization of the population in the pre-violent stage but it may continue even during the violent stage.

Anti-government sentiments are raised to a very high pitch in this phase as the grievances highlighted by the sponsoring organizations or states are easily identifiable by the people. Mass mobilization of the people against the government is planned to destabilise the system and set the stage for insurgency and terrorism. If the motivation or anti-government sentiments are not found strong enough among the masses a religious or ideological facade is given to the movement. Religious orientation provides a kind of protective umbrella to the sponsors. During religious functions the plight of the people and the oppressive nature of the regime are emphasised and highlighted. Ted Gurr in his work: 'Why men rebel,' established that people rebel if: "they are deprived of some expected value and they are made aware of this deprivation."[3]

The psychological polarization of the people is achieved by making them conscious of various material and spiritual deprivations. A 'we and they' syndrome is created that presents the government and the security forces as instruments of oppression. The people are also made to believe that resorting to violence is the only way open to deal with a oppressive regime and overthrowing of such a government is their religious and political duty.

The Proxy War

In Kashmir, Pakistan gradually manipulated public opinion in favour of a violent movement in four distinct stages: (i) raising of anti-establishment sentiments and giving it a religious bias; (ii) undermining and subverting the state authority and penetrating the security apparatus; (iii) induction of sophisticated weapons and infiltration of mercenaries and *jihadis* to wage a proxy war. Pakistan during all these stages had surreptitiously dumped large quantities of arms and explosives for the violent stage of the movement. Numerous bomb blasts, and mob violence heralded the beginning of the violent phase in 1988-89.

Sponsorship of armed groups to perpetrate acts of terror and employment of surrogate forces to gain political objectives was an integral part of the Pakistan game plan. Employment of lumpen elements to break the cohesion within the society and to subvert the Kashmiri culture through surrogate forces was a safe method of waging war in the nuclear era. Radical Islamic groups based in Pakistan operating under different names like Lashkar-e-Toiba or Hizbul-Mujahideen, etc., were mobilised to fight this kind of war. Disparate terrorist groups may not be capable of capturing power but they have successfully diverted critical and limited resources of the state from constructive tasks.

Besides terrorism, Pakistan also wages another way that may termed as social warfare. After the advent of nuclear weapons in the subcontinent social warfare has become a preferred method of waging covert wars with the aim to assault a state on the social and moral planes. This kind of war is particularly effective if the targeted state already suffers from internal dissensions and conflicts. The objective is to exploit and create cleavages, disrupt social cohesion and political mobility. These methods prove extremely effective in conjunction with insurgent terrorism. It is easier to achieve destruction of the adversary if social forces can be harnessed and converted into political or military power. Pakistan has lately been waging this kind of war by exploiting religious cleavages in India with the main focus on Kashmir. The ultimate objective is to create conditions which would start ethnic and religious polarisation and undermine the democratic, socio-economic and administrative system of the state.

The sponsored political violence and terrorism in Kashmir and some other parts of India, however, threaten peace in the entire South Asian region as the threat of an India-Pakistan war looms large behind this threat. The emergence of radical Wahabi-Sunni groups in Pakistan has added a new dimension to the India-Pakistan confrontation as it has now become a part of the global *jihadi* movement. The ethnic and religious affinity on either side of the border and the porous terrain of the border areas provide tailor-made conditions for infiltration of terrorist and insurgent groups to operate in India. Brutal violence against unarmed civilians and ethnic cleansing of certain areas to change the demographic balance has lately become a special feature of Pakistan inspired movements. Kashmir is not the main problem as is generally believed because radical religion is now being used by Pakistan to attain its politico-strategic objectives of weakening and destabilizing several parts of India.

Instruments of Terror and Violence

The mindset and the *modus operandi* of various fanatical groups operating in J&K has been discussed here but subversion is now being spread by such groups in various parts of India by manipulating radical Hindu and Muslim groups.

Markaz-e-Dawa, Mektab-e-Kadamat, and Al Qaida located in Afghanistan and Pakistan provide facilities of military training and financial support for *jihad* in Kashmir, most of these *jihadi* groups were previously involved in Afghanistan war. Those who carry out terrorist attacks on Indian soil come from Pakistan and some other Muslim countries. There is therefore always a large reserve available to carry out attacks and replace the casualties incurred in Kashmir. The motivating forces behind these groups are the recruiting network, social workers, religious journals and Madarassas of Pakistan which constantly pour venom against India. The terrorists group operating from Afghanistan, Pakistan and PoK are given the required military and material support by the Pakistan government. No organization is in a position, to infiltrate inside Kashmir or wage war without support from Pakistan Government.

A 21-day course for terrorists called 'Daura-e-Aama' creates the required motivation and initial military training. A three-month course called 'Daura-e-Khasa' trains selected groups in guerrilla warfare and ambush techniques besides special operations. Another spell of training in commando operations is conducted in remote areas of J&K to give an opportunity to the recruits to watch the Indian security forces at a close range. All newly enlisted fighters acquire Arabic nick-names, (called 'Kuwait',) of Islamic heroes or companions of the Prophet of Islam. Intensive indoctrination creates a new Islamic personality in recruits. This transforms an ordinary man into a fanatic who is ready, (even eager) to become a *shaheed* -(martyr).[3]

The shadow of Osama Bin Laden looms large behind the clamour of religious fanatics for 'Jihad' against the infidel rule in Kashmir. Colourful posters carrying emotional messages for the young members of the Muslim Ummah (community) are published in the name of Bin Laden, some of which proclaim: "You have seen that at the moment the US is the greatest terrorist In the world. By attacking Sudan and Afghanistan (refers to air-missile strikes), the US has blown the trumpet of war against the Islamic world. As far as we are concerned boundaries are meaningless, all land belongs to Allah". These posters are interspersed with others exhorting Muslims to wage Jihad in Kashmir to free it from Hindu India.[4]

Jihadi movement has lately acquired strong transactional capabilities. Mujahideen training camps located in Afghanistan and PoK have been sending insurgents and terrorists to Kashmir and Central Asia for many years. Insurgents operating in Kashmir are highly indoctrinated war veterans who believe that Islamic war can be won in Kashmir and the Indian army will be finally defeated by them.

The supply of sophisticated weapons by the CIA during Afghan resistance against the Soviet army to the Afghan Mujahideens had changed the complex of war there. Due to this the Mujahideens even acquired capability to strike beyond Afghanistan borders in the North and East. The active support of Pakistani religious parties for whom Jihad in Kashmir was the main agenda linked the Afghan war with Kashmir. Terrorists and insurgents became the main instruments of coercion in Kashmir. Jihad in Kashmir is however, proving rather costly as more than 1000 foreign mercenaries known as the 'guest Mujahideen' have already lost their lives and many more are destined to die here.

Holy war (Jihad) cannot be justified in Kashmir as Kashmiri Muslims are not facing religious persecution and there is no danger to Islam. The 'Jihad' in Kashmir is an ISI ploy to give its designs a Pan-Islamic character. The proxy war launched by Pakistan has caused the maximum number of casualties among the Kashmiri Muslims and the collateral damage caused by guerrilla tactics and terrorism sponsored by Pakistan has been immense.

The Terrorist Groups Active in Kashmir

Lashkar-e-Toiba (LET)

It is the militant wing of the 'Dawa' which inducts armed groups into Kashmir. A majority of Lashkar's Jihadi's are from Pakistan. Their number depends on the attrition rate and the type of work assigned to them in Kashmir.

The LET cadres are fully trained in guerrilla warfare, sabotage and subversion. They are indoctrinated by the LET to believe that they would go straight to heaven if they are killed in Kashmir. Those killed in encounters in Kashmir are not mourned, on the other hand their families are congratulated on the martyrdom of their wards. An organization, 'Tehrik-e-Minhajul Quran' and *Mija-ad-Dawa* its widely circulated Jihadi publication, adopt a hard stance against 'satanic practices' which they believe are common among the Muslims of the subcontinent. They are also against the Sufi or mystical Islam practised in Kashmir. LET is perhaps the most motivated among the terrorist outfits which are operating in Kashmir.[5]

Harkat-ul-Ansar (Now Mujahideen) HUM

The Harkat-ul-Ansar was declared a terrorist organization, by the US in 1997 after the reported killing of four Western tourists in Kashmir in December 1994. Thereafter, it changed its name to Harkat-ul-Mujahideen. The Pakistani nationals play a major role in Harkat's activities, incidentally a majority of militants killed in the US missile attack on Khost belonged to Pakistan. The organization works in close cooperation with the Taliban. In Afghanistan, Harkat activists are known as 'Pakistani Taliban'.

Pakistan Government supports this group with material and financial aid. Harkat is a highly motivated terrorist group and is ruthless in its methods. They are responsible for many brutal acts committed against the Kashmiri minority communities and non-cooperative Muslim groups.

Hizbul Mujahideen (Afghan)

The Hizbul Mujahideen lost its base in Afghanistan after the Taliban captured Kabul in September 1996. The Hizbul Mujahideen (HM) still operates in Kashmir because of their close links with the Jamaat-e-Islami of Pakistan. It draws its recruits from the Islami Jamiat-e-Talaba of Pakistan; members of the Hizbul Mujahideen are well educated and highly motivated. This group also enlists Kashmiris, however, lately many Kashmiris are not coming forward to join their ranks.

Al Badr is the latest addition to the Pak-sponsored forces trained in guerrilla warfare and subversion. Besides the above, more than a score of terrorist groups which have been active in Kashmir are:

AJF	Al-Jehad Force
AMF	Al-Mujahid Force
AMLF	Al-Mustafa Liberation Fighters
AUM	Al Umar Mujahideen
HUJI	Harkat-ul-Jehad-e-Islami
HM	Islami Inquilabi Mahaz
IJT	Islami Jamaat-e-Tulba
ISC	Islamic Students League
IUM	Ikhwan-ul-Mujahideen
JKLF	J&K Liberation Front (not active at present)
JKSLF	J&K Students Liberation Front (not active at present)
JUM	Jamait-ul-Mujahideen
KJF	Kashmir Jehad Force
MJC	Mutahida (United) Jehad Council
MJF	Muslim Janbaz Force
MM	Muslim Mujahideen Op. Balakote
PL	People's League
TEHK	Tehrik-e-Hurriat-e-Kashmir
TJI	Tehrik-e-Jehad-e-Islami

Pakistan and Afghanistan remain the training ground of all Islamic fanatical groups who consider any settlement or compromise with the infidels a sin. These Jihadi groups consider democracy un-Islamic and an evil introduced by the Western world to subvert Islamic culture. The groups sponsored by Pakistan into Kashmir have a pre-determined political agenda set by the ISI which has nothing to do with Islam.

People in Kashmir, in general find it increasingly difficult to accept the politico-religious dictates of Pakistan-sponsored terrorists because they have caused unbearable damage to the Kashmir ethos and socio-economic infrastructure. Jihadis have lost the battle of hearts and mind, and they no longer enjoy support of the local population. India should be able to counter Pak-sponsored political and religious propaganda by well focused political social and economic programmes, only the armed terrorists should be taken care of by the security forces.

Counter Measures in Kashmir

In case of Kashmir where a proxy war is being waged by Pakistan certain immediate steps are required to be taken. The aim should be to :

- Achieve moral and physical isolation of mercenary and foreign terrorists through a combination of psychological and political methods.
- Persuade and coax the regime in J&K to reach down to the people through pro-active socio-political programmes. Active and positive action to wean away people from the separatist political groups is urgently required.
- Introduce People's Armed Militias which are trained for self-defence, territorial and sector-defence schemes.
- Mobilise hard hitting paramilitary forces to put the terrorists on the defensive.
- Introduce innovative economic programmes to lift the state from its financial morass.
- Sanitise important tourist centres from terrorist threats to revive tourist trade, which is the main lifeline of the poor classes of the valley.

8 Improve supply of electricity, transportation system and industrial infrastructure to boost trade and industry.

Concluding Observations

Pakistan has institutionalized low-intensity conflict and is using it for, attainment of its foreign policy goals. Rather than relying on conventional warfare based on the notions of balance of power, the concept of correlation of forces has been adopted by Pakistan. The concept of correlation of forces includes "existence of reliable socio-political allies among other states, national contingents of congenial classes, mass international movements and other political forces active in the world".[6]

Pakistan considers correlation of forces' in South Asia favourable and ripe for exploitation. It plans to use the disgruntled and secessionist elements of the targeted countries as combatants and provide them with support organisations to subvert secular and democratic ethos of these countries. Pakistan has been offering training techniques, weapons and finances to anti-national elements to destabilise targeted countries in South and Central Asia. All this is being done while preaching peace and promises of non-aggression. This model can however provide the means of studying the nature of Pakistan's surrogate warfare, under the umbrella of nuclear weapons. Afghanistan and Pakistan are the two centres of radical Jihadi movement in South Asia and their covert designs have to be watched carefully.

The most important thing for India is to realize that it is facing a multi-pronged threat from Pakistan in which diplomacy, economic and socio-political factors also play an important role. Besides it is facing serious military threat through state-sponsored terrorism and it is not merely a law and order problem. Hence, it is necessary to ascertain the true nature of this threat to counter it effectively. India must decide and determine the military and political threats to its integrity and initiate effective counter measures to defeat Pakistan's designs of destabilising and weakening the country.

In a democratic country like India, mobilization of population is the first necessary step for defeating the terrorist threat. India cannot allow, divisive and radical forces among its own people to widen factional, ethnic or religious divides. All radical groups whether left or right must be disciplined in national interest. This however, should be done through mobilising popular support and not through coercive methods.

The other important step would be to initiate diplomatic, political and military measures to destroy Pakistan's covert political and military infrastructure which threatens India. Long-term strategic objectives and campaigns combining diplomatic, political and military initiatives have to be accurately determined. Planning on ad-hoc basis by a few officials or an initiative for short-term political gains cannot prove effective. The Government of India has to adopt a long-term policy seeking suppression of Pakistan's belligerent designs besides short-term measures to counter Pakistan's immediate threat. Political will and determination are necessary ingredients for defeating the combined threats of sponsored terrorism and social warfare which has been launched by Pakistan.

REFERENCES

1. Hanle Donald J : *Terrorism the Newest Face of Warfare*, New York Pergamon-Basseys International Defence Publishers Inc., 1989, pp. 193-95.
2. Buzan Barry : *People, States and Fear: The National Security Problems,* University of North Carolina Press, 1983, pp. 38-39.
3. Allahs Armies: *The Herald*, Karachi, 1998.
4. *Ibid.*
5. *Ibid The Herald* Annual January, 1998.
6. Sergiyev A : Leninism on the Corelation of Forces as a Factor of International Relations : *International Affairs,* 1975, p. 103.

CHAPTER 8

Pakistan and Afghanistan as Sources of Terrorism in the Region

Kalim Bahadur

Many countries in the Middle East, Central and South Asia have been facing political developments which are attributed to the rise of militant Islamic movements in the region. These militant groups have been giving calls for *jihad* against a variety of perceived enemies more specifically identified as Western imperialism and its predatory economies and ideologies. *Jihad* is a vague term and has been interpreted differently by Islamic theologians. What is called as Jihad has more often in recent times taken the form of senseless campaigns of murder and mayhem. Thus, the so-called jihad has in most cases degenerated terrorism against innocent citizens, threatening to destabilize established regimes. This wave of terrorism and violence has the official patronage of the ruling regimes in Afghanistan and Pakistan. The terrorist groups hava a nexus with cross-border arms peddlers and drug traffickers in the region.

The popularity of *jihad* among large sections of the Muslims in many countries is the result of the growth of Islamic fundamentalism. The term fundamentalism is not indicative of any set of Islamic concepts and ideas. In fact, a variety of political and social movements are labelled as Islamic fundamentalism. The popular upsurge among the Muslims in the countries of North Africa, Middle East, South and South-East Asia is given the label of Islamic fundamentalism. These movements are inspired by ideologues belonging to different sects of Islam and differ widely over the details of Islamic theology. The historical setting, political evolution and civilizational background in each country is different and yet the broad aim everywhere is the same; the setting up of an Islamic state.

Islamic fundamentalism has been defined as a movement for going back to the sources and the roots of Islam. It means adherence to the original principles of Islam contained in the Quran and their literalist interpretations. The principles transcend time and space. Thus, the text is unchanging and unchangeable and applicable at all times, in all cultural environments and across all social and economic transformations.

Islamic fundamentalism in its traditional form is refusal to innovate and an acceptance of the principle of imitation whereas reformist fundamentalism is critical of tradition, the commentaries, the popular practices and superstitions. The traditional fundamentalism supports *status quo* and feudal system. The reformist fundamentalism is also called militant Islam; its followers are aggressive and radical and believe that the present ruling elite will not bring any change.

While there are differences among the revivalist movements in each country they share common Islamic heritage and opposition to Western political and cultural imperialism. The three leading ideologues of Islamic fundamentalist movements have been Ayatollah Khomeini, Abul Ala Maududi and Syed Qutb. They have been leaders of three leading Islamic fundamentalist parties in their respective countries. They shared the belief that political power was essential to the establishment of an Islamic society. They were agreed on Muslim supra-nationalism and belief in *jihad*. The most radical of them, Syed Qutb called for the forceable removal of all leaders. He was the main proponent of the use of violence and terror for the achievement of the pure Islamic society. Khomeini also believed that Islam was the religion of militancy that was dedicated to truth and justice. He called for *jihad* against imperialism. Syed Qutb also advocated *jihad* to fight against imperialism and anti-Islamic forces to establish an Islamic system. According to Maududi, the most significant type of *jihad* was the use of violence as an element of strategy.

From the one end of the Muslim world to the other, a large number of motivated and inspired groups are fighting a variety of enemies in the name of Islam. Their philosophy of life and their world-view was inspired by those three leaders who belonged to three different parts of the world. The Jama'at-i-Islami of Pakistan led by Maulana Maududi has carried on a relentless campaign for Islamisation of Pakistan through all the ups and downs of Pakistan's history. It was only during General Zia-ul Haq's regime that Islamic fundamentalism got the official patronage of the establishment. His intervention in Afghanistan's civil war abroad and Islamisation at home strengthened the fundamentalist parties and exacerbated the sectarian strife in Pakistan. It was during the Afghanistan's war where fundamentalist parties, called the Mujahideens were fighting against the Soviet army, that there developed close links between the Mujahideens and Pakistan's fundamentalist parties. In fact, fundamentalism in Afghanistan owed its origins to the Muslim brothers of Egypt but the ideas of Maulana Maududi had also influenced them. The various fundamentalist parties though formally committed to Islamic tenets represent some region, ethnic community or a distinct theological tendency. After the withdrawal of the Soviet army from Afghanistan in 1989, followed the collapse of the Najibullah regime, in the bitter civil war which erupted among those groups.

Pakistani regimes in the earlier period had made several attempts to bring about among the Mujahideen groups an agreed government to oppose the Kabul regime of the Khalq party but all agreements among the Mujahideen groups used to break down even before the ink on them was dried. In the early nineties, Pakistani agencies organized students from the *madarsas* which had been set up in the Afghan refugee camps by the factions of the Jamiat-ul-Ulama and the Jama'at-i-Islami of Pakistan. They were trained and inducted into Afghanistan to fight the various warring factions of the Mujahideens. This group is called the Taliban. This force bought its way through intrigue and bribes and some fighting and soon was in control of almost ninety per cent of the territory of the country.

During the course of the Afghan civil war, scores of militants, mercenaries and soldiers from across the Muslim world had flocked to Afghanistan responding to the call for *jihad* against the Godless communists. They were mainly financed by the United States agencies and Saudi money. The border towns in NWFP and Baluchistan in Pakistan had become the staging ground for these volunteers going to fight in the holy war. Once the war in Afghanistan was over the Islamic soldiers stayed put, in Pakistan. Some of them were later sent to Kashmir. Others went to Egypt, Algeria, Chechnya, Dagestan, Sinkiang, etc. With the money coming from the United States agencies and the Saudi's drying up, new sources of funds were found for those militants and terrorists. These new sources were the flourishing drug trafficking in the Afghanistan and Pakistan region which became the major source of financing the terrorist camps and groups in the countries around the region. The notorious Arab terrorist Osama Bin Laden is also one of the major financier of the militants.

The nexus between drug trafficking and terrorism in the Golden Crescent has become a major reason for political and social instability in the region. The neighbouring Central Asian Republics have also been dragged into this cauldron. It is only recently that Pakistan has realized the gravity of the situation created by the production of illicit drugs and its sale at home and export abroad. The drug barons of Pakistan have enriched themselves because the State had laws which allowed drug money to be converted into white money easily. In Afghanistan, the tribal leaders during King Zahir Shah's regime and the Mujahideens during the ups and downs of the political fortunes in the Khalq regime later fueled the country's economy on drug trafficking. Afghanistan during the last decade has emerged as the second largest producer of the drugs in the world. In 1998, the Taliban controlled 80 per cent of the country's territory and over 95 per cent of the area where opium poppy is cultivated. Chemicals which are used to produce heroin and morphine in the laboratories in Afghanistan are imported from Europe, China and India. Morphine, and heroin are sent across the porous borders of Afghanistan into Pakistan, Iran and the Central Asian Republic of Tajikistan.

Taliban believe that growing poppy is not against Islam but its consumption is. Therefore they refuse to control poppy cultivation unless the international community offers development assistance and also political recognition. Except for a token destruction of a ton of poppy which has not been verified, Taliban has taken no action against traffickers or local dealers. In 1999, the production of heroin and morphine was estimated to be 4,500 tonnes. Talibans impose a tax of 10 per cent on production and a tax of Rs. 500 per kilo on the finished product. This forms a major source of country's revenue income.

Pakistan also produces almost 65 metric tons of opium. But because of the neighbouring country Afghanistan emerging as the second largest producer of narcotics, Pakistan faces a major threat of the free flow of drugs from Afghanistan to Pakistan. The country has also become a transit point of drugs being exported to western countries. Powerful drug mafias have emerged in Pakistan particularly in tribal belt of NWFP and Baluchistan. These mafias are linked to powerful leaders across the political spectrum.

Both in Afghanistan and Pakistan it is reported that a large portion of drug money finds its way to militant and terrorist groups which comprise fundamentalists and mercenaries from Arab countries, Central

Asian Republics, Afghanistan, Pakistan, Chechnya, Sudan, Algeria and Egypt. There are reports about some militants even from the UK and USA finding sanctuary in these camps.

The Golden Crescent is not only the centre of drug trafficking but is also a training ground of Islamic militants who come here to get training in use of weapons, explosives, etc., which they cannot get in their own countries. Many militant groups like Harkat-ul-Mujahideen, Hizbul Mujahideen, Al Badr are located in Pakistan but are active in trans-border terrorism in Kashmir and some of them indulge in attacks on minority sects in Pakistan. Osama Bin Laden, the notorious Arab millionaire has been running several camps in Afghanistan for training militants for action in Kashmir, Africa and Arab countries and in Central Asian Republics. The well-known Pakistani terrorist Riaz Basra, linked to Sunni group Sipah Sahaba and charged with the murders of scores of Shias is now living in Kabul.

The South-West Asian states face serious threat from the fundamentalist groups who in the name of *jihad* are involved in challenging political stability and economic development in the region. Terrorists trained in Pakistani camps have been involved in the Xinjiang region of China, in Chechnya, in Egypt and even in the Philippines. The Taliban which controls Afghanistan now was trained and armed by Pakistan's intelligence agency, the ISI. Even sectarian killers in Pakistan find sanctuary in Kabul.

Muslim terrorists influenced by the *jihadi* groups in the fundamentalist parties will continue to pose a threat to integrity, harmony and security of the States in the South-West Asian region, for a long-time to come. The concern displayed now in Washington about the growth of nexus between the drug trafficking and fundamentalists and terrorists in the region is rather belated. During the eighties, the United States intelligence agencies had been patronizing an assortment of Islamic militants and terrorists providing them with the latest weaponry to carry on fighting against the Soviet army in Afghanistan. Some of the terrorist camps which are now being used by Osama Bin Laden, for training his bands of terrorists to carry on attacks against the United States interests and for fighting in Kashmir had originally been set up by United States agencies. The Afghan Mujahideens had been running the flourishing drug trade even then but the Western agencies had turned a Nelson's eye to that. The United States had not realized the social and political implications of the emergence of the Taliban on the Afghan scene. It was presumed in Washington that the Taliban under the direction of Pakistan's ISI would bring a modicum of stability in Afghanistan and serve its interests. This assessment of Washington has proved wrong and the region is paying a heavy price for it.

The civil societies in the South-West Asian region already facing problems of economic development, social reform and democratic governance have been embroiled in the growing threats of cross-border terrorism and violence. Pakistan has recently suffered the fourth military coup reversing the democratic advance of the past years.

CHAPTER 9

Transformation of Pakistan and Afghanistan as Spring-Boards of Cross-Country Terrorism in the Region

Shri Prakash

In analyzing the rise of terrorism and secessionism with special reference to Jammu and Kashmir there are two issues concerning which efforts have to be made to build a consensus. The first concerns a definition of terrorism and secessionism and the second one is related to establishing the period during which these forces emerged as a distinct and noticeable political tendency. It is noteworthy that even though Jammu and Kashmir had been facing invasions after 1947 by the Pakistani Army to invade and annex Kashmir, they were not accompanied by the rise and functioning of terrorist organizations like the Harkat-ul-Ansar later renamed Harkat-ul-Mujahideen, Lashkar-e-Toiba, Hizbul-Mujahideen, Al Faran until the 1980s. These terrorist organizations consist of hardcore fanatic cadres who have been indoctrinated in the extremist ideology of waging a *jihad* or a Muslim holy war against Hindus with a view to expelling them from Kashmir and capturing power through military means. Their political counterparts like the All Party Hurriat Conference and the Jammu Kashmir Liberation Front do not recognize the Indian Constitution or J&K's accession to India and live on in the hope of establishing an independent state of Jammu and Kashmir with Western aid and some support from Islamic States especially Pakistan, Saudi Arabia and Afghanistan. The rise of both these tendencies corresponds much more with Pakistan's reassessment of its ability to ever win a conventional war against India (the last one it lost decisively, during the formation of Bangladesh) than it does with any theory about a sudden deterioration of economic conditions of the people or a rise in unemployment. In fact, if a simple cause and effect relationship were to be said to exist between the rise of terrorism and secessionism and the persistence of mass poverty as well as unemployment then it gets discounted because there are many areas in India much worse off than Jammu and Kashmir e.g., Rajasthan and Orissa where there is no terrorism or secessionism.

Even in areas like Bihar and some districts of Andhra Pradesh and Madhya Pradesh where unbearable social and economic inequalities have coalesced to produce protest movements like Naxalism these have not demanded political separation or secessionism. In the case of the secessionist groups in Jammu and Kashmir, clearly expectations of support for secessionism from political groups in Pakistan and Afghanistan have encouraged the groups wanting political power to demand the formation of an independent nation state, instead of trying for power as a constitutional opposition through elections, which many opposition parties in the centre and the states have done successfully.

In order to understand what differentiates the situation in Jammu and Kashmir from the Mujahideen led anti-Soviet and subsequently the successful Taliban campaign to capture power in Kabul we have to first of all understand the different place occupied by the anti-Soviet war in Afghanistan within the global calculus of power like USA, Saudi Arabia, Pakistan and their allies. The anti-Soviet war represented after the US defeat in the Vietnam war, a chance to tie down the Soviets in a costly conflict which served as far as the huge Soviet military expenditure was concerned to be the proverbial last straw on the camel's back. The USA was able to secure vast public funds from the Congress for its proxy war against Soviet Communism. The direct costs of the Afghan conflict for USA in the 1980s have been put at US $5 billion which was about 50 times the yearly aid that had been given till 1979. American aid started at about $ 30 million in 1980 for the Afghani resistance going up to $ 50 million in 1981 and 1982.

Under the Reagan Administration this jumped to $ 80 million in 1983 and $ 120 million in 1984. The US Congress doubled the Administration's requested funds to $ 250 million plus an extra allocation for anti-aircraft weapons in 1985. This figure climbed to $ 470 million in 1986 and $ 630 million in 1987 remaining thus through 1989. With Saudi aid matching US contributions total aid to the Afghan resistance since 1987 exceeded one billion a year until 1995. Total aid from all sides had been put by other sources as around $ 8.7 billion between 1986-1990 far exceeding the legal weapon imports of most countries during the same time period. By the end of 1992 there were enough small weapons within Afghanistan to equip the armed forces of both India and Pakistan.[1]

In addition to the aid meant for the Mujahideens in Afghanistan, during the 1980s because the pro-West Government of Shah had collapsed in Iran, Pakistan became in American eyes the lone state that would be the spring-board to protect the Persian Gulf besides providing a convenient location to "keep an eye on what the Soviets were up to". Pakistan got a $ 3.2 billion aid package, a blind eye to its nuclear programme and what is less known the weapons and finance that allowed it to wage its own proxy war in the region. To raise more money for their so-called *jihad*, Pakistan allowed itself to become a nodal centre of an entire network of drug syndicates that flourished within the country even as they systematically used the conflict in Afghanistan to make it the second largest producer of opium in the world. Since the late 1970s, the pace of drug cultivation can be assessed from the fact that between 1986–1988 alone drug cultivation in the region nearly doubled.[2] A UN Report points out how despite Islam's forbidding the use of drugs, the Taliban have expanded drug cultivation in Afghanistan. In 1996 alone a 33 per cent increase in drug cultivation was noticed in the areas under the control of Taliban.[3]

First the massive monetary aid from various sources in the West and Middle Eastern countries and secondly the income from drug cultivation became the basis for the organization of a myriad of "mujahideen" groups, armies, cartels of men and weapons—essentially private mafias subject to no law except their own and those whom they considered useful or more powerful than themselves. On an average during the 1980s it has been estimated that there were 1,50,000 to 2,00,000 armed guerrillas on active service inside Afghanistan. This worked out to a ratio of one-and-a-half Mujahideens to two fighters for every member of the security forces. By contrast, in the Malayan counter insurgency campaign, the British authorities reached a stage where they could deploy 30 security forces personnel for every guerrilla or communist terrorist as the insurgents were called.[4] By comparison as a Pakistani newspaper *The Herald* reported in November 1994: "Today, estimates available from the three major religious groups involved in the Kashmir conflict—the Jamaat-e-Islami, the Jamiat-e-Ulema-e-Islam and the Jamiat-e-Ahl-Hadees put the total number of Pakistani mujahideen fighting in Kashmir at 5000".[5]

Today, the sources for recruiting Mujahideens are kept alive by the presence in Pakistan of nearly 3 million Afghan refugees who have not gone back to Afghanistan. They get lower wages than Pakistani labourers and live in abysmal conditions since international aid has been stopped once the civil war in Afghanistan has been deemed to be officially over.

Another reason for the rise of hi-tech terrorist groups was the involvement of an increasing number of countries who were supplying weapons to the Mujahideens. The Mujahideens moved on from the .303 they managed to cull from the Pakistani arms bazaars on the frontier in the early 1970s to assault rifles and rocket launchers. Often weapons were bought from East European countries and upgraded in American factories. The Saudis supplied the 7.62 Kalashinikov (AK-47) as well as the 5.55 mm Ak-74. Evident also are G-3's, a few M-16's, a wide variety of pistols and revolvers, the Egyptian 'Sakr' shoulder-fired missile, the British Blowpipe, the Igala, Strela and anti-personnel mines from China, Czechoslovakia, Egypt, the US, USSR and Yugoslavia. Chinese mortars and RPG's together with the RPK and RPD Russian heavy machine guns (HMG) were also sold.[6] It was an arms bazaar with global linkages operating on a cash and carry basis.

It is obvious that the Governments in Pakistan and Afghanistan have to do something to retrieve illegal weapons, register the bonafide ones and restrict the supply of weapons to extremist groups. The international community has to agree to come down heavily on the supply of arms to Pakistan and Afghanistan. Recognized terrorist groups have to be banned. The Government in India has to make it absolutely clear that it will do everything in its powers to take a series of steps namely:

(a) Make clear to Pakistan and to the rest of the world that they cannot win a military victory in Kashmir and therefore no military solution is possible.
(b) To make clear to the terrorist groups that not only will it seal the borders in J&K as it has done in Punjab to make infiltration

costly, it will never negotiate under the threat or impact of sectarian and communal violence.

(c) That the militant groups who want a share in political power have a better chance of running the government if they fight elections as a constitutional opposition in Kashmir. Alternatively, they face a bleak future in total political wilderness. There are no solutions outside the Indian Constitutional framework and all discussions have to be within it, including those about autonomy and human rights.

(d) To convey to the world community that India is here to stay as a secular country which has the second largest number of Muslims after Indonesia of which only 4 per cent live in Kashmir. The Muslims are an integral and respectable part of the Indian system and face no formal restrictions on their religious life and social practices. Inequality, poverty and development are experienced by them too in the same way as they are experienced by others. Hence, there is no real basis for arguing a separatist case on religious grounds.

REFERENCES

1. Cf. Focus on Afghanistan, *Strategic Analysis* Jan–Feb. 1997.
2. *Ibid,* p. 1397.
3. *Ibid,* p. 1410.
4. Cf. *Contemporary Conflicts and Brutality,* Centre for International and Strategic Studies, 46 Miremont, Geneve, Switzerland, p. 31.
5. *Ibid,* p. 113.
6. C.f. Focus on Afghanistan, op. cit, p. 1399.

CHAPTER 10

The Face of the Proxy War in J&K

Brig. Chandra B. Khanduri

The Trend

During the 1990s, internal security threat to the country manifested and further exacerbated in its worst ever form since Independence. The Nagas kept up their tirade against the nation. Manipur too threw up several disparate anti-national groups. The rise of ULFA and Bodos in Assam was the direct manifestation of this threat. So also were the Gorkhas in Darjeeling Hills who created an anti-national Gorkha National Front.

That the situation in Jammu and Kashmir in general, and in the Kashmir Valley in particular, took a drastic turn for the worse from January 1990 are known facts. It saw battalions of the Indian Army and other security forces (SF) fight on two fronts: on the Line of Control, and in the hinterland in Jammu and Kashmir itself. Some were moved from Nagaland and others had their peace tenures truncated. The intervening years saw the severest form of low intensity conflict (LIC) in J&K. Initially, the Jammu and Kashmir Liberation Front (JKLF), generally a moderate group, only was operating. By 1992-1993, hardcore, fundamentalist, pro-Pakistani groups had proliferated. They included; Hizbul-Mujahideen, Al Burg, Harkat-ul-Ansar, and Lashkar-e-Toiba. All these had 20 to 25 per cent Afghan guerillas and were controlled completely by Pakistan from the PoK.

But the SF fought a grim battle in the strife torn Kashmir Valley and retained the national integrity and unity against well trained and motivated anti-national elements, the ANEs, as these secessionists came to be called. ANE is a politically motivated soft semantic substitute for secessionists and hostiles, especially coined as the proxy war began in J&K in 1990s. Elsewhere, they were being called as 'Hostiles' and even 'Undergrounds'.

A proxy war, is a war fought by an adversary without his direct involvement, often disguising his efforts through indigenous means and resources. Its larger form was the Korean War (1950-1953), where USSR made North Korea fight its war against the US led UN forces. The fight by the US-led Western powers' against the USSR in Afghanistan (1979-1989) is another example of proxy war.

So, alongside terrorism in Punjab still continued to keep the Army occupied. Operation Rakshak was really begun here and it attempted at beating the terrorists in their own game, while also attempting to restore confidence of the civilian population to the fair systems and ways of the Army in Punjab. By 1996, the operations by the SF combined with other national efforts saw the end of militancy and terrorism in Punjab. A series of civil actions were conducted by the Army in Punjab besides Operation Rakshak I : Operation Avert, Operation Goodwill, Operation Wood Rose, and so on, which organized medical and veterinary camps, recruitment rallies, ex-servicemen's welfare, besides sports and entertainment.

Militarily, Operation Rakshak in J&K was a continuation of the operations in Punjab. These were sometimes referred to as Operation Rakshak I and Operation Rakshak II respectively.

It would be suffice to say that the units of the SF conducted themselves exemplarily and with a sense of purpose. Their approach to the problem was humane. Half their battles were won as soon as they demonstrated their sincerity. Concurrently, they gave a hard knuckle and pursuit to the ANEs, the 'Hostiles', the 'Undergrounds', and every hue of disruptive forces. So pervasive has been the commitments of the Army to the CI area that 'CI Operation Allowance' has been accepted to be paid to all ranks. According to this, Lieutenant Colonels and above are entitled to Rs. 1,300; Majors, Rs. 1,200, Captains, Rs. 1,100; Lieutenants, Rs. 1,050; JCOs, Rs. 900; Havaldar, Rs. 600; and ranks below, Rs. 500 per month each. These figures are being mentioned to highlight the small but the growing cost of fighting CI in J & K. And as a rough estimate while the Siachen sector costs Rs. 3 crores a day or so, the CI operations' cost is almost the same. That is in addition to the PMF—the Paramilitary Forces, and the CPO—the Central Police Organisations, which get paid almost 70 to 80 per cent extra salary in all the CI areas including the North-East. The cost is turning excessive, if not prohibitive.

Conduct or Modus Operandi of the Guerrillas

Pre-Kargil Period

The guerrillas coerced the support of the local Kashmiris, especially the inhabitants of the valley; garnered afresh the political support of the various anti-national factions; and sought and acquired a larger monetary support from Pakistan besides the Muslim countries. The groups then created nuclei of resistance in the villages and towns including down-town Srinagar. They incorporated students, local Muslim leaders, religious zealots and even businessmen. The proliferation of this nuclei grew into larger organizations. With infiltrators across the Line of Control (LoC), arms training was carried out clandestinely and the SF were targetted as often as possible.

It is interesting to note that not only Afghans but also the LTTE were brought into the Pakistani camps in PoK to train the selected men in use of IEDs, and for operating Stinger missiles and signal equipment of various makes and usage. All this time Pakistan conducted a well-planned 'psychological warfare' to alienate the locals against Indian Government and win them over to the so called Pakistani propagated cause of *Azadi,* 'Plebiscite', and so on. They had a mixed bag of results.

With the proliferation of the nuclei, the intelligence gathering, target acquisition and targetting began to be controlled by the Afghanis and the Pakistanis. The ISI also spread its tentacles in the Valley and around the Jammu and Poonch areas. Because the Kisthwar-Doda areas were initially free of militancy, they also moved into them.

They targetted equally the Hindus while leaving the Sikhs untouched. By adopting this dirty trick they had hoped to acquire a tacit support of the Kashmiri Sikhs to their nefarious cause. The Sikhs however, refused to join them, opposing them more vigorously as the time passed. The Chattisingpora (in the Anantnag district) massacre of 35 innocent Sikhs on the eve of President Clinton's visit to South Asia on March 20, 2000 climaxed this stratagem.

While in the initial stages in 1990s, infiltration and ex-filtration of the guerrillas was primarily over the Pir Panjal and Keran, in subsequent stages the jungles of Tithwal and Kupwara provided sanctuaries to the guerrillas; and in some cases they operated with large degree of successes.

All this time, the targets were the long stretches of unmanned lines of communications in the hinterland, convoys of the SF and civilians. Efforts were also centred at political assassinations. So this technique adopted by the guerrillas created uncertainty in the minds both of the SF and the politicians. However, by mid 1995-1996, continuous CI operations neutralised to a very large extent, the operational capabilities of the ANEs. Towards this effort, the overall unity of command, contribution of local anti-ANE organizations, was reasonably supportive. There was distinct decline in their ability to 'rule the roost' as tourists returned to the Valley and the business revived. This led to the 1996 elections and a semblance of restoration of democracy in J&K.

Post-Kargil War Scenario

Operation Vijay, where the 3rd and the 8th Divisions took active part in evicting the Pakistani Army from the heights of Drass-Kargil-Chorbatla involved a thinning out of regular troops from the Valley. The Pakistanis accepted the defeat and the remnants were forced to withdraw into PoK. It was a matter of humiliation and the Army found it difficult to 'stomach' it despite the impossibility of holding on its area of occupation. Seething with anger generated out of its helplessness, it began to resort to larger guerrilla warfare, calling it a *jehad.* In a way, the Indian Government helped the guerrillas. For, its intention to reduce the Army component from the CI force in the Valley, the transfer of that responsibility to the PMF and CPO besides RR was covertly conveyed as a stance both of overconfidence and lackadaisical gesture. It certainly led to a sort of void in the force level in the Valley.

The void created in the Valley led to a spurt in offensive actions by the ANEs, who calling themselves *Jehadis,* selectively struck at targets such as Corps Headquarters, RR posts, BSF Headquarters, and so on. The aim of these actions was clearly to show that they were active and the cause of secession had not been given up. Politically, organizations like the All Party Huraiyat Conference, also played on these incidence in banner news. Another factor that is significant is that, since October 12, 1999 when General Pervez Musharraf replaced the civilian Government in Pakistan through a *coup d'etat,* the ANEs have been thus further emboldened; the same being exacerbated by a mishandled hi-jacking of an IA plane 'Flight 814' from Nepal to Kandhar via Amritsar.

Integration and Boldness—An Immediate Necessity

It is often said that insurgency is the cheapest form of fighting a clandestine-cum-proxy war against an enemy. The Pakistan promoted proxy-war in J&K seems to prove it. They began the tribal warfare in J&K in 1947. A repeat of it was attempted through Operation Gibraltar in 1965. In 1990s it has carried the 'War' for almost a decade and continues its threats and intimidation combining them with its nuclear strikes. It is, therefore, essential for India to devise a strategy that would liquidate the Pak-backed proxy war, once for all. It is worth then especially for senior Army commanders responsible for CI operations in J & K, to read the British experiment in Malaya and Israeli *modus operandi* in Palestine and emulate them, if not in their entirety, then at least imbibe their larger lessons.

One of the reasons for larger degree of ANE violence in the post-Kargil period was absence of an integrated command in the Valley. And as intelligence has often been casualty in J&K and elsewhere, the ANEs have been in a position to strike at their targets with ease. The need of integration of all resources has been once again highlighted.

In J&K there are virtually three Corps of the Army stretched from Jammu in south, Leh and Demchok in the north-east. In between, there is a Brigade group in Siachen. This force is entrusted with defending the LoC, ensuring security of the hinterland and being poised for offensive tasks. In addition there are 30 battalions of RR and few battalions of Assam Rifles besides over 50 battalions of BSF. The additional force in form of Police, ITBP is also available to bolster up the defence efforts. Truly, 2,00,000 men in uniform is a very large force which calls for greater degree of co-ordination and very firm operation control.

Strategically, it is absolutely clear that unless the following objectives are achieved there cannot be lasting solution to the LoC:

First, a demilitarized zone of at least 10 kms about the LoC would have to ensure that the entire area is de-populated and the SFs retain operational freedom there. That would also facilitate adequate counter-infiltration measures.

Second, a degree of strategic flexibility to be available to the SF to strike at targets inside PoK; carry out raids into various establishments; and grievously hurt the Pakistanis in PoK and elsewhere.

Third, as a nation India is capable of escalating its overall efforts to eventually 'bankrupt' Pakistan in its proxy war against India. History serves a useful lesson here. The proxy war that the USA and its allies fought against the Soviet Union in Afghanistan is one such example. Also the USA's role in dismembering the former Super Power Soviet Union is fresh in memory. Perhaps India should evolve its overall strategy, incorporating those lessons.

At the tactical and operational levels, the need is now felt for a reorientation of effort. In this, the first step is to look afresh at the gaps in intelligence—its planning, acquisition and dissemination. The three C's, i.e., command, communication, co-ordination along with intelligence, also needs to be reviewed afresh. It is time that whole of J&K is divided into CI zones corresponding to administrative districts and all resources are placed under command of the man responsible for CI operations. Overall, while the Chief Minister/Governor remains the overall in charge, the CI commander should be provided freedom to devise his plans and execute them.

Politically, the Prime Minister has even gone to the extent of expressing a desire to cross over into PoK to complete the 'unfinished task of history'. Calling the latest attack on the Kashmiri Sikhs, as an act of 'ethnic cleansing', he reiterated the Government's intention and will to eliminate the Pak-proxy-war in J&K. Perhaps Pakistan has provided adequate cause for turning this task into a mission.

It is probable that this proxy war might inevitably turn into a regular war.

CHAPTER 11

Islamist Extremism and Terrorism in Kashmir

K. Warikoo

The success of the Khomeini revolution in Iran and the dissemination of the ideology of Islamic revolution did influence the Muslim peoples in Asia, but it was the Soviet armed intervention in Afghanistan (December 1979) which brought home to them the threats still looming over the Islamic countries. It was in these circumstances of Islamic victory and despair, that the Jamat-i-Islami and other Muslim fundamentalist groups of Kashmir like Students Islamic Federation, Islami Jamiat Tulba, Muslim United Front, etc., through their sustained efforts of indoctrination and preaching in mosques, *madrassas,* Friday congregations and social and political assemblies ignited the Islamic passions among the majority of Kashmiri Muslims and built the "youth cadres to achieve the objective of Islamicising of Kashmiri society".[1] The situation was ripe for Pakistan and its President, General Zia-ul-Haq to launch the operation of fomenting insurgency and subversion against India in Jammu and Kashmir, what has come to be known as the 'Operation Topac'. The Islamic fundamentalist indoctrination of Kashmiri Muslims was channelised against India and anything that symbolised Indian culture, society and polity. Now slogans of *jehad* (holy war) against the secular and democratic order of India and for the establishment of *Nizam-i-Mustafa* (system based on Islamic Shariat laws) were raised in Kashmir. Thus, started the first phase of terrorism in Kashmir in 1989. Pakistan, having failed to wrest Kashmir from India by means of direct armed conflicts in 1947-48, 1965 and 1971, now opted for a low cost proxy war against India, by sponsoring terrorism in Jammu and Kashmir.

During the past eleven years, the phenomenon of terrorism in Jammu and Kashmir has manifested in coercive intimidation of civil population, introduction of radical Islam in society and culture, violation of human rights and restrictions on freedom of religion, expression and life, destruction of properties, ethnic-religious cleansing of Hindu minorities, hostage-taking, attacks on security forces, mines and bomb-blasts, subverting the legitimate civil and political authority in the state and undermining the democratic and pluralistic socio-political order based on the principles of equality and peaceful co-existence.

During the first phase of militancy in Kashmir which started in 1989, the Islamist militant groups strived to "bring structural changes at cultural levels of Kashmiri society",[2] seeking to Islamicise the socio-political set-up in the Valley to bring it in tune with the Islamic state of Pakistan and the Muslim Ummah. There were open calls for establishment of an Islamic order. The liquidation of central government officials, Kashmiri Pandits, liberal and nationalist intellectuals, social and cultural activists which followed, was described as necessary to rid the Valley of its un-Islamic elements. Simultaneously, all cinema houses, beauty parlours, wine shops, bars, video centres, use of cosmetics, etc., were banned by the militant groups. Al Barq issued a ban order on selling of cigarettes.[3] The Peoples League asked Kashmiri girls not to take part in any cultural programmes outside the Valley.[4] Allah Tigers threatened to throw bombs on houses where women would refuse to wear veils.[5] The militants through terror of their gun, coerced the local newspapers to highlight their activities. The Hizbul Mujahideen imposed a ban on the circulation of national and Jammu newspapers in Kashmir Valley. The Wahdat-e-Islami even banned the entry of Mark Tully, the former New Delhi Bureau Chief of the BBC into the Valley and asked the people to "stop listening to the BBC".[6] Offices of daily newspapers like *Aftab, Alsafa* and, *Srinagar Times* were attacked with bombs and even set on fire. Several prominent media persons including Mohammed Shaban Vakil, editor of *Alsafa,* Station Director of Doordarshan Lassa Kaul, Srinagar, P.N. Handoo and Syed Ghulam Nabi, both senior officers in the States information department were gunned down for not toeing the militant line. The terrorist groups used both terror tactics and Islamist ideology to control the local press, which now projected the Islamist viewpoint on society, politics, governances and laws, etc., as superior to the so-called corrupt and anarchic practices in the democratic and secular order prevalent in India. Various Islamist groups like Jamat-i-Islami and its militant wing Hizbul Mujahideen, women's wing Dukhtaran-i-Millat, Jamiat-ul-Mujahideen, Allah Tigers, Jamiat-ul-Ulemmi Islam, etc., proclaimed the objective of their struggle as Islamicisation of socio-political and economic set-up, merger of Kashmir with Pakistan, unification of Ummah and establishment of an Islamic Caliphate.[7]

The Islamist orientation of insurgency in Kashmir became more pronounced. The extremist and terrorist organizations like *Hizbul* Mujahideen, Jamiat-ul-Mujahideen, Harkat-ul-Ansar, Lashkar-e-Toiba, *Markaz Dawal-al-lrshad*, which launched a religious crusade against the non-Muslim minorities, have been publicly taking pride for killing Hindus in the name of *jehad*. The Islamist extremists launched a malicious campaign against the Kashmiri Hindus through periodic write-ups in local newspapers and through sermons in mosques. And the final ultimatum was given to this minority community through press on 14 April, 1990 asking them to leave the Valley within two days or face retribution and death.[8] About one thousand members of the Hindu minority community were brutally murdered and the entire community of about 300,000 forced out of their hearths and homes. The terrorists resorted to most brutal means of killing by hangings, strangulation, beheadings,—skinning alive, blowing the bodies by tying dynamites, slitting of throats, nailing and gunning down the innocent victims. This minority community which is lying scattered in camps in Jammu, Delhi and other parts of India, is agonising in its eleventh year of displacement from its indigenous habitat in Kashmir. Terrorism and religious extremism has had devastating consequences for the socio-psychological, physical, health and demographic profile of these displaced persons. More than 30,000 houses belonging to Kashmiri Pandits, hundreds of their business establishments, educational, cultural and religious institutions have been destroyed or burnt with the object of decimating all traces of the 5000 years old history and culture of this non-Muslim minority in Kashmir.[9] This displaced community is a victim of sinister design unleashed by Pak-sponsored terrorists to deprive the ancient and indigenous Kashmiri Pandits of their right to the territorial locus in the Indian State of Jammu and Kashmir so that its social and political order is altered to a mono-ethnic, Islamist and extremist agenda.

The forced displacement of almost the entire Kashmiri Pandit indigenous minority who were terrorised, killed and hounded out by the

Islamist terrorists and mercenaries, presents a classic case of ethnic-religious cleansing with long-term implications for the composite socio-cultural set-up and secular polity in Kashmir. The Islamist mercenaries have even resorted to targeted killings of the few remnants of Kashmiri Pandits who could not move out of the Valley due to various constraints. On March 21, 1997 seven such Kashmiri Pandits were forcibly taken out of their hearths in Sangrampura village of Budgam district and gunned down. Another 23 members of this miniscule minority including 10 men, 9 women and 2 infants were huddled together in dark cold night of 26 January, 1998, at Wandhama village in Ganderbal and mowed down by terrorists. The killings were done with a clear objective of ensuring that the Indian State of Jammu and Kashmir is cleansed of non-Muslim minorities. More recently one Brij Nath was kidnapped at gunpoint from his home at Brari Angan in Achabal in Kashmir Valley and later put to death on 4th March, 2000, the day of Shivaratri the most auspicious religious festival of the Kashmiri Pandits.

Having cleared Kashmir of the Hindus, brought the media to heel and crippled the administrative and political structures, the terrorists now started bringing the local Muslims under their control. Thousands of young Kashmiri Muslims were coerced to cross the LoC (Line of control) to undergo training in arms and sabotage in various training camps set-up in PoK, Pakistan and Afghanistan. Select groups of such recruits were taken for advanced training to camps on the Pak-Afghan border and inside Afghanistan. Thousands of local youths who resisted were tortured and even killed. In this phase of militancy, it were the local Muslims who bore the brunt of atrocities by the Islamist terrorists and mercenaries. Thousands were killed in this process. Series of assassinations and bomb attacks on social and political activists belonging to nationalist and liberal sections of Muslim society in Kashmir were enacted in a bid to destroy the established political structures and to thwart the process of restoration of democracy in the State. These terrorists were only following the dictats of their Pak sponsors. The Amir of Lashkar-e-Toiba, Hafiz Mohammad Khan went on record saying: "Democracy is among the menaces we inherited... These are all useless practices and part of the system we are fighting against. If God gives us a chance, we will try to bring in the pure concept of an Islamic Caliphate."[10]

The brutal killings, extortions, kidnappings, rape of women, destruction of properties and holy shrines, both Hindu and Muslim, by the Islamist terrorists and mercenaries caused revulsion among the common people in Kashmir against the Jamat-i-Islami brand of fundamentalism. This was more so because the Islamist groups like Jamati-i-Islami and Jamiat Ahl-e-Hadith directed their efforts to eliminate the traditional social and religious practices prevalent among the Kashmiri Muslims. These Islamist groups exhorted the Kashmiri Muslims to banish such un-Islamic practices as visiting ancient holy shrines of Sufis and Rishis. The people of Srinagar even resisted the attempts by some militant groups to stop the celebration of annual Urs at Batmol Rishi.[11] Then followed the burning down of a part of Baba Rishi shrine near Tangmarg. In Aish Muqam, there was a bloody clash in which a few people got killed, when "militants tried to prevent the local villagers from celebrating the Urs of Baba Zainuddin Rishi".[12] And on May 11, 1995 the Islamist mercenaries from Afghanistan and Pakistan led by Mast Gul, destroyed the ancient holy shrine of Sheikh Nooruddin Rishi at Chrar-e-Sharif, 35 kms. from Srinagar.[13] This shrine had been a centre of pilgrimage for lakhs of devotees both Hindus and Muslims, over the past six hundred years. In early July 1998, the terrorists made an abortive attempt to blow up the nearly 700 years old shrine of Naqshband Sahib in Srinagar.[14] Similarly Hizbul Mujahideen and other such outfits have been holding out public threats against participation by Hindus of Kashmir and from other parts of India in the annual pilgrimage to holy Amarnath cave. These holy shrines of Kashmir have been targetted by the Islamist terrorists and mercenaries in order to obliterate the indigenous ethno-cultural and spiritual heritage of Kashmir and the traditional ethos of religious tolerance, harmony and peaceful co-existence, and to usher in the fundamentalist and radical Islamic practices.

The Islamist extremists have also committed atrocities against the women of Kashmir, using rape, kidnapping and murder as their weapons to subjugate the people to their will. Much against the Kashmiri Muslim tradition, the local women are being forced to adopt the fundamentalist way of life, wear the veil *(burqa)* and discard modern lifestyle. Some time back three young girls were shot and injured in Srinagar for wearing jeans. The heads of some girls were shaved just because they sported a modern hairstyle. The terrorists have forced the hapless young girls and their parents to what are known as "command marriages." Hundreds of such victims have been visiting Udhampur and Jammu for abortion of unwanted pregnancies. Gun culture has snatched freedom of choice in marriage. Girls are forced to marry gun-totting militants, lumpens, and people twice their age. Many of these marriages have led to desertions, divorces and torture-killings of women. There are at least 10,000 widows in Kashmir. According to a study conducted by the Sociology Department of Kashmir University, the widows in Kashmir have been experiencing severe problems particularly "emotional stress, denial of inheritance rights, sexual harassment, social undesirability, mismanagement of home affairs, losing control over children, loneliness, physical insecurity, overburden of work and compulsion for remarriage."

Children in Kashmir have also been the victims of violence perpetrated by the Islamist extremists, who resort to various means to Islamise the Kashmiri society .Schools, school going children and school teachers are directly facing the brunt of the atrocities of these terrorists who want to deprive the children the benefits of modern scientific and secular education as they want only medieval .extremist Islamic education to be imparted to these children. On 11th May, 1999, the biggest school in Banihal town of Doda district was destroyed in a bomb blast triggered by these mercenaries throwing the education of hundreds of children in jeopardy. Similarly on 23 October 1999, three students were injured in two bomb-blasts set off by terrorists in a school at Sangla near Surankot at a time when the students had assembled in the compound for their morning assembly. In a related incident, five gunmen entered the house of Mohd. Amin Shah, a school teacher at village Didikot in Kupwara district in Kashmir on 12th May, 1999 and opened indiscriminate fire on the inmates killing Mohd. Amin Shah, his wife Sharifa, three-year-old daughter Sanober and his brother's wife Zareefa. The only crime of Mohd. Amin Shah was that he continued to teach at the village school despite several warnings by the terrorists. In another incident of a similar nature Sarfaraz Ahmed, the only teacher in the primary school at village Neoch in Mahore Tehsil of Rajouri District was killed by the militants on 22nd April, 1999. The killing eventually resulted in closure of the only school in the village, the aim that the terrorists had sought to achieve. Besides thousands of children belonging to the minority communities in the State of Jammu and Kashmir have been rendered orphans because of the relentless killings of the minority communities by the Islamic terrorists. These orphan children are carrying the scars of such atrocities and their childhood as well as adulthood is being adversely affected. More than 30,000 orphans are thus suffering denial of normal childhood and are growing in an atmosphere of deprivation, discrimination, in midst of horror of death and destruction of their dear ones.

The possibility of establishing a new Islamic Caliphate running from Kashmir to Pakistan through Afghanistan, Iran and Central Asia was being discussed by the Islamist extremist groups in Kashmir at a time when the Soviet troops had withdrawn from Afghanistan and the Muslim Central Asian Republics emerged as independent states following the disintegration of USSR. They were echoing the ideas of the Amir (Chief) of Jamat-i-Islami, Pakistan, Qazi Hussain Ahmed, who speaking on Kashmir Solidarity Day in Rawalpindi in February 1992 declared that "a great Islamic state, spreading from Kashmir to Central Asia would emerge after the independence of Kashmir."[15] Soon after new groups like Tehrik-i-Ahyay-e-Khilafat (the movement for revival of Caliphate) and Tehrik-e-Khilafat-e-Islamia (the movement for Islamic Caliphate) announced their presence in Kashmir.[16] They propounded the ideology of transnational Islam and the Caliphate. TKI asserted that "Islam did not recognize nationalism or territorial patriotism. The slogans based on ethnicity, race, gender or nationalism were false... The real Islamic ideology was the ideology of Caliphate... The slogan that future of Kashmir would be decided by Kashmiris has given rise to an evil, which was distorting the Islamic identity of present movement, and reducing it to a mere democratic movement".[17] It is against this backdrop that there emerged close linkage between the Islamist insurgents from Kashmir and the Afghan Mujahideen, with the pan-Islamic ideology binding them together. That thousands of such Kashmiri militants exfiltrated to Pakistan and Afghanistan to undergo training in arms and guerilla warfare, with some of them later fighting alongside the Afghan Mujahideen, lent new dimensions to the ongoing militancy in Kashmir. Now the insurgency in Kashmir was not only losing its indigenous character, but was also being simultaneously taken over by the Islamist radicals and Afghan and Pak-mercenaries as part of the new Pakistani strategy .

The marginalisation of Kashmiri militant outfits like JKLF was deftly brought about by Pakistan after failing to sustain the euphoria among

Kashmiri Muslims about their movement against India. This was achieved by propping the radical Islamist terrorist groups like Hizbul Mujahideen, Harkat-ul-Ansar, Markaz Dawa-al-Irshad and its armed wing Lashkar-e-Toiba in Kashmir, their cadres being drawn from heavily armed and battle hardened Afghan, Pakistani and other Islamist mercenaries all maintaining close linkages with the Jamat-i-Islami in Pakistan and Kashmir.

Hizbul Mujahideen (HM) which was established in late 1989 as the militant wing of the *Jamat-i-Islami,* Kashmir, soon gained prominence after the Jamat-i-Islami and Islami Jamat-e-Tulaba of (PoK) provided liberal arms, funds and cadre support to the HM. This pan-Islamic group gained exclusive control over the terrorist operations in Kashmir in 1990 by diluting the influence of JKLF, by eliminating such Kashmiri secessionists considered inimical to the pan-Islamic ideology and interests of Pakistan, by maintaining hegemony through sufficient arms strength and by utilising the infrastructure and apparatus of Jamat-i-Islami in Kashmir, PoK and Pakistan. The HM has been following the technique and model of Afghan insurgency against the Soviets, and its cadres are mainly drawn from foreign Islamist mercenaries particularly from Afghanistan and Pakistan, mostly veterans of the Afghan war. The Afghan Mujahideen loyal to the Hizb-e-Islami of Gulbadin Hekmatyar were first to join the HM in mid-1991. And following the fall of Najibullah regime and the establishment of Islamic state of Afghanistan by the Mujahideen, the influx of Afghan mercenaries into Kashmir increased. Mercenaries from other Islamic countries like Saudi Arabia, Egypt, Sudan, Algeria, etc., have also joined them. The HM and its mercenaries who are specialised in improvised explosive devices, laying mines, ambush, operating heavier weapons like rockets (anti-aircraft guns) and other lethal weapons, have fanned out in the Jammu region and even in some parts of India to stage acts of terrorism.

Harkat-ul-Ansar (HUA) is another deadly radical Islamist terrorist group with its headquarters in Islamabad. HUA was established in late 1993 in Pakistan and soon after in Kashmir also with the merger of two pan-Islamic outfits, Harkat-ul-Jehad-e-Islami and Harkat-ul-Mujahideen, sponsored by Jamat-ul-Ulemah Islam and Tableeg-ul-Islam—the Pakistani Islamic fundamentalist groups. HUA which aims at 'liberating the Muslim majority areas and establishing the supremacy of Islam, has its operations extending to Kashmir and other parts of India besides Bangladesh, Pakistan and the Central Asian Republics. This organization has been recruiting students from Muslim theological schools for arms training being given in Elaka Gair and Khost areas of Afghanistan. The HUA strategy is to achieve its Islamist objectives by means of *tableegh* (religious discourses), publicity and *jehad* (holy crusade). Most of the Harkat-ul-Ansar mercenaries infiltrated into Jammu and Kashmir have been esconsed in the hilly areas of Baramulla, Anantnag, Udhampur, Kishtwar and Doda from where they extend their reach to adjoining Himachal Pradesh as well. The HUA cadres have been conducting their operations against Indian security forces besides targeting the Hindu minorities in Kashmir and Jammu region, in tandem with the Hizbul Mujahideen. Being equipped with heavy and long-range weapons and sophisticated wireless communication system, the HUA mercenaries have played the key role in terrorist activities including gruesome massacres of Hindu minorities in Jammu and Kashmir since 1997.

Markaz Dawa-al-Irshad (MDI) which was established in 1980s in Muridke near Lahore in Pakistan is an international Islamist fundamentalist and terrorist centre, maintaining close links with Al-Gamaa-al-Islamiya of Egypt, the Ikhwan-ul-Musalmeen and the Islamic radical groups of Algeria. MDI took active part in the Afghanistan war against the Soviet troops. After the successful culmination of *jehad* in Afghanistan, the MDI focused its attention to Kashmir and started recruiting Islamist volunteers from various Muslim countries including Afghanistan and Pakistan for *jehad* in Jammu and Kashmir. Markaz Dawa-al-Irshad has been propagating pan-Islamic Wahabi ideology, and it receives support from centres in Sudan and Saudi Arabia. During the sixth annual convention of MDI held at Muridke, Lahore from 3-6 November 1993, Hafiz Mohammad, its chief declared that Kashmir was not the final destination of the Mujahideen of the Markaz but only a gateway to India. He asserted that *jehad* would be extended to entire India.

Lashkar-e-Toiba which is the armed wing of the Markaz Dawa-al-Irshad, has of late, been trying to establish a foothold in Jammu and Kashmir. Two to three thousand Islamic terrorists belonging to the Hizbul Mujahideen, Harkat- ul-Ansar and Lashkar-e-Toiba are reported to be active in Jammu and Kashmir engaging Indian security forces in long drawn clashes and indulging in subversive activities. And to facilitate the infiltration of Islamist mercenaries, Pakistani forces resort to firing at Indian pickets along the LoC, to divert attention so as to provide cover to the armed intruders.

The pattern of Islamist mercenary activities in Jammu and Kashmir during the past few years suggests that their infiltration and terrorist operations have increased both in breadth and intensity, with the corresponding decline in the local support and popularity of militant groups in Kashmir. Restoration of the democratic process and establishment of the duly elected government in the State in September 1996, delivered a big blow to Pakistan in its proxy war in Kashmir. Now Pakistan intensified its efforts to induct mercenaries into Kashmir to carry out sabotage, targetted killings and attacks on security forces. The Pak-sponsored mercenaries have been employing the local Hizbul Mujahideen cadres for securing hide-outs, logistics and also to act as local guides in their terrorist operations.

These Islamist terrorists have been training their guns on the Hindu minority in Poonch, Rajouri, Udhampur and Doda districts of Jammu province. These terrorists have masterminded mass killings of more than 300 Hindus, women and children, young and old in several parts of this region. The gruesome massacres of Hindu families at Prankote (18th April, 1998), Chapnari (24th June, 1998), Thakrai (29th July, 1998), Bafliaz (3rd August, 1998), Moraputta, Bariyara and Bilala (20th February, 1999), Ari, Poonch (2nd July, 1999), Lahati-Thathri (19th July, 1999), Shindra, Poonch (20th July, 1999), have resulted in forced exodus of about 8000 surviving members of Hindu minority community from their habitat in search of safer places.

More recently, the Islamist terrorists belonging to the dreaded Lashkar-e-Toiba and Hizbul-Mujahideen targetted the minority Sikh community in the Kashmir Valley. On the night of 20th March, 2000 a group of Islamist terrorists and mercenaries, descended on the small village of Chittisinghpora Anantang District of Kashmir Valley. After assembling all the male members in two groups, they gunned 35 of them in cold blood. The aim of this massacre was to force the Sikh community, which had stayed put in the Valley during all these years of terrorist violence, from their homes so that these Islamist zealots can realise their objective of converting the Indian State of Jammu and Kashmir into a theocratic Islamic state.

The challenges posed by Islamist extremists, terrorists and mercenaries need to be confronted and tackled firmly. In order to achieve positive results in the battle against terrorism certain guiding principles need to be followed :

(a) Legislative and criminal proceedings related to different types of terrorist crimes should be set in motion to ensure expeditious trial, prosecution and deterrent punishment of terrorists.

(b) Trans-border and international terrorism be dealt with effectively by ensuring extradition and prosecution of the terrorists.

(c) Principle of non-use of the territory of one state for terrorist activity against the other be applied strictly.

(d) Steps be taken to apprehend and destroy the terrorist groups, and even follow a policy of hot pursuit when these terrorists are operating from their bases in other countries.

(e) Media should strike a balance in their coverage of terrorist activities, in order to contain rather than facilitate the spread of terrorist activities and ideologies.

(f) The society needs to galvanise, its social support to the law and order machinery and create a social milieu in which such terrorist activities are not tolerated.

(g) And at the international level, the UN bodies and states should come out openly against terrorist activities without getting dictated by their own political priorities and compulsions.

REFERENCES

1. Riyaz Punjabi, "The Concept of an Islamic Caliphate: The Religious and Ethnic Pulls of Kashmir Militant Movement," *Journal of Peace Studies,* Vol. 1, No. 1, Nov.-Dec. 1993, p. 42.
2. *Ibid.,* p.43.
3. D.P. Kumar, *Kashmir : Pakistan's Proxy War,* New Delhi, Har Anand, pp. 149-50.
4. *Ibid.*
5. *Ibid.*
6. *Srinagar Times,* 23 September, 1992.
7. Daily *Afaq,* 16 November, 1992; Daily *Nida-i-Mashriq,* 30 January, 1993; Daily *Srinagar Times,* 23 June 1993; Daily *Srinagar Times,* 6 May, 1993.

8. See *Alsafa,* Srinagar, 14 April, 1990.
9. Ghulam Mohammad Sofi, a renowned Kashmiri journalist and editor of Daily, *Srinagar Times* confirmed in a press interview that about 32,000 Kashmiri Pandit houses have been burnt since 1990. See *Times of India,* 19 November, 1997.
10. The *Herald Annual,* Karachi, January, 1998.
11. Riyaz Punjabi, Charar-e-Sharif Tragedy: The Ideological Complexities; *Bulletin of Himalayan Research and Cultural Foundation,* Spring 1996, pp. 16-18.
12. *Ibid.*
13. A Pakistan mercenary, Abdul Rahman confirmed in an article in *Urdu Digest* of Lahore that the shrine of Charar-e-Sharif was destroyed by Pakistani mercenaries led by Mast Gul. Cited in *The Hindu* and *Indian Express,* 2 March, 1998.
14. *The Hindu,* 12 July 1998.
15. Riyaz Punjabi, *op cit.,* p. 46.
16. Daily *Alsafa,* Srinagar, 13 March, 1993.
17. Daily *Srinagar Times,* 18 July, 1993 cited in Riyaz Punjabi, *op.cit.,* p. 45.

CHAPTER 12

Militancy in Jammu and Kashmir: A Study of Actors, Objectives and Strategies

G.M. Shah

Introduction

The origin and evolution of militancy in Jammu and Kashmir State is deeply rooted in the frustration of those anti-Indian political forces within the state who wanted Kashmir to become either an independent country in itself or preferred to see it as a province of Pakistan. The anti-Indian elements were in fact very much present in Jammu and Kashmir even before the actual partition and freedom on 14-15 August, 1947. The political parties like Jammu and Kashmir Muslim Conference, Jammu and Kashmir Kisan Party and the sympathies of Mohammad Ali Jinnah's Muslim League were all opposed to the accession of Jammu and Kashmir to the Indian Union.

When, Maharaja Hari Singh, with the approval of Jammu and Kashmir National Conference led by Sheikh Mohammad Abdullah signed the Acession of Jammu and Kashmir with India with respect to three areas. i.e. defence, foreign affairs and communication, on 26 October, 1947, following the tribal raid from across the border; the hardcore section of the 'anti-India campaign' in the state could not adjust itself to this new political development.

The provisional acceptance of accession by the Government of India and making the finalisation of accession subject to a free and fair plebiscite to ascertain the wishes of the people; subsequent UN Security Council resolutions on Kashmir for holding the plebiscite; dismissal of Sheikh Abdullah from Prime Ministership in 1953 and erosion of the autonomy of the Jammu and Kashmir became the strong factors that broadened the popular base of those political organisations that felt maladjusted with the Indian Republic.

The present phase of militancy in Jammu and Kashmir is the extremist face of anti-India political organisations that have their own sources of inspiration, strategies, financial backing, and other infrastructural facilities for operationalising their plans and programmes. The present study is an attempt to understand the genesis of ongoing phase of militancy in Jammu and Kashmir with all objective to suggest most appropriate policy measures to bring permanent peace to the troubled state of Jammu and Kashmir.

The First Phase of Militancy

The present phase of militancy in Jammu and Kashmir is the third one of its kind in the state during the present century. According to Victoria Schowfield who has thoroughly researched the phenomenon of militancy in Kashmir, the first phase of armed struggle against the Maharaja Hari Singh's government was launched in Spring 1947. Out of over 70,000 soldiers of the state who fought World War II more than 60,000 were from the recruiting grounds of Poonch and Mirpur. Once the war was over, the ex-soldiers requested Maharaja to recruit them in his army but the Maharaja partially for lack of financial resources to pay their salaries and partially due to the fear of overpowering his non-Muslim armed strength refused to take them in his service.

Once these ex-soldiers returned to their fields, they found them not useful for the heroes of the war but for the fresh taxes. With the result they launched 'no-tax campaign' against the Maharaja's government. The Maharaja's government brutally crushed their movement and asked them to hand over their arms to the government. But once these arms passed into the hands of the Dogra, Hindu and Sikh army of Maharaja, the Muslims became very angry over this. They established contacts with the people of North West Frontier Province which was a traditional arms manufacturing base in their immediate neighbourhood. Once the news of armed struggle against the Maharaja's government and the tyranny of Maharaja's forces towards the Muslims of Mirpur and Poonch reached the tribals and subsequently when they learnt about the murder of Muslims in East Punjab and Bengal, the communal passion was heightened with the result on 22 October 1947, Afridis, Mahsuds,

Turis, Bittanis, Khattacks and other tribes crossed the Jhelum river and after a long fight eventually managed to take away (PoK) and Baltistan. The Gilgit Scouts after hearing the Maharaja's accession with India revolted against the Dogra Governor Gansara Singh with the blessings of British officer Major William Brown.

There is a big controversy over the tribal raid of 1947. Pakistan has maintained that the Government of Pakistan was unaware about what was going on in the tribal areas but the Indian government believed that tribal raid was made on the behest of Pakistani regular army. However, one cannot ignore the fact that the Muslim Mirs and Raja's in Gilgit Agency and Mirpuries and Poonchies were not willing to be a part of a state which was likely to accede to India.

The Second Phase of Militancy

Inspired by the Algeria's successful struggle against France and Vietnamese resistance against the United States, the exiled Kashmiri nationalists in Pakistan came to the conclusion in the mid-60s of the twentieth century that, 'there can not be freedom unless we shed our own blood as well as that of our enemy' said, Amanullah Khan[1]. To secure the freedom of Jammu and Kashmir, Amanullah Khan, Maqbool Bhat and several others had joined together in 1965 to form a political party known as Plebiscite Front in PoK. The armed wing of the Front was called Jammu and Kashmir National Liberation Front (JKNLF). As Bhat later recounted, 'Interestingly, Amanullah Khan and several others in my group had seen eye to eye with my proposal favouring an Algerian type struggle to free Kashmir from Indian occupation.[2] Bhat who had first come to Pakistan in 1958, crossed back secretly to the Valley in June 1966. For four months he trained local workers for sabotage and set-up secret cells.

In September 1966, Bhat clashed with the Indian army during an exchange of fire in Kunial village, near Handwara. As the group captain of 'OID' (Operation against Indian Domination) Bhat and several others were charged with sabotage and murder. Bhat and another activist were sentenced to death in September 1968, but before the sentence was carried out they escaped from the Srinagar Central Jail and fled across the cease-fire line to PoK.[3]

During the five year period from January 1965 to January 1971, not less than 80 underground cells and espionage rings operated including

Al-Fateh, Al-Baro and Al-Kashmir. During this period 281 (.303) rifles, 309 guns, 8 sten-guns, 4 light machine-guns, 44 revolvers, 431 hand-grenades, 66 (2") mortar shells, 5 automatic rifles, 65 bayonets, 117 detonators, 30 bombs, 2 rocket, launchers, 3 wireless sets and 1600 lbs. of explosives were recovered by the police.

The period following the Tashkent Declaration after India-Pak war in 1965, was dominated by the organisation called Al-Fateh. This organisation commenced its activity in 1966. By 1969, it had become a full-fledged organisation with a political wing and with a well planned strategy of economic and militant subversion. 'Al-Fateh' derived its name from an Arab guerilla organisation committed to the liberation of Palestine. The organisers also drew inspiration from such diverse elements and movements as the Hungarian struggle for independence, the Cuban revolution and the Che Guevara tactics. The Al-Fateh had about 200 recruits on its list, 40 of whom were extremely active and highly motivated.

The main organiser and leader of Al-Fateh was Ghulam Rasool Zehangir. He also secured the support of the Syed Sarwar founder of Students Revolutionary Council, Fazal-ul-Haq Qureshi and Nazir Ahmad Wani. Al-Fateh drew substantial support from the Plebiscite Front Leaders of the Valley, particularly Mirza Afzal Beg. The youth wing of the Front worked in close liasion, with the Al-Fateh's special organisation-Youngmen League and Student Federation. Mirza Afzal Beg clandestinely remained in touch with Ghulam Rasool Zehangir.

According to Indian authorities the top leaders of Al-Fateh were guided, trained and motivated by officers of Pakistan Intelligence—Major Habibullah, Major Qaiser Qureshi, Major Tufail, Major Asgar and Zafar Iqbal Rather. They crossed the border several times and also remained in touch with Pakistan Embassy to secure guidance and help. The primary objective of Al-Fateh according to the official version was to indulge in espionage and bomb explosions, dacoities and other acts of subversion. Its strategy included destruction of holy places such as 'Maqdoom Saheb-Ke Ziarat' and arouse communal passion. It also brought out posters under the caption' Red Kashmir 'and gave a call for Independent Kashmir.

Al-Fateh was responsible for three major incidents of militancy in Kashmir, namely (I) attacking and killing of Constable Charan Dass of B.S.F. at Nawa-Kadal bridge on 3 February, 1967, (ii) dacoity on 1 April,

1970 at Tehsil Education Office Pulwama, from which about Rs. 72,000 was looted, and (iii) Hazratbal bank dacoity on 2 January, 1971 during the course of which Rs. 97,000 was looted.

It was during the Hazratbal bank dacoity case that police was able to find a clue which led to the detection and ultimate arrest of most of the members of the organisation. The investigation also revealed that a large quantity of arms had been kept by one Saleem Jahangir at Charar-e-Sharif. When his residence was raided by the police 12 sten-guns, 13 (.38 bore) revolvers and large number of bags containing ammunition were recovered. The investigation also revealed that there was a diabolical plan of kidnapping and assassinating VIP's including Chief Minister and Ministers, who would become easy targets during 1971 elections[4].

Most of the activists of Al-Fateh were provided with government jobs according to their educational qualification under the scheme of rehabilitating 'misguided youth' but some among them like Fazal-ul-Haq Qureshi reappeared on the scene during the present phase of militancy in Kashmir.

The Transitional Phase

In January 1971, an Indian Airlines plane 'Ganga' en route from Srinagar to New Delhi; was hijacked by two Kashmiri youths one among them was Hashim Qureshi. The plane was diverted safely to Lahore. Maqbool Bhat came into limelight by meeting the hijackers and claiming responsibility for the hijacking. But when Maqbool Bhat returned again to the Valley in 1976, he was caught and imprisoned for the murder of a bank clerk. After Bhat's re-arrest, Amanuallah Khan moved to England and changed his militant organisation to a political one called Jammu and Kashmir Liberation Front (JKLF) and for ten years Amanullah Khan operated out of Birmingham[5].

In February 1984, Ravindra Mahtre, the Assistant High Commissioner in Britain was kidnapped and the kidnappers asked for one milion pound ransom and the release of several prisoners held in India, including Maqbool Bhat, who was awaiting execution in Tihar Jail after India's re-introduction of death penalty. The Kashmir Liberation Army (KLA) believed to be associated with Amanullah Khan's JKLF, was held responsible for the kidnapping and subsequent murder of Mahtre. When Maqbool Bhat was executed on 11 February, 1984 in Tihar Jail, a strike was held in Srinagar and some other towns of the

Valley to mourn his death, which again demonstrated the potentially subversive leanings within Kashmir.

In September 1985, over a year after the murder of Mahtre in 1984 Amanullah Khan was arrested in England. The charge brought against him was possession of some illegal chemicals which the prosecution alleged could be turned into explosives. Khan protested that they were insecticides for his back garden. He was acquitted in September 1986 but was deported three months later. Khan maintained that he and a Sikh extremist were traded off in return for India's purchase of some British helicopters[6].

Amanullah Khan took refuge in Pakistan from where he began to direct operations across the Line of Control (LoC). He had realized that if his movement was to gain momentum, he had to attract support from the Valley. Four young Kashmiris were recruited and brought to PoK known as the 'Haji' group their names were Ashfaq Majid Wani, Sheikh Abdul Hamid, Javed Ahmed Mir and Mohammad Yasin Malik. They received arms training from across the border and returned back with arms and ammunition to launch the armed struggle against the Indian Establishment in Kashmir.

The Third Phase of Militancy

In March 1987, State assembly elections were held in Jammu and Kashmir and Farooq Abdullah administration was charged with rigging the election. In May 1987, the first major act of violence was perpetrated against Farooq Abdullah when his motor car was attacked on the way to the mosque. Throughout the year sniper attacks became more common which clearly indicated the increase of arms in the Valley. The Valley began to feel the impact of armed militancy in 1988. There were continuing disturbances which disrupted daily life quite frequently. There were two major bomb blasts which just missed the Central Telegraph Office and Television Station in Srinagar.

In an interview to a Pakistani paper on 31 July 1988, Amanullah Khan said, 'uprising had become an armed struggle'. In September, there was an attack on the Director General of Police, Ali Mohammad Watali and a retired session judge, who had sentenced Maqbool to death. The Jammu and Kashmir Liberation Front (JKLF) claimed their first martyr Ajaz Ahmad Dar, who was killed during police firing on 27 October, 1988.[7]

Worse was to follow in 1989. A strike was called for India Republic Day on 26 January. The fourth anniversary of Maqbool Bhat's execution on 11 February provided an early start for anti-Indian demonstrations in the Valley. At the eve of 13 July which is being observed as 'Martyrs day' in Kashmir since 1931, two CRPF jawans were killed at Saraf Kadal by the militants. On 7 July, JKLF made a formal announcement, claiming responsibility for attack on CRPF. It declared, "such attacks would go on till the Indian tyranny and imperialism are ended". After a few days another militant organization Hizbullah Islamic Jamhoria-made similar announcement. It also gave a stern warning to the pro-India politicians of Kashmir labelling them as 'traitors' and said they would be given exemplary punishment. The other organizations which issued anti-India posters include Hizb-e-Islami and People's League.

On July 20, there was a bomb explosion in the ladies toilet of Khyam Cinema indicating the participation of woman in the militant activities. On July 29, acid was thrown on two young Muslim ladies, who were moving about without 'Burqa'. It was intended to serve as a warning to those who did not pay heed to the 'instructions' issue by some of the fundamentalist organizations to the women to observe strict 'purdah'.

On 14 August, Pakistan's Independence Day was celebrated with gusto and gaitey. On 15 August 'hartal' was observed on the call of various militant organizations. At night the lights were switched off. On August 17, a state government bus was hijacked near Tangmarg at pistol point and blown up after ordering the passengers to alight. On August 21, Mohammad Yusuf Halwai a National Conference leader was shot dead near Safal Kadal. A placard on Halwai's body identified the JKLF as responsible for his death. Sheikh Abdullah's death anniversary on September 8 was observed as a deliverance day 'Yome-e-Najat'. A near total 'hartal' was observed in Srinagar, Anantnag, Baramulla, and other towns of the Valley. Effigies of the Sheikh Abdullah were burnt. At night a 'black-out' was observed. On September 14, Tikka Lal Taploo, first Kashmiri Pandit and BJP leader was killed. Neel Kanth Ganjoo, who had been fired upon earlier was shot dead in a Srinagar street on 4 November. Repeated bomb attacks on Mujahid Manzil, the Srinagar headquarters of National Conference indicated that some militant organisations regarded it as their main enemy.

By 1989, a significant number of militant groups had begun to operate throughout the Valley, mainly centered in the towns of Srinagar, Anantnag, Baramulla, and Sopore their objective was either complete independence or unification with Pakistan. The Jammu and Kashmir Liberation Front directed from across the LoC by Amanullah Khan was best known and had the oldest cadres. It was committed to independence rather than joining Pakistan. After the militant campaign had assumed the character of full-fledged insurgency, Amanullah Khan told 'Newsline' of Pakistan in February 1990:

'We basically stand for reunification of our Motherland which has now been divided into four parts: Indian Kashmir, Azad Kashmir and Baltistan which are currently with Pakistan and Aksai Chin under the Chinese. We want these parts to be reunified and made a completely independent state what we are struggling for is independence from both Pakistan and India[8].

In another interview to the Karachi *Herald*, Amanullah Khan reiterated the demand for independence and said it was spreading rapidly in Kashmir. When asked how he worked with groups who wanted Kashmir to accede to Pakistan, he replied that they were all agreed that Kashmiris should be given the right to choose among India, Pakistan and Independence. He also reiterated the secular character of the JKLF and insisted, with little evidence, that some non-Muslims were sympathetic to the campaign that it was waging in the Valley.

Several of the Muslim political parties, who had been component of Muslim United Front (MUF) had formed militant wings. The militant group, Al Barq, had links with Abdul Gani Lone's Peoples Conference, Al Fateh, led by Zainul Abdeen, a former contestant in the 1987 elections was the armed wing of one faction of Shabir Shah's People's League. Both parties had also come out in support of the independence movement. Another armed faction of People's League was Al Jehad[9]. Additional groups aimed at the formation of a 'theocratic' state, the Allah Tigers, in particular forced the closure of bass video shops, beauty parlours and cinema halls, as being anti-Islamic. The Kashmiri women who are not attached to the 'burqa' were asked to veil themselves. They were supported by Asiya Andrabi's fundamentalist women's organisation, the Dukhtaran-e- Millat (Daughters of Islamic Nation). Women were even threatened that acid would be thrown on unveiled faces. The JKLF did not approve of such activities. In the early days of the insurgency, the Hizbul

Mujahedin founded in 1990 based in Sopore within Kashmir and regarded as the militant wing of Jamat-i-Islami aimed at the unification of Kashmir with Pakistan. The smaller groups believed to favour Pakistan were Hizbullah, Al-Umar Mujahideen, Lashkar-i-Toiba, Ikwanul-Mujaheddin, Hizbul Momineen, Tehrik-ul-Mujaheddin, as well as other numerous splinter groups.

Azam Inquilabi had transformed his Mahaz-i-Azadi (Independence Front) into Operation Balakote. His objective was to provide a united front between the rival groups to fight for liberation of Kashmir from Indian rule. 'India and Pakistan must recognise our right to self-determination so that the two parts of Jammu and Kashmir be allowed to annex with each other. Then the people must be able to decide whether they want to remain free or join with Pakistan. We want to be able to determine political future for ourselves'[10].

Many of the militants were the disappointed political workers and traditional opponents of the National Conference in the 1987 elections. Young men aged between sixteen and twenty-five, came from the towns of Srinagar, Anantnag, Pulwama, Kupwara and Baramulla. Unlike their forebears, who had campaigned for education and political rights in the 1930s, the majority were well educated, doctors, engineers, teachers and policemen who had become alienated by Indian government policies towards Kashmir. Their grievances were as much economic as political. Older militant leaders, like Amanullah Khan of JKLF, Ahsan Darof of Hizbul-Mujaheddin and Azam Inquilabi of Operation Balakote, provided the motivation and historical context in which the struggle was being waged; 'we kept struggling for a peaceful resolution of the dispute but failed, said Inquilabi, so this young generation has opted for active resistance and it has gained momentum and it will continue to gain momentum come what may'.

On 8 December, 1989, the militants belonging to JKLF kidnapped the then Union Home Minister Mufti Mohammad Syed's daughter Dr. Rubaiya Sayed, an intern at the Lal ded Memorial Womens Hospital Srinagar. The kidnappers demanded the release of five militants, including JKLF leader Sheikh Hamid, and the brother of Maqbool Bhat in return for her freedom. Journalists and bureaucrats became involved in the negotiations to free Rubaiya and on 13 December, the militants were ultimately freed; two hours later, Rubaiya Sayeed was also released unharmed. The releasea militants were taken out in a triumphant procession through the streets of Srinagar.

On 13 February 1990, Lass Kaul, the local director of Doordarshan was murdered by militants in Srinagar on his way home. The militants blamed the state administration for pressuring Kaul into broadcasting pro-Indian government material, thus indirectly bringing about his death. In April, Kashmir University Vice Chancellor Prof. Mushir-ul-Haq, his secretary, Abdul Ghani and the general manager of Hindustan Machie Tools watch factory, H.L. Khera were kidnapped by the, militants. They demanded release of their jailed militants but this time government did not meet their demands and the militants killed all the three hostages.

On 21 May, Mirwaiz Maulvi Farooq who had a traditional following in the valley, was shot dead at his residence but his death remained a mystery as none of the militant organisation claimed the responsibility for his assassination.

After the JKLF's earlier successes, their leaders found that the Hizbul Mujahedin was finding more support in Pakistan at their expense. Amanullah Khan complained that his recruits were being coerced to join the Hizb and other groups. In December 1991, at a press conference in Islamabad, Khan regretted that the pro-Pakistani Hizb was killing JKLF workers. The JKLF also accused pro-Pakistani supporters of providing clues to the Indian security forces regarding JKLF hideouts, which made them easier to catch. In 1992, Amanullah Khan made repeated attempts in February, March and October to demonstrate that JKLF did not recognise the line dividing 'the motherland of Kashmir'.[11] Although thwarted in his objective, the publicity did boost his support and demonstrated that the JKLF was prepared to pursue its independent objectives in the face of opposition from the Pakistan Government.

The JKLF staged a comeback, writes Balraj Puri, and the slogan of 'azadi' returned to the Valley at the expense of pro-Pakistani sentiments. Puri believes at this stage the Kashmiri People began to shed many of their illusions about Pakistani support for their movements[12].

Under Governor G.C. Saxena, the government also worked to improve its intelligence gathering operation and counter insurgency measures in the Valley. Those militants who could not withstand torture under interrogation, were 'turned' and use as 'Cats' (Concealed Apprehension Tactics) to identify fellow militants. 'Operation Tiger', launched in August 1992 was the first in a series of security forces operations code named 'Shiva', 'Eagle', 'Cobra'. Their aim was to suppress the various militant groups through a 'catch and kill' policy[13].

In February 1993, thirty-two anti-India political parties grouped together to form an umbrella organisation known as the All Parties Huriyat (Freedom) Conference (APHC). Maulvi Farooq's teenage son and Mirwaiz of Jama Masjid Srinagar became its Chairman. The common objective of different political parties within APHC was that the people should be given the right to choose among India, Pakistan and freedom.

In October 1993, the mosque at Hazratbal attracted international attention. Since the spring, the militants had been parading openly in the streets nearby. The area was cordoned off by the security forces leaving about a hundred militants and more civilians inside the mosque. Negotiations took place and after thirty-two days the militants were given a safe passage by the government.

During the year 1994, political process and normalisation became the key phrases of the Indian Government to hold elections for Jammu and Kashmir state legislative assembly. The militant's response to such initiatives was negative. The murder in March 1994 of Wali Mohammad Yattoo, a National Conference leader and former speaker of the J&K legislative assembly, was taken to be a warning against attempts to revive political process in the state. At India's Independence Day celebrations on 15 August 1994, Prime Minister Narasimha Rao formally announced that a political process would be initiated for the normalization of the affairs in Kashmir. In order to commence its dialogue, the government released some of the top political activists including Shabir Shah, Syed Ali Shah Gilani, Abdul Ghani Lone, Yasin Malik had been already released on bail on May 1994; moreover 276 detainees were also released. At the end of October, however, the militants further attempted to derail the election process by stealing the electoral rolls for Sringar from a government building and setting them on fire[14].

The Presence of Mercenaries in Kashmir

The presence of foreign militants also called as 'mercenaries' was felt in Kashmir as early as in 1992. But the Charar-e-Sharief episode highlighted their presence in large numbers in the troubled state of Jammu and Kashmir.

In March 1995 Mast Gul, former shopkeeper from Pakistan's North West Frontier Province, trained during the war in Afghanistan occupied the mosque at Charer-e-Sharief, which is revered for its association with Nund Rishi, the patron saint of Kashmir. Amongst his followers were what the government referred to as about seventy 'mercenaries'. The militants claimed to have liberated the area from the Indian security forces, but the forces responded by cordoning off the area. The mosque was destroyed by fire on 11 May, 1995 which the militants blamed on security forces, who in turn blamed the militants for it. Although, over forty people were killed, Mast Gul escaped to Pakistan[15]. The burning of the nearly 600 year old shrine caused a serious resentment among the people against the government machinery for mishandling the situation. The elections for state assembly, tentatively planned for July 1995 were postponed in the wake of Charar-e-Sharief incident.

By 1993, the JKLF appeared to have lost its military ascendancy to the Hizb-ul-Mujahideen, although politically, the organization claimed to have retained 85 per cent of the people's support. When Yasin Malik was released from jail in May 1994, he renounced the armed struggle and made an offer of political negotiations. In 1995, Azam Inquilabi of Operation Balakote left his base in PoK and returned to Srinagar, where he declared himself in favour of working towards a 'political solution'. The Hizbul Mujahideen, whose active strength was assessed by the Indian authorities at around 2500 was able to gain its ascendancy militarily in the middle 1990s. Since the militants had adopted a strategy of killing the surrendered militants many among them were compelled by the circumstances to rejoin the militant organisations after release from the jail but nearly a 1000 with the support of security forces formed Ikhwanul Muslimoon under Mohammad Yusuf alias Kukka also code named as Jamsheed Sheerazi, whose objective was to liberate Kashmir from the control of militant organisations. In order to boost the morale of militants fighting against Indian forces and provide them leadership the mercenaries appeared on the scene.

The Harkat-ul-Ansar which was formed in 1993 by reuniting Harkat-ul-Jehad-e-Islami and Harkat-ul-Ansar in October 1993 started operating alongside Hizbul Mujahideen, Al-barq and Al-Jehad in the mountainous districts of Doda, Poonch and Rajouri, Later Laskhar-e-Toiba whose headquarters are at Muridke near Lahore also started operating in the mountainous districts. With the passage of time the recruitments of Kashmir youth started showing a decreasing trend and the proportion of mercenaries and those of non-Kashmiri's went on increasing. The control of the militant organisations like Harkat-ul-Ansar, Lashkar-e-Toiba and Al-Badr remained under non-Kashmiri militants and mercenaries. It is believed that presently two-third majority of the militants active in Jammu and Kashmir are mercenaries'.

Following the Lok Sabha elections in May 1996, State Legislative Assembly elections in September 1996 in Jammu and Kashmir and Lahore Bus Yatra of Prime Minister Atal Bihari Vajpayee in February 1999, an atmosphere of future peace and normalcy in South Asia in general and Kashmir in particular was created. But neither Pakistani army nor the militant organisations operating in Jammu and Kashmir were willing to promote bilateralism without separating Kashmir from the Indian Union with the result Kargil frcnt was opened by the Jammu and Kashmir Jehad Council stationed at Muzaffarabad in PoK as well as Pakistan regulars in Spring 1999, soon after melting the snow in Drass, Mushkoo, Batalik and Turtuk sectors. Though after fierce fighting along the LoC, the militants were compelled by the Pakistani Government to retreat the post-Kargil strategy of militants active in Kashmir proved highly disastrous for security forces. The death squads called 'Fidyeen' who sneaked in from across the border blew up many army bunkers in Kashmir, thereby creating a huge damage to the security sytem in the state.

Following the release of Hurriyat leaders by the Central Government and the announcement to hold talks with the separatist leaders within the constitutional framework of India, the Hizbul Mujahideen blew up the vehicle of State Power Minister Ghulam Hassan Bhat in early May 2000 in which five persons including Mr. Bhat were killed. The attack was a warning to those political leaders in Kashmir who may have in some way given an indication to negotiate Kashmir issue on table. Though the killing of 35 Sikhs at village Chhatisinghpora and 11 Shia Muslims at Pattan are the examples of elevated terror in recent months, but the militants did not claim any responsibility for these incidents.

The Magnitude and Impact of Militancy

Both, the magnitude and impact of militancy in Jammu and Kashmir has been of an enormous proportion. The official figures indicate that between 1989 and 1995 as many as 13,427 AK-47's, 756 rocket launchers, 1682 rockets, 54 light machine guns, and 735 general purpose machine guns were recovered by the security personnel from the militants in Kashmir. On an average the government claims to recover 4000 weapons a year of varying sophistication[16]. In 1995, it retrieved 587 bombs compared with 300 in 1994. During the militancy of last one decade hundreds of schools, bridges, and official buildings were damaged due to militancy in Kashmir. Nearly 50,000 people were killed and nearly one lakh families were directly affected due to militancy in one way or the other. About four lakh people were compelled by the circumstances to leave Kashmir due to political instability in the Valley. The period from 1990 to 1991 was the peak time of militancy in Kashmir during which nearly 10,000 militants were active in the state. Nearly, 50 militant organisation were active in Kashmir during this period. The militant organisations presently active in Jammu and Kashmir are Hizbul Mujahideen, Harkat-ul-Ansar, Lashkar-e-Toiba and Al-Badr. All these militant organisations are pro-Pakistan ones. Only Hizbul Mujahideen is under the control of a Kashmiri militant leader Maulvi Yusuf Shah alias Syed Salahuddin. All others are run by non-Kashmiri militant leaders.

According to 173rd Report on 'Prevention of Terrorism Bill 2000' submitted to the government by Indian Law Commission, the ISI sponsored terrorism and proxy war had resulted in the deaths of 29,151 civilians and 5,101 security personnel and 2730 explosions Security related cost in countering ISI activities was around Rs. 64000 crores[17]. Though the militants active in Jammu and Kashmir deny any link with ISI and call their activities as *'jehad'* and 'indigenous freedom struggle' it is obvious that the arms training and the financial support they receive is not indigenous.

According to a recent study conducted by the Institute of Defence Studies and Analysis, New Delhi more than 50 per cent funding for the militancy in Jammu and Kashmir comes from poppy cultivation in NWFP and Afghanistan. Around 5 to 10 crores a month are spent on the salary of the militants. Each new recruit gets a salary of Rs. 10,000 to 15,000 a month. The top militant leaders are paid Rs. 15 to 20 lakh a month as a salary for their militant operations in Kashmir[18].

8. Conclusion

From foregoing study it becomes clear that the militancy in Jammu and Kashmir is deeply rooted in the contemporary history of the state as well as that of the India-Pak relations. The political and militant forces active in Jammu and Kashmir need a patient hearing by both India and Pakistan to resolve the Kashmir crisis permanently. The bilateral engagement between India and Pakistan could not bare fruit unless the people from different shades of Jammu and Kashmir are involved in the process of conflict resolution. The unilateral initiative by the Government of India to hold negotiations with Hurriyat Conference and other representatives of the people of Jammu and kashmir will not pave the way for permanent peace in the state unless Pakistan and the militant organisations are involved in such a process. Keeping in view the mountainous topography of the state of Jammu and Kashmir, it is not possible for the Indian security personnel to stop cent per cent infiltration into Kashmir and as long as infiltration is not stopped, permanent peace cannot be brought about. The only option left with the Government of India is to secure the goodwill of Pakistan and militant organisation at the most minimally affordable cost in terms of economic, and political bargaining. The Indian official stand to talk to Pakistan only when it stops the cross-border terrorism indirectly amounts to help the suffering of the people of Jammu and Kashmir in cross-firings, bomb blasts, and other sorts of armed violence.

REFERENCES

1. Kak. B.L. *The United Story of Men and Matter;* Jammu 1987, p. 76.
2. *Ibid,* p.77
3. Schowfield, Victoria; *Kashmir in the Crossfire,* Viva Books Pvt. Ltd., Delhi, 1997, p. 209.
4. Jagmohan; *My Frozen Turbulence in Kashmir,* Allied Publishers, New Delhi, 1991, pp. 150-61.
5. Akbar, M.J., *Kashmir: Behind the Vale,* New Delhi, 1991, p. 173.
6. Schowfield Victoria; *Kashmir in the Crossfire;* 1997, No. 3, p. 232.
7. Desmond Edward; 'The Insurgency in Kashmir (1989-91)', *Contemporary South Asia,* 1995, Vol. 4, No. 1 pp. 6-7.

8. Bhattacharjea, Ajit; *Kashmir the Wounded Valley,* New Delhi, 1994, p. 259
9. Schowfield, Victoria, *op.cit*, p. 239.
10. *Ibid.*, p. 240.
11. Anwar Iqbal; *The News,* 8th February 1992.
12. Puri Balraj, *Kashmir: Towards Insurgency;* London, 1993, p. 67.
13. Schowfield, Victoria; op.cit, p. 252.
14. Tim McGirk; *The Independent,* 31 October, 1994.
15. Shaheen Akhtar, 'Reviving Political Process in IHK: Problems and Prospects' in *Regional Studies,* Islamabad, Pakistan, 1999, p.5.
16. Indian High Commission, London, February, 1996.
17. Legal Correspondent, *The Hindu,* 28 April, 2000.
18. Kshitij Prabha; 'Narco-Terrorism, The Case of Pak-Sponsored Terrorism in India' paper presented in the National Seminar on '*Rise of Terrorism and Secessionism in the Region*' organised by International Institute for Asia-Pacific Studies, New Delhi on 30 April, 2000.

CHAPTER 13

'Cross-Border' Terrorism in Punjab

Satya Pal Dang

The term "cross-border terrorism," if I am not mistaken, began to be used after a combination of political parties headed by the BJP came to power in India and in relation to Jammu and Kashmir. In any case, I cannot recall this term having been used by anyone who mattered in discussing the nearly 15-year long period of terrorism in Punjab. I think it was proper and correct that this was so.

There is no doubt that forces beyond India's borders did play a very significant role in fuelling terrorism in Punjab. However, terrorism can flourish nowhere unless there are internal factors giving rise to it. Terrorism is not like ordinary crime. It requires some mass support, at least benevolent and sympathetic neutrality of a section of the people on the basis of their real or imagined grievances. The terrorists may give voice to these grievances in correct forms or in some distorted forms. From this it follows that even cross-border terrorism needs to be fought not only on the law and order front and against the forces across the border fuelling it, but also politically inside the country, in order that sections of the people sympathetic to or supporting the terrorists may be won over. The term 'cross-border terrorism' would tend to suggest a strategy that neglects the need of a political fight inside the country or region where the terrorists are operating. I think the strategy of the present Indian Government in relation to Jammu and Kashmir terrorism suffers from this great defect. This, however, does not fall within the scope of this study.

For terrorism in Punjab too, both external and internal factors were responsible. The external factors were the following:

1. Pakistan has a common border with Indian Punjab (and with some other states in India). It was asserted that the Sikhs in Indian Punjab

were being oppressed and that 'their' demand for Khalistan a sovereign theocratic state with Sikhism as its official religion) was justified and deserved to be supported. Of course, the rulers of Pakistan were not so naive and ignorant as to believe that India was a very soft state and that the establishment of Khalistan was a practical proposition. They would also have known that the demand for Khalistan did not have the support of the majority of the Sikhs in Punjab and in India as a whole. Their real aim was to create such a situation in the Indo-Pakistan border areas of Amritsar and Gurdaspur districts as would help them to seize Kashmir, with no one in these border areas of Punjab to help the Indian Army. This, of course, does not rule out the possibility of some Pakistani Army officers really believing that they would be able to disintegrate India through terrorism and thus take revenge against a country which they considered responsible for the disintegration of Pakistan by establishing an independent sovereign Bangladesh.

The help that terrorism in Punjab got from across the border came in many forms, including the following:

(a) Training of youths smuggled into Pakistani Punjab from Indian Punjab as terrorists and supplying them weapons, including some very sophisticated ones.
(b) Weapons were smuggled into India for Khalistani terrorists.
(c) Allowing leaders of the Punjab terrorists to stay in Punjab to help the ISI and others in their work and to guide their followers operating on the Indian side of the Wagah border. Even today there are not a few people in Pakistan with whose help efforts are being made to revive terrorism in Punjab.
(d) Propaganda, mostly false or based on distorted facts.

At a later stage possibly, some Punjabi speaking Pakistani youth turned into "Sikhs" with a good knowledge of Sikh religion/ and fully trained as terrorists were also sent to Indian Punjab.

It is reported that there exists a press in Lahore which prints Punjabi books about Sikh religion and Sikh history in Gurmukhi script. Sikh gurdwaras in Pakistan were also used for Khalistani propaganda whenever a large number of Sikhs from India visited Pakistan on such occasions as Guru Nanak's birth anniversary.

The Government of Pakistan apart from the ISI and the Pakistan Army) was itself involved in helping Khalistani terrorists, though it was never admitted—just as in the case of Kashmir today. How close was the liasion between the terrorists in India and the Pakistan Government would be clear from the following single incident.

DIG Police Atwal, a Sikh, who was in plain clothes, was shot dead just outside the main gate of the Golden Temple, from where he had just come out. He was shot by terrorists from within the premises of the Darbar Sahib. Pakistan radio was the first to broadcast the news; and it did this when the dead body of the police officer was still lying where it had fallen after the bullets hit the target.

2. US imperialism and its allies too played a significant role in fuelling terrorism in Punjab. The aim was to weaken India as much as possible since its anti-imperialist foreign policy of non-alignment and friendship with the erstwhile USSR was a big troublesome thorn in their side. While the Pakistani hand was all too obvious, imperialism acted mostly from behind the scene and in a clever and sophisticated manner. The banner of "human rights" was, of course, exploited in a big way. Violation of human rights by the police, paramilitary forces and the army in India was alleged and grossly exaggerated day after day, while for a very long time not a word was said about the grossest violation of human rights by the terrorists. The sympathy and support given to Punjab terrorism by the imperialists was not such as could not be seen. Sometimes it became all too obvious. For instance, the US media once reported about a number of Sikh youths being trained as Khalistani terrorists in the USA. When asked, the then US President tried to befool the people by saying he had no powers to stop such training camps being run by private agencies. Despite all this, no one except the Left in India raised an accusing finger at the US ruling classes for a very long time. Terrorism in Punjab received help from Britain, Canada and West Germany too.

3. The Punjab terrorists received considerable help from a section of Sikhs living in the USA, Canada and other countries, led by men like Ganga Singh Dhillon. They grossly misused Sikh gurdwaras in these countries for the purpose. Some of the leaders dreamed of Khalistan as a lucrative market for their goods. Ganga Singh Dhillon himself had close links with the rulers of Pakistan. At least one Indian bank actively helped in the transfer of large amounts of money from abroad to Punjab terrorists. This matter was raised in the Parliament too.

As we have already said, without the internal factor, Punjab would not have had to go through more than a decade-long night of terrorism, something that makes one shudder to think even today. The following in my opinion are the main internal causes:

(a) The autonomy provided to the states in the Indian Constitution had been eroded. India needed to be more federal. This was necessary to ensure India's unity in diversity in the new situation (considerable development on capitalist lines after India became independent). This was denied and this encouraged separatist tendencies. In Punjab capitalist landlords (gentlemen farmers) and rich peasants (*kulaks*) dominated the economy of the state. Economically, this was the most powerful class in the state. It wanted to dominate politically too. Almost all these gentlemen happened to be Sikhs. The programme and leadership of the Akali Party represented the interests of these gentlemen.

The refusal of the Government of India to make the country more federal in nature and even the erosion in the quantum of autonomy for the states provided for in the constitution, helped the terrorists on the one hand, and the Akali leadership, on the other, to distort the justified urges for more power for the state of Punjab into increased support for a Sikh theocratic state within India *a la* Anandpur Sahib resolution, or for Khalistan, as demanded by the extremists and terrorists. It is noteworthy that at no stage could the majority of the Sikhs be won over for Khalistan and even for a theocratic state.

The facts noted above, and the issue of more powers for the states including Punjab, suitably distorted, gave birth to the Anandpur Sahib resolution adopted by the Akali Party. The resolution, in fact, demanded a theocratic Sikh state within India with a very weak Centre which, if conceded, would lead to a sovereign Sikh state. This resolution united the moderates and the extremists in the Akali Party. Undoubtedly, it brought plenty of grist to the mill of the Khalistani terrorists.

(b) Some genuine grievances of Punjab, relating to the division of surplus waters of the rivers of the erstwhile pre-1967 Punjab province, and to territory (both distorted as Sikh issues), helped the terrorists.

(c) A number of imagined grievances were created and were widely aired, the aim being to make the Sikhs believe that they were second class citizens in India. This was done even by moderates like Parkash Singh Badal who even burnt copies of the Indian Constitution in public.

The Akali Dal as a whole had accepted the false thesis that 'Sikhs are a nation'. This helped the separatists, who drew the obvious conclusion that Sikhs must have a separate state.

(d) A factor that played a very big role was the vote bank policies pursued by the political parties in Punjab. The Congress and the Akalis were (and still are) the two main parties in Punjab—rivals for power in the state and for bigger representation in the Indian Parliament. Both played the terrorist card as part of their strategies to achieve their power related objectives. Jarnail Singh Bhindranwale, the chief of the Khalistani terrorists, originally a Sikh priest, was brought into politics by the Congress which encouraged him to raise extremist slogans. The Akalis, in gross violation of Sikh *maryada*, installed Bhindranwale and his bodyguards in the Akal Takht. They converted the Darbar Sahib into an armed fortress. Arms were allowed to be freely taken into the Golden Temple by the Congress government, while the Akali leaders denied that there were any arms in the temple even when machine-guns could be seen on the outer walls of Darbar Sahib. A DG Police once asked, "How can you fight terrorism when everyone wants to play the Bhindranwale card?" Bhindranwale himself said in an interview once, "Some people say that the Congress is using me. The fact is that I am using the Congress." He could justifiably have said, "I am using both the Congress and the Akalis".

(e) Hindu communalists too provided considerable support to the terrorists. The terrorists' strategy was to provoke Hindu-Sikh riots. Severed heads of cows were thrown in front of some Hindu temples. In retaliation, Hindu communalists threw cigarettes into gurdwaras.

Competing economic interests of Hindu and Sikh traders also played a part. Against the demand for Amritsar being declared a holy city, Hindu fundamentalists demonstratively and provocatively asserted their right to smoke. The model of the Golden Temple outside the Amritsar railway station was destroyed.

There are other, secondary, factors which helped the terrorists in Punjab. One of these was provided by police excesses. Many Sikh youths were subjected to torture again and again by some police officers on mere suspicion. Many of them were left with no other choice than joining one terrorist group or the other. Unemployment (and especially the non-availability of the types of jobs desired by the Sikh youths) on the one hand, and the huge amounts offered to them and their families by the terrorist groups, on the other, was another factor, besides some others.

Punjab terrorism was not linked with nationalism, as in Assam, but with religion, as in Kashmir. Inevitably, religiosity played a big role in strengthening terrorism in Punjab.

Terrorism all over the world would have a number of common features, such as: killings to create terror and to prove that terrorists are stronger than the state, kidnappings for ransom, prescribing codes of conduct, dress, etc. At the same time there are country-specific and even region-specific features too. I do not want to deal with all these aspects of terrorism in Punjab, not only for reasons of space, but also because by now they have been discussed at length in a large number of books and other writings by some of those who were in Punjab during the days of terrorism, by Punjabis living in Delhi and by many others, including academics. However, I think it necessary to refer to some specific issues.

Sikh Community in Punjab and Terrorism

There is no doubt that the majority—even a large majority of Sikhs in Punjab from the beginning was opposed to the demand for Khalistan and also terrorism as a method to achieve it. Support and sympathy in the earlier stages came from some sections of the land owning peasantry and some sections of the urban middle classes. Agricultural labourers as a class were strongly opposed to it from the beginning, as also Sikh industrial workers as part of the working class as a whole. There are cases of even Sikh middle-class youths risking and even sacrificing their lives to protect their Hindu brethren. Attempts to provoke Hindu-Sikh riots failed miserably, though it cannot be said that the gulf between the two communities did not increase.

It is extremely unfortunate that Operation Blue Star was undertaken. It should and could have been avoided. The responsibility for it lies on Bhindranwale on the one hand, and the Congress and Akalis, on the other.

Role of Police in Punjab

In the initial stages, only some police officers fought terrorism in Punjab. The police force as a whole did not fight it. Its hands were tied by the ruling party which was seeking to use the terrorists for narrow political gains. It also seemed to some police officers that some leader from amongst the terrorists might become the Chief Minister of the state as a result of a deal between the politicians and the terrorists. A police officer once told me, "When such a deal comes through, our IPS officers will go to the other states. We of the Punjab police will then be at the receiving end from the new rulers of Punjab if we fight terrorists as we should."

The police as a whole started fighting against the terrorists with full determination only when the terrorists began targeting policemen and after there was a change of policy, brought about by Chief Minister Beant Singh from "Catch them if you can, but don't shoot to kill them" to "All out fight against the terrorists on the law and order front."

Even amongst the topmost officers there were different approaches. Julio F. Rebeiro did an excellent job in motivating the police force. He ended the rift between the Punjab police and the CRPF. Rebeiro was known as an upright officer. He was by no means soft, but allegedly his slogan "a bullet for a bullet" was misunderstood and misinterpreted. Before he took over, there was no realization amongst the top brass that the fight against terrorism needed to be waged on the political front as well. There was Shri Chaman Lal, who banned anything not strictly legal. The police were told that anything illegal done by any police officer or official would attract deterrent punishment. There was also the "super-cop" K.P.S. Gill—a Punjabi Jat Sikh with experience of dealing with terrorism in Assam, and much more. He did not succeed when the job was entrusted to him first because his hands were tied. When he became the police chief in Punjab after Beant Singh became the Chief Minister, he was given a free hand to the extent that Beant Singh himself could not transfer even an SHO. K.P.S. Gill's role in fighting terrorism should not be underestimated, but his negative side must be seen too. He did not try to ensure that no innocent person became a victim. He believed that "everything is fair in love and war". Some of his instructions to his subordinate officers gave them a free hand to commit atrocities and indulge in torture of the worst type. As a result there were many avoidable excesses.

Officers of the lower ranks too were not all of the same mould. Some used the most heinous methods for even personal revenge, etc. There were also some who took care that as far as possible no innocent person was killed. And even if some innocent person did get killed, unavoidably or as a result of some bona fide mistake, they took measures to ensure adequate compensation for the family.

As regards corruption, I should like to reproduce here two conversations. A friend of mine told me after he had returned from a trip abroad, "Some of the terrorists have built huge properties in some foreign countries." I requested him to prepare a list for me. His reply was, "I will do that. And I will also prepare a list of police officers who have done the same thing." Unfortunately, he drifted, and failed to prepare the lists he had promised.

There were fewer complaints against the paramilitary forces. As far as the Army was concerned, its help was sought twice. During the first stage, there were complaints of excesses. During the second stage, however, the behaviour of the Army was on the whole good and positive.

Extra-constitutional methods were definitely used by the police. To some extent these had become unavoidable because the vote bank politics of some parties had allowed terrorism to become too strong.

Role of Political Parties

Apart from what has already been said, the following needs to be noted.

(a) Beant Singh was one Congress leader who was active against terrorism throughout. He, however, believed wrongly and repeated many times that terrorism was only a law and order problem.

(b) Differentiation between the extremist and the moderate sections of the Akali Party has to be made, even though they took some common positions too as we have already said before. The moderate section of the Akalis was not in favour of a sovereign Sikh state, though Badal had signed a memorandum with the UNO demanding Khalistan out of fear and cowardice. The moderates, however, were also not averse to using Bhindranwale to get better terms. Longowal had even described him as "our *danda*" (our stick) to beat the Congress with.

The Akali Party as a whole and especially the moderate Akalis stood to gain from terrorism in another way. Many sections of the Sikhs have been opposed to the Akalis due to class reasons as well as because of their secular traditions. The Akali party, therefore could not be sure of winning the majority in the Punjab Assembly on its own, despite Punjab being a Sikh majority state. Terrorism in Punjab under the banner of Khalistan would lead to large scale migration of Hindus from Punjab. Its repercussions outside Punjab would result in the migration of many Sikhs to Punjab. Such a two-way migration and the circumstances leading to it would tend to benefit the Akalis electorally and make it easier for them to come to power.

The percentage of Sikhs in the total population of Punjab increased from 60.75 in 1981 to 62.95 in 1991, while that of the Hindus decreased from 36.93 to 34.46 in the same period. Compared with the 1971 Census figures the change would undoubtedly be bigger.

(c) The BJP did oppose terrorism. However, as is well known, the BJP is controlled by the RSS. The declared objective of the RSS is the establishment of Hindurashtra India, i.e. a Hindu theocratic state. Also, the RSS asserts that "Sikhs are Hindus". Both these positions of the RSS were fully exploited by the terrorists to strengthen themselves.

(d) The Left (the CPI and the CPI-M) has been the most consistent fighter against terrorism. The CPI campaigned against terrorism from the very beginning, and was later joined by the CPI-M. The activists of all political parties were killed by the terrorists. In the case of the Left, however, its activists and leaders were targeted because the Left alone, and in particular the CPI, carried on a mass campaign against terrorism even in the rural areas which were the stronghold of the terrorists.

In the earlier stages the Left as a whole very much underestimated the need for fighting on the law and order front, on the ground that the problem was only political.

It needs to be noted that from the Left to the BJP, an all-parties campaign against the danger of Hindu-Sikh riots and even to denounce terrorism, was also there. The initiative in this respect was generally taken by the Left, and especially by the CPI.

Role of Women

The terrorists had in their ranks some women too who worked mostly as couriers. But a large section of women, including Sikh women, participated in the campaign against terrorism. The role of the Punjab Istri Sabha (affiliated to the National Federation of Indian Women-NFIW) is particularly noteworthy. The Istri Sabha won national recognition for the work done by it in collecting funds for and rendering immediate and prompt help to families of victims of terrorism, including persons injured by the terrorists. Subsequently, the Punjab Istri Sabha set up the Punjab Istri Sabha Relief Trust, a registered body with Mrs. Oshima Raikhy as Chairperson, Mrs. Vimla Dang as Secretary and Shri Kulwant Rai Gupta as Joint Secretary-cum-Treasurer, which has been doing remarkable work, especially in the matter of giving stipends to children of terrorism-affected families to ensure their education. The Punjab Istri Sabha also worked hard for enhancing the government's relief package and for its implementation.

Prof. Laxmi Kanta Chawla of the BJP too won laurels for her work against terrorism and in connection with relief measures.

Some people confuse terms like "fundamentalism", "theocracy". "militancy", "terrorism", etc., and even think that they all mean more or less the same thing. In fact, militancy is quite different from terrorism. To call terrorists "militants" is to give them respectability while defaming the militants. Theocracy, religious fundamentalism and terrorism can help each other and may in some cases—but not always—go together; they are quite different.

Terrorism is a method to try and achieve some objectives, which may be good or bad. The method is best understood by what happened in Punjab.

Innocent people were shot dead at random by firing upon individuals, by spraying bullets on passers by and shopkeepers in streets, by entering houses and killing whole families from 80-year-old grandmothers to little children and pregnant women. Not to speak of villages, no one dared to walk on the streets and in bazars after sunset even in cities like Amritsar. Mothers could not be sure if their children would return safely from their schools. Kidnappings for ransom were the order of the day. The terrorists would enter any house and order the inmates to supply them food and rooms to sleep in, and so on. Later on, there were many incidents of rape, forced marriages, etc.

Even when the objectives of the terrorists may be just, terrorism cannot but lead to their own moral degeneration, especially if it is not given up soon.

As everywhere else, there were rivalries amongst different terrorist groups and even mutual killings. There was reliance on anti-social elements from the very beginning. Bhindranwale himself took help from smugglers. In course of time, many other anti-social elements joined in. The terrorists too degenerated with the passage of time. However, the conclusion that some academics have sought to derive from such facts, that the whole "struggle" was the result of some gun-loving and trigger-happy youth is not at all correct. The "struggle" had its ideologists from the very beginning.

I was asked by many people how it happened that, after an all-out fight against the terrorists was started by the government on the law and order front in 1992, the terrorists were very much down, though not out, by the beginning of 1994, i.e. in a short period of two years. This happened because by that time the terrorists had lost whatever sympathy and support they had. In Amritsar district a section of the land owning peasantry would say during the first phase, "The boys are fighting for us." During the second phase they began saying, "The boys are doing some bad things, but they are for us." (This was when money began to be extorted not only from Hindu and later on the Sikh-traders, but also from well-off rich peasants too). The third stage arrived when large-scale rapes and also forced marriages began to take place. Now the earlier sympathy turned into hostility and information began to be given to the Army about the terrorists. This helped the government to achieve big successes quite quickly.

The fact that political issues were not resolved was not without effect. The danger of terrorism re-emerging in Punjab, though in a different way, remains. Efforts to revive it continue to be made by the ruling circles in Pakistan as well. The setting up of a Pakistan Gurdwara Committee, headed by a former ISI chief, to control gurdwaras in Pakistan is a part of such efforts.

The Left, democratic and patriotic forces must exercise the utmost vigilance and remain alert.

CHAPTER 14

Islamic Factor and Fundamentalist Threat in Central Asia

Devendra Kaushik

Independence (Azadi) of the five former Soviet Central Asian Republics as a consequence of the sudden and unexpected dissolution of the Soviet Union witnessed a prolonged debate among the policy-making and concerned academic circles in India on the likely impact of the Islamic factor on the region and the danger of fundamentalist threat. A realistic and informed assessment of the situation in these republics was of crucial importance to India as Pakistan which has been fomenting trouble in the Indian state of Jammu and Kashmir in the name of religion was not likely to miss a perceived opportunity for acquiring a strategic depth in Central Asia inhabitated predominantly by people professing Islam.

The author recollects how several Indian observers of Central Asian scene dismissed out of hand the "exaggerated" fears about Islamic fundamentalists ever posing a serious threat to the new post-Soviet region. The basic thrust of their argument was that the seven decades of modernization under the Soviet rule urbanization, industrialization, emancipation of women, mass literacy, etc., were going to act as an insurmountable barrier for the Islamic fundamentalists' efforts to gain ascendancy. The lack of knowledge of Arabic language even among the Central Asian clergy and the weak hold of Islam over the largely nomadic composition of the Kazakhs, Kyrgyzs and Turkmens, it was pointed out, would further deter the rise of fundamentalists Islam in Central Asia.

The author, who did not agree with the view, summarily rejecting any possibility of emergence of the fundamentalist threat in the region, had taken the stand that under conditions of social tensions caused by problems of transition to a free-market economy and multi-party democracy, a danger of easy conversion of "religious-Islam" into "political Islam" and through exploitation of the latter by vested interest and internal opposition, into "fundamentalist Islam" cannot be totally ruled out. The decay and disappearance of the Soviet ideology left a vacuum in the belief and value system. As belief in communism began to decay during the Brezhnev period, search for an alternative ideology acquired a mass dimension. Thus, Islam began to acquire a deeper roots among the masses in Central Asia much as orthodox Christainty became widely popular in Russia. The Islamic revivalism in Central Asia gained a wide sweep involving millions of people. Islamic revivalism was, of course, not Islamic fundamentalism but it had far-reaching implications in terms of Islamsation of public life.

The renewal of interest in Islam after the collapse of the Soviet regime was not surprising despite the right to freedom of conscience and worship enshrined in the constitution. Communist party in power conducted a vigorous anti-religious propaganda.

Nevertheless, notwithstanding this anti-religious propaganda, Islam persisted as a key element in every day life of the Central Asian people who adapted themselves to the new circumstances. Even party members did not completely disown their Muslim identity while celebrating birth of a child, solemnising wedding or offering prayers after burial of the dead. Rituals like *Nikah* and circumcision were widely practised and religious festivals like *Id* were popularly celebrated. Inability to go to Mecca for Haj pilgrimage resulted in performance of little Haj in the form of visits to graves (*mazars*) of the Muslim dividers. Thus, a typical Central Asian could be described as *Homo Islamicus* in as much the lifestyle and traditions followed by him were in many cases based on Islam. Families were large and close-knit. Marriages were early and divorce rates were low. The population growth rates (201.9% for Tajiks, 177.4% for Uzbecks in comparison with the 36.8% average for the Soviet Union during the 1959-89 period) created large labour crises and consequently high unemployment particularly in the rural areas, cancelling out all Soviet attempts at biological or cultural assimilation. Even in the urban areas, the *Mohallah* or community feeling continued to dominate and allegiances were shaped by native neighbourhoods[1].

The activization of the Islamic factor in Central Asia passed through several stages. It was conditioned by a whole range of complex socio-economic and political factors. The growing ties with the developing Islamic countries and the projection of Central Asian Republics as a socialist model of development for the Third World countries also helped the Islamic renewal. It was under such conditions that Wahhabism began to acquire a foothold in the Fergana valley of Uzbekistan as far back as the seventies of the last century. While some observers of the Central Asian scene tend to view the rise of Wahhabism as a purely indigenous movement advocating return to "pure" Islam, others attribute its appearance to the decay of Saudi Arabian support. The decay of communist ideology during the latter period of Brezhnev's rule created an ideological void among the popular masses which they tried to fill up with religion.

Islamic renewal received further impetus during the Perestroika period of Gorbachev who followed a policy of glasnost or openness. If previously Islam was blamed for backwardenss, it was now sought to be used for fight against such social evils as bride preppies, alcoholism and as wasteful expenditure incurred on lavish wedding celebrations: the need to counter the spreading influence of the Iranian Islamic revolution through glorification of local Central Asian religions, traditions also helped the renewal of Islam. The relaxed atmosphere created by the glasnost policies led to rise of opposition to official Islam. The Central Asian Mufti who was an appointee of the Soviet regime was accused of following an un-Islamic way of life. Public agitation against Mufti Shamsuddei Bobokhan resulted in his replacement by a new Mufti, Mohd. Yusuf. The new Mufti promised a copy of Koran for each family and larger opportunities for Haj pilgrimage.

More and more new mosques and *madrassas* which began to the constructed in the Central Asian Soviet Republics were another manifestation of renewal of Islam. These mosques and *madrassas* were built not by wholly indigenous resources. Liberal financial assistance from Saudi Arabia, Iran and Libya, and also human resources to run these institutions made possible their large-scale construction. Turkmenistan which had just four functioning mosques before 1991 had many more under construction after that. The number of mosques in Uzbekistan grew from 300 to 5000 in 1993. In Kyrgyzstan there were 1000 mosques by 1995. In Tajikistan there were over 2000 mosques during 1989-1991 period including 130 large Friday prayer mosques. A large number of *madrassas* for religious education including some exclusively for women also appeared in Central Asia[2]. Thousands of Central Asians went for Haj pilgrimage to Mecca. Most of them, the author was told during his visits to Tajikistan in 1989 and 1990, were handsomely rewarded in cash by the Saudi authorities.

As noted above, change in government policy during the late 1980s under M. Gorbachev also helped the renewal of Islam in Central Asia. From 1989, a more conciliatory policy towards Islam was followed. If previouly Islam had been blamed for acting as a roadblock for social and economic progress, it was now acclaimed as having many progressive features which could be harnessed for accelerating social progress. The government acceded to the public demand for changing the old Central Asian Mufti and transferred the Koran of Caliph Usman to the custody of the Muslim board of Central Asia. The importance of the Islamic factor also grew in conditions of an ideological vacuum which threatened social implosion in the aftermath of disintegration of the USSR. The ruling Central Asian elite took the course of promoting Islam as the basis for the new state ideology and its own legitimization. The Soviet ideology was dismissed as temporary aberration and indicted for undermining public morality. President Akayev of Kyrgystan and President Karimov of Uzbekistan took their Oath of Office on both the Constitution and the Koran. The Central Asian Presidents Niyazov of Turkmenistan, Karinov of Uzbekistan and Nazarbayev of Kazakhistan made a beeline to Mecca for Haj. Signboards in Arabic script appeared on shops in the Fergana region of Uzbekistan and demands for adoption of local languages as the official language of the state and change over to the Arabic script began to gain popular momentum.

This emergence of Islamic renewal in the late eighties and early nineties also known as the "folk Islam" was a product of the complex socio-economic and political conditions discussed above. To some extent it was a reaction to the anti-religious measures undertaken during the Soviet period which grew apace in the liberal atmosphere of the Gorbachev rule. Outside influence encouraged by the events of the seventies and the eighties in Iran and Afghanistan (the Khomeini Revolution and Soviet military intervention in Afghanistan), education of the future clergymen abroad, delegation to Islamic countries and increasing number of Haj pilgrimage also contributed to this new phenomenon.

Uzbek scholar Ablakul Bazarov has aptly analysed this phenomenon of sudden spurt of "folk Islam" during the late eighties and early nineties and the process of its transformation into fundamentalist Islam in the Fergana region which is now trying to expand into other parts of Central Asia through terrorists methods[3]. According to him, initially it began through conversations and speeches in mosques and *chaikhanas* (teahouses) which focussed on declining living, standards, price rise, shortage of essential products, corruption of party and government elite, etc. Islam began to be projected as the only alternative to this decline in quality of life. Criticism of the officially appointed *Imams* and clergy was voiced. Self-appointed religious leaders seized the functioning mosques and opened new mosques. This moment was seized by the Wahhabis who were followers of a fundamentalist movement for restoration of the "pure Islam" which appeared in Arabia in the mid-eighteenth century under the leadership of Muhammad Alwahhab. The spread of Wahhabe doctrine was greatly favoured by the events of the 70s and 80s in Iran and Afghanistan. Imam Khomeni was the most popular figure among the Wahhabies in Uzbekistan.

References to Koran were made while indicting the party leaders and the official clergymen appointed by them. Ideal of equality and justice as embedded in true Islam were lauded. The Islamic factor, writes Bazarov, thus became actively involved in the struggle for political and economic power that was waged following the disappearance of the Soviet power. The Islamic parties which emerged accused the official Islamic clergy of apostasy while the latter denied the necessity for Muslims to set-up political parties and underlined that all true believers represent a single entity, the charter of which is Koran and the programme is Sunna.

The appearance of extremists notes in the speeches of the leaders of the newly emerging political parties and movements alarmed the Government of Uzbekistan. It also came to know about the contacts between the Afghan Mujahideens and the followers of Islamic renewal in Uzbekistan. Under these circumstances it took the decision for re-registration in Uzbekistan, of parties and organizations registered earlier in Moscow. The all-union Islamic Renaissance party which was founded in June 1990 at a Congress of the Muslims held in Astrakharr with three regional structures, including the one for Central Asia was meant to be the only political organization for the Muslims in the Soviet Union. Its objective was to enable the Muslim population of the former Soviet Union to live according to the requirements of the Koran and advance humanistic ideals and equal rights for all nations. According to the programme adopted by it, the Muslim people of the Soviet Union who had ceased to be real Muslims need to be educated about the Islamic way of life, about Islamic customs and traditions, the IRP aimed at forming a federation of Muslim governments within the Commonwealth of Independent States founded after the dissolution of the Soviet Union and gave a call for supporting strong Islamic movements that emerged in Pakistan, Sudan, Algeria and the Middle Eastern countries, these movement were represented as parts of one great whole since they rejected secular regions[4].

The Tajik branch of the IRP had close connections with the Afghan Mujahideen both before, during and after the civil war in Tajikistan and extended support to each other on several occasions[5]. As early as February 1990, the new President of Afghanistan Burhanuddin Rabbani lent open support to the Islamist demonstrators in Dushanbe[6]. Both Hekmatyar and Masood trained the Islamist militants in their camps in Afghanistan. After the civil war in Tajikistan many of the IRP leaders including Davlat Usman, Mohd. Sharif Hirmmatzoda and Akbar Tirrajonzoda fled to Afghanistan and continued their opposition activites with the help of the Afghan Mujahideen[7]. Ahmad Shah Masud is known to have trained some 7,000 Tajik rebels in Kunduz province of Afghanistan. According to the KGB officials, Hekmatyar armed 400 IRP militants during the Spring 1992 demonstrations in Dushanbe[8]. The Mufti of Uzbekistan Mohammad Sodiq, Muhammad Yusuf transferred 200 thousand dollars from charity fund to the Moscow Industrial Bank for purchasing weapons for Tajik Muslim Koziyat headed by his personal friend Turajonzoda[9]. This led to the dismissal of Mufti Sodiq by President Karimov, making the end of the latter's brief honeymoon with the new Mufti whom he had appointed to placate popular opposition to the continuation of old Soviet appointed Mufti Shamsuddin Bobokhon. Mufti Mohd. Sodiq was charged with the misappropriation of money derived through sale of copies of the Koran donated by Saudi Arabia[10]. The Islamic fundamentalist movement appeared in the Fergana region of Uzbekistan where several Wahhabis had been active during the late eighties. The first manifestation of militant Islam in the Fergana valley was in the form of violent demonstrations at the time of President Karimov's visit to Namangan in early 1992. The Islamist fundamentalists demand for setting up an Islamic state in Uzbekistan was turned down by Karimov. About one-third of the total population of Uzbekistan. The unemployment rate is about 35% of the workforce, this provides an ideal incubator for growth of religious extremism. Operating from mosques and *madrassas* led by Saudi largesses, about 15,000 students, a potential Taliban type force of militant Islamists were trained in Fergana, the Imam of Nawangan Abdul Ahad, was reported to have declared: "first Fergana, then Uzbekistan, and then the whole of Central Asia will become an Islamic state". The militant Islamists organised vigilante groups of young volunteers to force women to wear the veil and to seek justice through the shariat courts. They also started collecting local taxes in the name of *zekat,* traditional Islamic payments for the welfare of the people. The Wahhabis also started spreading their influence to the nearby city of Osh in Kyrgyzistan. In December 1997, the militant religious extremists beheaded the Namrangan militia Deputy Chief and hung his head to a pole in a public square. They also put a packet of currency notes in his mouth to justify their killing of a corrupt official.

In early 1992, a group of militants calling itself *adolat* or Justice Party appeared in the Namargan district in the Fergana Valley. It projected itself as a group fighting against encroachment on property of honest working people, bribery, narcotics, prostitution, etc., and initially received some public support and laudatory references in the local press. But the Adolat followers began to change with the passage of time and started taking the law into their own hands. Their ex sses led to public resentment and demand for ban on their functioning. In Kazakhistan too xenophobic nationalist party *Alash* advocated return to Islamic precepts. However, both the Adolat and alash found few new supporters and soon disappeared from the scene. The IRP was not registered as a political party not in Uzbekistan on the ground that it sought to exploit religion for political ends. It is however, legal in Tajikistan where the Islamist opposition is a part of the national coalition ruling the country. Its fluence in Tajikistan is however, declining as evidenced by its poor performance in the recent Presidential and Parliamentary polls.

As discussed above, the influence of Islamic factor in Central Asia has undergone several stages. Towards the end of the eighties, it was characterized by a non-conflictual expansion of its reach and role of Islam in both, the day-to-day public life as well as state ideology. It was followed by a second stage in 1991-1993 which witnessed factorization of non-governmental Islamic movements in the Fergana valley and split in the spiritual administration against the backdrop the bloody civil war in Tajikistan which forced Tashkent to take some active measures to prevent its spillover into Uzbekistan. In the post-1993 period, a degree of stabilization was achieved in the situation with regard to Islam under conditions of considerable socio-economic progress in the Republic of Uzbekistan. By 1995, the Islamic "religious boom" wars over. Construction of new mosques almost came to a halt and many mosques were left incomplete. The enrolment of students in the Mir-Arab madrassah in Bukhara fell sharply[11]. Traditional Islam however, continued to occupy an important place in the socio-cultural life of the Republic.

But in 1996, the stage of de-politicization of Islam which had just begun in 1994-95 was again interrupted by the Taliban takeover of Kabul and the fallout of the first Chechen war which emboldened the religious extremists in Central Asia. As already mentioned above, religious terrorist groups became active in the Namangan district of the Fergana region in December 1997 and early 1998 killing of the police chief. In a statement Komilov foreign minister of Uzbekistan, accused the extremist religious organization in Pakistan of training Uzbek forces from the Fergana valley in Wahhabism and armed combat. Komilov charged these Pakistani organizations for encouraging subversive trends in Uzbekistan by sending the trained militants through Tajikistan and Kyrgyzstan. But he did not blame the Pakistani Government which according to him had no knowledge of these activities. Obviously, Uzbekistan does not want to spoil relations with a country through which it hopes to have access to the sea. For some time Tashkent also tried to keep the Taliban in good humour, hoping to cope with the threat posed by them to its security by moving further closer to the United States through its active participation in the partnership for peace programme of the NATO. It also started distancing itself from Moscow in the process of bringing about national reconciliation in Tajikistan and changed its earlier hostile attitude towards the Islamist opposition in that Republic. Uzbekistan unlike Tajikistan did not show any enthusiasm for invoking the provisions of the 1992 Tashkent Collective Security Agreement concluded between the four

Central Asian Republics and Russia from the Taliban threat. Instead, it actively participated in NATO military exercises in Central Asia and served notice of its intention to withdraw from the Collective Security Agreement with Russia in February 1999. It vocally supported the United States in the United Nations against what it called the "Cuban Terrorism".

A change in the assessment of the Islamist fundamentalist threat in Uzbekistan could however, be noticed beginning with the year 1997 in the aftermath of the northward drive of the Taliban. Karimov's book *Ubzekistan on the Threshold of the 21st Century"* published in early 1997 listed fundamentalism as serious threat to security and stability of the Republic. This was followed by the law on religious organizations, which in its amended form adopted in May 1998 governs the administration of religious affairs in Uzbekistan. This law guarantees freedom of religion subject to reasonable restrictions in the interest of public health, morality and order. A religious organization can own land and other property. Registered religious organization can have central organs but their leaders can only be citizens of Uzbekistan and non-citizens can be leaders only with the permission of the Ministry for Religious Affairs. Article 5 of the Law on Religious Organizations prohibits prosyletization just as it is the case with the law in Armenia, Lithuania and Russia. This provision is meant to protect the traditional religions. Article 14 which is opposed by the fundamentalists prohibits religious followers warning in public, of dress or of beard being identified with a religious sect. The Article prohibits imparting of military training to followers of any religious organization, import and export of religious literature and objects is also to take place in accordance with procedures laid down by law. The stand taken by President Karimov in his book mentioned above is that the use of religious slogans for intervention in politics, economy and jurisprudence is not permissible as it poses a threat to stability. Karimov however, supported the role of Islam in exhorting people to follow higher spiritual and moral values. He has established by a Presidential decree a scientific centre for the study of Islam in Tashkent.

The five bombs that went off in Tashkent on 16 February 1999 signalled a new upsurge of religious terrorism. Two explosions took place inside the building of the Interior Ministry, one near the Uzbekistan National Bank and one on the Independence Square where government headquarters are located. President Islam Karimov himself escaped narrowly as one of the bomb exploded just 150 metres away from his car which was stopped by the commander of the Presidential Guards. Addressing the diplomats in Tashkent on 23 February, President Karimov stated that not only the Wahhabis but members of Hezboolah were also involved in planning the explosions in Tashkent. On 1 March, the Uzbek Television named the President of the banned opposition Party Erk, Mohd. Solih as a suspect in these explosions. The Interior Minister of Uzbekistan Zakir. Almatov pointed the accusing finger at "Uzbek citizens with their mentors from elsewhere" and mentioned the responsibility of Wahabism, Hezb-e-Jahriri, Islamiya and Islamic movements in Pakistan for this crime[12]. *The Kommersant* daily published from Moscow reported in its issue of 3 March that Uzbek authorities were investigating the possibility of involvement of Osma Bin Laden who has reportedly spent 150 million dollars in Central Asia for subversive activities.

Islamic militants not only exploded bombs in Tashkent on 16 February, 1999 killing 15 people and injuring more than 100, they also started taking hostges by hijacking buses. Thus, a bus was hijacked on the Tashkent-Urgenh route on 30 March 1999. During the operation to free the hostages, three officers of the Uzbek national security service and an officer of traffic police were killed. The Uzbek television report on 31 March points to the casualty figure at nine dead and several wounded. The Khorezm regional court tried a group of 16 people for this crime. They were charged with the offence of attempting to illegally overthrow the constitutional system of the Republic of Uzbekistan and turning the country into a state dependent on the banner of a single Caliphate. The evidence in the case showed that they had been active over the past several years, purchasing arms with money obtained by means of robbery and sending young people for military training in Chechnya. The court sentenced on 6 July, two of the accused to death and the rest to imprisonment for 6 to 20 years and ordered confiscation of their property[13]. On 26 July, a Karkalpak court sentenced three young men to 15 year imprisonment for subversive activities. They had illegaly crossed over to Tajikistan and Turkmenistan for receiving training in use of arms and also went to Iran. They were arrested while returning from Iran with narcotics and religious propaganda material[14]. Twenty two person were tried in July 1999 for the 16 February explosions in Tashkent and six of them were sentenced to death. In August 1999, six more people including the two brothers of Erk Party Chairman Mohd. Solih were also tried for the Tashkent explosions. The trial of 22 people for the bomb attack in Tashkent was described in a Meshed radio broadcast from Iran, carrying statement of Mohd. Solih as a framed attempt to silence the opposition. Solih alleged that the accused on trial in Tashkent were arrested in Turkey ten days before the bomb blast by the Deputy Chairman of the National Security Service who had gone there to arrest them with the permission of the Turkish authorities. He also stated that his two brothers had been falsely implicated[15]. The Uzbek opposition leader declared terror as an "unaceeptable action for us even for motherland, nation and religion".

In May 1999, The Islamist terrorists hijacked another bus taking 26 passengers as hostages. Two passengers and four policemen were killed while freeing the hostages. The terrorists who hijacked the bus were trained in Chechnya[16]. On 15 November 1999, the Islamist terrorists attacked a police station in Yangiabad district of Tashkent killing three police officers and three local residents. It is suspected that these militants numbering 15 to 20 infiltrated from Kyrgyzstan.

The biggest armed operation launched by the militants after the Tashkent explosions was in the southern Kyrgyzstan district of Batken. Trouble started when a group of 21 armed militants mostly ethnic Uzbeks crossed over to the southern Kyrgyzstan district of Batken from northern Tajikistan and took four hostages including the head of the Batken district National Security Directorate, towards the end of July 1999. On 31 July, the Defence and Interior Ministers of Kyrgyzstan flew to Batken to conduct negotiations for the release of the hostages. A 200 strong Kyrgyz force was deployed to encircle the militants. The militants who entered Kyrgyzstan from Tajikistan were led by a field commander Aladulaziz of Uzbek origin. They asked for a large ransom payment indoors for the release of the four hostages and permission to enter Uzbekistan[17]. The Uzbeck TV on 17 August reported on the basis of the statement given by the Uzbek Foreign Minister. A. Komilov, that the Uzbek air force bombed the militants' camp in Batken with the permission of the Kyrgyz authorities to prevent them from entering Uzbekistan[18]. The Radio Russia reported the release of the hostages on payment of ransom money and promise of safe passage to Jirgator district in Tajikistan[19].

But, instead of going back to Tajikistan the militants took 120 people as hostages and demanded food. They seized three villages and took four Japanese geologists along with one interpreter as hostages on 22 August. They also held up the Commander of Kyrgyz Interior Troops, Major General Anarbek Shamkeyev after killing his driver. The Security Minister of Uzbekistan, Kyrgyzstan and Tajikistan met on 23 August to discuss the hostage issue. The Uzbek Foreign Minister A. Komilov accused the Tajik Islamist opposition of having links with the militants trying to enter Uzbekistan through the territory of Kyrgyzstan[20]. The Tajik President's Press Secretary Zafar Saidov denied the collusion of the United Tajik Opposition with the militants in Southern Kyrgyzstan. He called them a bandit formation led by; one Juma Nomassgoni who belonged to the Islamic Rebirth Movement of Uzbekistan.

The interesting thing about this large-scale armed operation by the Islamist militants in Southern Kyrgyzstan is its timing and pattern which coincided with incursion of armed Chechen terrorists into the territory of neighbouring Dagestan. The Russian news agency Itar-Tass reported from Dushanbe on 24 August that the Tajik secret service took a number of serious measures to prevent attempts by envoy Shamil Basayed, a leader of Chechen terrorists, to recruit mercenaries from the ranks of the Tajik Islamist opposition to resume fighting with the Kyrgyz forces. This resulted in the further seizure of 20 Kyrgyz soldiers as hostages on 27 August, 1999. This discomfiture of the Kyrgyz defence forces led to the declaration of emergency in the Osh region where 1,000 armed Islamists were engaged in fighting the Kyrgyz government troops. Kyrgyzstan requested Russia for military and technical assistance. Moscow agreed to provide Kyrgyzstan all possible military and technical help excepting the direct involvement of its troops in fighting the terrorists. The fighting resulted in the exodus of about 4000 Kyrgyz villagers as refugees. On 28 August 1999, the four Central Asian states convened a meeting of their defence and foreign ministers in Osh which resulted in the adoption of a joint declaration signed by their foreign ministers. This declaration noted that terrorism and religious extremism were becoming an international phenomenon and expressed confidence that the world community would support their joint efforts to fight them. The Russian Defence Minister Igor Sergeyev discussed the situation with President Islam Karimov. Russia and Uzbekistan formed an operational group of specialists to localize the conflict, on 30th August both the Kyrgyz and Uzbek planes conducted air strikes on the Islamist militants hideout in southern Kyrgyzstan[21]. On September 2 1999, the Iranian Radio reported that the Japanese authorities had approached Abdullo Nuri, the leader of Islamist opposition of Tajikistan, to use his good offices for release of the four Japanese hostages[22]. Seven Kyrgyz soldiers were killed and seven wouded in an encounter with the terrorists. On 17 September, the Uzbek Foreign Minister Komilov again blamed the United Tajik Opposition for helping the bandits in the Batken district. He termed Nuri's denial of links with the terrorist, in southern Kyrgyzstan as "deception"[23].

The Russian daily *Kommersant* of September 25 reported that several groups of terrorists succeeded in crossing into the Fergana valley of Uzbekistan using the Kyrgyz peasants as human shields. They broke through in groups of three or four men and tanks sent to capture them proved powerless against their tactics. Having ensconced themselves in the Uzbekistan mountains the Islamist guerrillas now could take on both the Uzbek and Kyrgyz forces from there. The Japanese hostages were however, finally released. It is believed that the Islamists opposition on Tajikistan played an important role in arranging for their release. It is alleged that some ransom money was paid to procure the release of the Japanese hostages. The Kyrgyz authorities also put no obstruction in the way of the return of Uzbek Islamist militant force led by Jarna Nomangoni to its hideout in northern Tajikistan sometimes in early October 1999. Subsequently, to prevent estrangement in relations with Uzbekistan, Nomangoni with hundreds of his followers was allowed to leave for Afghanistan under a deal negotiated with the Taliban by the Islamist opposition of Tajikistan.

With the movement of a strong contingent of Islamist Uzbekistan to Afghanistan the threat of sponsored-terrorism to the security of the centrally located Republic of Uzbekistan has increased. This republic on account of its geographical location has common border with all other Central Asain republics—Tajikistan, Turkmenistan, Kazakistan and Kyrgyzstan provides the key to the spread of terrorism across the whole region. President Akayev of Kirghizea has recently expressed the fear that up to 2000 Islamic militants might attempt an incursion this year[24]. A combined onslaught of Uzbek Islamist militants and the Islamabad-backed Taliban on the Republic of Uzbekistan from Kandahar in Afghanistan and the expected renewal of the Chechen rebels attacks from across the mountain gorges in Georgia has the potential of destabilizing the vast tract of the Eurasian land. The Indian state of Jammu and Kashmir is the other natural target of this fundamentalism driven cross-border terrorism, self-financed by the super profits from the narcotic trade.

India has suffered greatly at the hands of international terrorism right since the time it became independent. Terrorism has played havoc not only in the states of Jammu and Kashmir and Punjab in the north-west but also in the north-eastern states of Mizoram, Manipur, Nagaland, Tripura and Assam. The situation in the north-east has not improved much as Pakistan has taken over from China the sponsorship of terrorism and secessionism. Terrorists in these parts are operating with the help of international agencies which have become active in the bordering countries of Nepal, Bangladesh and Myanmar. India being a multi-cultural and multi-ethnic country, it is easy to stir trouble among the various religious cultural and ethnic groups. Political parties, too are generally not averse to exploiting the grievances, real or imaginary of the different groups in order to create their vote banks. Until recently, Indian foreign policy had not given much attention to the problem of countering terrorism globally by mobilising international opinion against it and achieving a degree of co-operation among the members of the international community. But, the heavy toll taken by the prolonged low-key undeclared war carried out by Pakistan through acts of cross-border terrorism has ultimately forced India to forge a proactive policy. New Delhi is now taking up a sustained diplomatic offensive to expose Pakistan's sponsorship of Islamic terrorism in Jammu and Kashmir. It is on account of this new activism in India's foreign policy that the United States and other Western powers are becoming increasingly convinced of the Pakistani role in perpetrating acts of terrorist violence across the Indian border through infiltrators and mercenaries. Yet it is still a long way before Pakistan is declared a terrorist state by the United States which regards its national interest as supreme and is reluctant to include Pakistan country among its list of "rogue states".

Besides, its active stance at the various international forums for setting up an international data base on terrorism, enhanced security at airports, increased surveillance over transfer of funds, elimination of supply sources of weapon and explosives and strengthening of anti-terrorist legislations of reinforcing of police cooperation and sharing of intelligence and experience, etc., India should also plead for a comprehensive review of all existing conventions relating to terrorism. It seems unlikely that the international community will in the near future reach a consensus for signing a more comprehensive convention for international cooperation towards eradication of terrorism. Hence, India should concentrate simultaneously on bilateral agreement with countries sharing its perceptions about international terrorism. Its agreements with Egypt, Russia and more recently Uzbekistan are welcome steps in the direction of building a suitable climate for international cooperation for fighting terrorism. Useful discussions on combating terrorism were held in the Indo-American joint group on terrorism before the visit of President Clinton. The visits of Russian Security Council head Sergei Ivanov and President Islam Karimov of Uzbekistan to India this summer also made their important contribution towards forging international cooperation for fighting terrorism. After signing the agreement for institutional cooperation between the Security Council of India and Russia, Sergei Ivanov pointed out in a press statement that the Security Councils of the two countries will now regularly analyse the military and political situation in South and Central Asia including ways to combat the scourge of terrorism which has infected this zone[25]. Containment of Islamic terrorism in Central Asia and Caucasia (the latter for its impact on the former) are of vital importance for both India and Russia. Since this international Islamic terrorism has a common nursery in the Taliban governed Afghanistan tended by Pakistan, a failed state looking to religious fundamentalism to sustain itself on the 'hate India' basis, it is only natural that the key states on the Eurasian continent come together to preserve their multi-religious and multi-ethinic secular states. A centre to fight terrorism in the CIS countries has been recently set-up in Moscow and the Central Asian states are seeking cooperation from China as well within the framework of Shanghi-5. The negative fallout of developments in Afghanistan on regional security was seriously discussed during the New Delhi visit of President Karimov in early May 2000. India fully shares Tashkent's concerns about the conversion of Afghanistan by the Pak-backed Taliban into a brigade for subversion of Central Asian Republics of Kyrgyzstan and Tajikistan besides Uzbekistan. In fact, due to continued infiltration of armed militants into Kashmir, Afghanistan has become a nerve-centre for subversion in both central Asia and South Asia. Russian Security Council Secretary, Sergei Ivanov's visit to New Delhi on the eve of President Karimov's visit and the holding of military exercise in Central Asia with Russian participation has signalled enhanced Russian interest in countering the subversion threat to Central Asia. Uzbekistan President's three visits to China and his discussions with the Chinese President Jiang Jemin about the threat posed by religious extremism during the latest visit, also indicate the Chinese desire to participate in the fight against terrorism.

Despite the recent upsurge of Islamic fundamentalism in some parts of Central Asia, it is highly unlikely that an Islamic state would be created in the near future in any of the Republics of the region. Absence of a strong and independent force of *ulema* or religious scholars, lack of popular knowledge about the basic tenets of Islam, and no historical precedent of a theocratic state in Central Asia are factors negating such a course of development. To say this is not to deny the increasing role of Islam in the process of spiritual renewal and rediscovery of the cultural heritage of the people of Central Asia. However, the danger of conversion of Islamic renewal into a fundamentalist threat due to exploitation of the problems caused by transition to market economy and democracy by outside forces and internal opposition cannot be ignored by the Indian and the world community.

REFERENCES

1. Alexandre Benningsen and Marice Broxup, *The Islamic threats to the Soviet State,* New York, 1983, p. 124; Donald Calisle, Uzbekistan and the Uzbeks" Problems of communism, No. 5, 1991.
2. Shirin Akiner, "Islam, the State and Ethnicity in Central, Asia in Historical Perspective", *Religion state and society*, Oxford, vol. 24, Nos 2/3 1996, pp. 90-132.
3. "Fundamentalism and social and political stability in Uzbekistan", *Ethnic and Religious Conflicts in Eurasia,* Moscow, 1997, pp. 112-29 (in Russian).
4. *Negavisimaya Gazeta,* 31 January 1992.
5. Pinase Akcali, "Islam as a common bond in Central Asia: Islamic Renaissance party and the Afghan Mujahideen, *Central Asian Survey*, 1998, 17 (2) p. 267-84.

6. *Ibid*, p. 280.
7. *Ibid*, p. 279.
8. *Ibid*, p. 276.
9. Ablakul Bazarone, *op.cit.*
10. Mufti Sodiq returned to Uzbekistan from his voluntary exit. Appearing on TV on the eve of Presidential election on January 9, 2000 he praised Karimov and asked for his forgiveness, *Central Asian Monitor*.
11. E.V. Abdullaeo and L.F. Kolesnikov, "Islam and the Religious Factor in Uzbekistan", E.M. Kozhokin (ed.), *Uzbekistan: obretenie novogo oblika,* T. 1, Moscow, 1998, p. 263.
12. Central Asian Monitor, No. 2, 1999, p. 20.
13. SWB, SU/3582, G/2 July 1999.
14. SWB, SU/3598, G/2, 28 July 1999.
15. SWB, SU/3598, G/3, 28 July 1999.
16. SWB, SU/3540, G/3, 21 May 1999.
17. SWB, SU/3611, G/1, 12 August 1999.
18. SWB, SU/3612, G/3, 13 August 1999.
19. SWB, SU/3614, G/3, 18 August 1999.
20. SWB, SU/3622, G/1, 25 August 1999.
21. SWB, SU/3627, G/1, 31 August 1999.
22. SWB, SU/3631, G/2, 4 September 1999.
23. SWB, SU/3645, G/1, 21 September 1999.
24. *Vechermy Bishkek*, 3 March 2000.
25. *The Hindu*, 28 April 2000, p. 11.

CHAPTER 15

Rise of Islamic Extremism in West Asia and North Africa

Jagdish P. Sharma

The post 1970s period has been rife with speculation about an imminent fundamentalist Islamic explosion in the West Asian and North African region. By 1980s, Islamic militancy or terror emerged as the leading vehicle of political opposition in West Asia and North Africa, regardless of official state ideology, political system and of leadership, whether in communist Afghanistan, military Pakistan and Sudan, socialist Algeria, revolutionary Libya, secular Tunisia, modernist Egypt, divided Lebanon or puritanical Saudi Arabia and Morocco. Elsewhere, in states as diverse as Turkey, Jordan, Kuwait, India, Indonesia, Malaysia, Philippines, Nigeria, Islamic groups strained the relationship between governments and governed. The fundamentalist call that has been sounding across the world promotes "the return to Islam" as an ideology for political action to remedy the malaise in the Muslim condition. Experts agree that extremism or militancy is the use of threat of violence, a method of combat or a strategy to achieve certain goals. It's aim is to induce a state of fear in the victim. It is ruthless and does not conform to humanitarian civil norms. It is, to some western observers, an abhorrent and unacceptable means of pursuing social, political, religious and military ends. In general, extremism or terrorism is interpreted as an illegitimate means of attempting to effect political change by indiscriminate use of violence and force. Recently the President of Uzbekistan, Islam Karimov, called for international cooperation against religious extremism, international terrorism and drug peddling. He also held Afghanistan as the main source of harbouring terrorist organisations.

After the collapse of Communism, religious extremism particularly

Islamic militancy is viewed as a major threat to world peace and new global order. The Islamists gained prominence as a reaction to what was perceived as the failure of Arab-African socialism, marxism, liberalism and capitalism. Islamists want a total revamping of society in which government and economy are Islamic. The family is projected as the central and most important unit of Islamic society. Women are to be confined to roles understood to be Islamic. It is seen as the bulwark that will keep Arab-African society from sliding into the abyss of pornography, drugs and vulnerable disease. The Arab-African world has not been a happy or successful place in the last fifty years, and the misery and disenchantment of the people has recently become acute. As one Arab Ambassador in London put it, "the people have lost faith in their governments." There is a sense of failure, which has opened a gap between the rulers and the ruled. It has led to a lack of self-confidence in Arab-African culture, and hostility to foreign influences. For years the Arab-African world has not been at ease with itself'. When he made these remarks the Ambassador, who represented Algeria, had particularly in mind the disastrous developments in his own country.[1]

The President of India, K.R. Narayanan and Prime Minister Atal Behari Vajpayee condemned the massacre of 35 innocent Sikhs in Kashmir Valley which occurred on the eve of President Clinton's visit to India and described it as "yet another vile example of cross-border terrorism". "Even as I extend my sympathy to the next of kin of those killed, let me express the hope that this latest instance will open the world's eyes to the sordidness of terrorism which does not mind spilling innocent blood in order to coerce civil society and make an impact on the world", the Indian President said in a message. Reacting to the terrorist massacre of 35 Sikhs by Islamic militants in the south Kashmir village of Chitti Singhpore, the U.S. President Bill Clinton, joined his Indian counterpart K.R. Narayanan, and other leaders in expressing outrage over the same. President Clinton said, "we share your outrage and our heart breaks over the last night's brutal attack in Kashmir".[2] He spoke emphatically against terrorism and warned Pakistan in vivid words: "cross-border terrorism must stop." It is surprising that those supposedly fighting for the rights of the people of Kashmir have no respect for the rights of others. Interior Ministers from Arab countries met in Algiers recently (Feb. 1-2, 2000) to discuss the phenomenon of Islamic militancy and the ways to combat it. For some years now, the Arab Interior Ministers, at their annual conferences, have been seized with the issue of fundamentalist terrorist violence and its nexus with the drug trade. It is not just the mayhem that these forces can unleash that makes them dangerous. Such forces also block the changes that are necessary if West Asian and Arab-African societies are to cope with modern times. Military departments of the countries of the Commonwealth of Independent states, or the CIS, have drafted a programme for combating international terrorism and other manifestations of extremism for the period up to 2003. That document was discussed at a recent closed session of the CIS Defence Minister Council in Moscow. In Morocco, the Government recently decided to introduce measures to improve the education of women and in Egypt the Government widened women's rights to seek divorce. South measures have attracted the ire of fundamentalist pro-militant parties. King Fahd of Saudi Arabia and his brother, Crown Prince Abdullah issued a joint statement at the end of the Haj pilgrimage denouncing militancy in the name of Islam. They emphasised that Islam is a religion of peace and there is no place for extremist violence in it. The former Prime Minister of Pakistan, Ms Benazir Bhutto has also called for a struggle against Islamic militarism and fundamentalism. A genuine secular liberation movement like the Palestine Liberation Organisation (PLO) finds the *Hamas* and *Islamic Jehad* as a major impediment in pursuing its campaign for an independent Palestinian State since the extremism of the latter legitimizes Israel's harsh and unbearable counter-measures in the eyes of the world.

The radical Palestinians regard Zionism as a particular manifestation of Western imperialism, neo-colonialism and globalism, and the existence of Israel as an extension of the West (especially of the USA) in Afro-Arab-Asian world. Moreover, in the contemporary international system of North African society, Islam stands as a symbol of legitimacy. It does have some influence on the configuration of domestic socio-politico and economic power of the Afro-Arab society. Islam embodies the system of values upon which the salvation and legitimacy of the political regime rests. In the absence of any other channel of voicing the socio-politico demands and economic justice, religious idioms, symbols and institutions remain the most potent channels of articulating public grievances in the Arab-African and Asian world. In this context, religious radicalism or

Islam as a transnational socio-economic and cultural ensemble, links domestic legitimacy with economic justice, social security and international prestige.

The Egyptian Scene : A Return to Jehad

Since the last three decades, Egyptian rulers have grappled with a resurgence of Islam that has significantly challenged the State. In the 1980s and 1990s, Egypt provides a primary example of the dynamic and diverse relationship of religion to society, its challenge to the state, and its impact upon the democratization and globalisation process. The Egyptian experience has witnessed radical revolutionary Islamic assertions and the institutionalization of Islam, socially and politically. Muhammad Abdul Salam Faraq, leader of the Egyptian Jehad organization in 1979, pronounced the government to be apostate and an entity to be fought through a holy war by believers; a return to Jehad was the only way to redemption.[3] The stridency and aggressive stance of these groups brought them into open conflict with the State, starting with the bloody attempted takeover of the Technical Military Academy in April 1974 by the Islamic Liberation Party. This was followed by the assassination of President Sadat in October 1981 by members of the Jehad Organization. The conflict has continued throughout much of the 1980s and into the 1990s.

India condemned the attack on the Egyptian embassy in Islamabad and the assassination attempt on President Hosni Mubarak's life by Pakistani trained militants in Ethiopia and reiterated its commitment to combat the "scourge of cold-blooded violence and terrorism that is directed against the constitutional order and spirit of tolerance in our societies." In a message to Egypt's President, Mr Hosni Mubarak, the former Prime Minister of India, Mr P.V. Narasimha Rao, offered support to Egypt and other like-minded countries in actively opposing the forces of terrorism.[4]

Indian Prime Minister Atal Behari Vajpayee, recently said that State-sponsored terrorism was a threat to democracies all over the world and the international community needed to formulate new strategies to combat it if democracies were to progress. At the recently concluded South Summit in Havana (April 2000), India has called for a concerted initiative against the looming spectre of terrorism and drug trafficking threatening civil society and democracy. India has been discussing with other countries the need for a new convention to effectively counter terrorist menace and

New Delhi wants the issue to be taken up in the next UN General Assembly session in September this year (2000).

Islamic militants blamed for a series of terrorist bomb attacks in France are also said to have received paramilitary training and fundamentalist indoctrination in Pakistan and Afghanistan. The newly chosen leader of Egypts most powerful Islamic movement The Muslim Brotherhood predicted his group would establish an Islamic mega-state within the next 30 years. "The goal of the Brotherhood is simple", the groups supreme guide Mostafa Mashour was quoted as saying in an interview with the London-based *Al-Hayat* daily. "We are working for the establishment of an international Islamic State before a century has passed since the group was set up 70 years ago," he added. The Egyptian authorities have cracked down hard on this moderate Islamic group, jailing its leaders and linking it to the Game al-Islamiya, which is trying to topple Mr Mubarak. The crackdown came after President Mubarak accused the Brotherhood of backing a campaign of Muslim militant violence which had left more than 940 dead in Egypt.[5]

Islamic resurgence in Egypt and the Afro-Arab world began with the formation of the society of Muslim Brothers or Islamic Brotherhood (*Jamiyyat al-Ikhwan al-Muslimin*) by Hassan al-Banna (1906-1949) in 1928. Al-Banna was a graduate of the College of Sciences and a school teacher of Arabic. Banna and the successive leaders were well-versed in religious scriptures and were products of modern Egyptian institutions. The most important legacy of the Islamic Brotherhood is that it has politicised Islam and injected it with a new religious dynamism which thrust it to the forefront of public affairs, a status that paved the way for the rise of Islamic militancy in Egypt. Indeed, today's militant extremist groups are rooted in the Muslim Brotherhood.[6] Egypt was the most logical place for such a movement to take root. The British occupation of Egypt in 1882 had symbolised the basic aspects of the intense confrontation between Western colonial imperialism and Islam. Another important fact about Egypt was the role it had played in Islamic affairs. It was not only the largest Arabic-speaking Muslim secular country but also the site of the most prestigious university of Islamic scholarship Al-Azhar.[7]

Hasan al-Banna's central concern was to analyse the reasons for the decline of Islam in Egypt and elsewhere and to arrive at a comprehensive and effective remedy. Though he admired the principles of Western democracy, he felt that the West itself had been corrupted by its preoccupation with individualism This had led initially to selfishness, class conflict, the breakdown of the family and its values and then to monopolisation of power and colonialism and imperialism. His immediate concern was to find an alternative way of extricating Egypt from its own predicament.

The fiction of the Arab-Palestinians and the establishment of Israel on Palestinian soil had deeply troubled Al-Banna and remained a concern of the Muslim Brotherhood thereafter. But during a trip to the United States in 1949, Sayyid Qutab (1906-1966), who succeeded Al-Banna, was shocked by what he perceived as a broad backing of Israel throughout the US and a generally negative opinion about the Arabs. His conclusion was that people in the West looked upon the Afro-Arab-Asian world and Islam with condescension and had little regard for the rights and dignity of Third World inhabitants. Sayyid Qutab interpreted Islam as the only liberating force and looked to a radical Islamic revival to wage *Jehad*, or holy war. The Jehad of Islam is to secure complete freedom for every man throughout the world by releasing him from servitude to other human beings so that he may serve God.[9] This applied even within secular and nationalist Islamic countries such as Egypt because "all the existing so-called "Muslim societies are also *Jahili* or ignorant societies."[10]

Because of the size of its population, Egypt seems to be vulnerable to this emerging radical Islamic movement. The mass appeal of Islamic radicalism has its roots in worldly frustrations and denials, and those frustrations and denials have been given a religious idiom. In Egypt, Algeria, Saudi Arabia, Kuwait, Jordan and elsewhere, Islamism is basically an indigenous response to prevalent socio-economic and political problems. Islamism here is a product of the failed modernization policies of the past 50 years, which have culminated in unmet expectations and consequent militancy.[11]

Egypt under President Nasser's socialist model was on the whole a positive movement from the point of view of social and economic development. In contrast, during the succeeding periods, there has been a drastic decline in the socio-economic sphere. The conspicuous characteristics of this decline are a major increase in dependency on external power, particularly the United States,[12] decreasing capacity for vital self-sustaining capability accompanied by social, political and economic instability and as a result of growing sense of insecurity and helplessness among large segments of the populace.[13]

An evaluation of the Egyptian society during the post-Nasser period shows an unmistakable reversal of the progressive trends due to causes indigenous to Egypt. Post-Nasser Egypt became open for invasion by private interests and corruption: During President Sadat's period, Sadat shifted to a more outward-looking "open door" development policy i.e. *Infitah*, designed to encourage domestic and foreign private investment. Closer economic, political and military ties were developed with the West and the United States in particular. But this policy proved unsuccessful. The distributed effects of Sadat's *Infitah* were instrumental in promoting class divisions and tensions in the society. The shift in power from President Sadat to President Hosni Mubarak's period continued the state of decline. President Mubarak today feels more under siege than ever before. His regime is tainted by increasingly conspicuous corruption, rising unemployment and insecurity. His long battle with the fundamentalists keeps getting worse, crippling the tourist industry that is vital to the flagging economy. A statement in the name of the militant *Gama' Al-Islamiya* (Islamic group) advised tourists to leave Egypt immediately because it was pursuing its campaign of violence against tourist targets.[14] Despite attempts to compromise with "moderate" fundamentalists and brief efforts at mediation with the radicals, the past years have seen a steady escalation of political violence.

The reality of Egyptian society, as indeed of many Arab-Islamic societies, today contributes to a climate in which the influence of Islam and activist organizations on socio-political development will increase rather than diminish. Egypt continues to exist in a climate of socio-economic crisis and political alienation in which many experience the failure of the State and of secular ideologies. The government and ruling elites or classes possess tenuous legitimacy in the face of mounting disillusionment and opposition, among whom Islamic activists remain the most vocal, best organized and most effective. The growing state centrism under President Mubarak, which has increased proportionately with the longevity of the regime—now in its fourth 'six-year term' has raised fears among the liberals Nasserists and Islamists about the prospects of democratic governance. Today, as President Mubarak wades through his fourth 'six-year term', hardly anyone believes that the radical Islamic militants pose a serious threat to the regime. Yet Islamic extremists are far from being extinct. The only way to stamp out the Islamic opposition is to remedy the painful economic conditions of the country.[15]

However, President Mubarak has adopted some alternative strategies to recoup the declining image of his country and to rehabilitate it not only in the Arab-Islamic world but in the world at large and thus is attempting to build a new Egypt. Mubarak's Egypt played and is playing an important role in the diplomatic efforts which led to the convening of a Middle East peace conference in Madrid, Spain, on October 30, 1991. Despite the procedural delays by Israel and slow progress of the negotiations, Egypt felt that the conference represented the best hope for a durable peace in the Afro-Arab-Asian region. President Mubarak has brought Egyptian diplomacy back to the centre, stage.

A multiplicity of social, economic and political factors outlined above contribute to the rise of traditionalist sentiments in the world today. Possibly the most important of these, which appears to be relevant to both industrialized and developing countries, is the increased search for communal solidarity and identification.

The threat of anomie is real in most societies. In western industrialized countries, the problem stems from an excessive degree of individualism and the growing feeling that socio-economic changes, represented by an advanced capitalist market economy and high-powered technological development have led to a growing abstraction of socio-economic changes, represented by an advanced capitalist market economy and high-powered technological development have led to a growing abstraction of socio-political institutions that mediate between individuals and society. A similar process seems to be at work in developing Afro-Asian countries with an even severe unsettling impact. Separation of individual from collective entities, resulting from rapid population growth and urbanisation, the rise of a centralized bureaucratic—military State and changing forms of economic and political activities is typical of the modernization process. The post-independence histories of many Asian and African states are replete with such efforts.[16]

Although occurring in markedly different socio-political environments, some manifestations of counter-modernist tendencies in the form of religious radicalism is a fact of life throughout the North African region.

Unlike Egypt, Algeria has no tradition of early Islamic revivalism. Nor does it have a deeply rooted or a well-defined Islamic identity. The country was moulded largely by France in the nineteenth century to suit its colonial interests. The colonization of Algeria was both long (1831-1962) and intense, seeking the assimilation and incorporation of the country as an integral part of France. The pervasive French cultural and educational influences were ascendant throughout much of Algeria's colonial existence. The French would not have tolerated any form of Islamic revivalism that might have threatened their rule. Hence Islam was largely devoid of an activist spirit.

Association of Muslim Ulema

It was only in 1931 that the Association of the Algerian Muslim Ulema was formed by Sheikh Abdul Hamid Ben Badis (1889-1940). Essentially reformist, its purpose was to deliver Islam from the corrupt innovations of the Sufis through a cultural and educational revival, with emphasis on original sources. The movement championed a reformed, *Salafi* (invoking ancestral heritage) Islam against the rural traditional Islam. The movement became more involved in the initial nationalist demands for equal rights and preservation of a distinctive Muslim identity.

The message of the reformers laid the foundation of an Algerian national Muslim consciousness and identity that would give stimulus to the Algerian Revolution in 1954, which initiated the War of Independence (1954-1962). As the revolution swept the country, the Islamic reform movement became a constituent part of the nationalist FLN (National Liberation Front), and by 1956, it was completely subsumed. The paramount position of the FLN, with its predominantly secularism-modernist orientation, established the supremacy of the mostly French-educated secular leaders. The FLN looked upon Islam simply as one important element of national and cultural identity. Its stance was far from a commitment to religion. Accordingly, the tradition of secularism continued after independence in 1962.

Although Islam was generally dormant during the decades of 1970s and 1980s, it underwent occasional moments of revival before the rise of the Islamic Salvation Front (FIS) thrust Algeria into the throes of Islamic militancy, that is, political Islam. Islamic radicalism surfaced toward the end of 1970s and in early 1980s as an outcome of Algerian President

Boumedienne's leftward socialist revolution and state bureaucratic elitism. His nationalization policies extended to seizure of private small businesses and expropriation of farmland, and the consequent disaffection of great numbers of Algerians took an Islamic form against FLN's state elitist socialism. Only after the death of Boumedienne in 1978 was there a sign of Islamic opposition with the rise of *Rabitat al-Da'wa al-Islamiyya* (the League of the Islamic call) in the early 1980s. In fact, the Islamic movement in Algeria is a product of worsening economic conditions in the 1980s. The effect of years of socialist economic mismanagement, official corruption, and bureaucratic fiat came home to roost during the successor regime of Chadli Benjadid: high unemployment, educational decline, agricultural failure and food dependency, over-population, rural migration and the attendant urban bloat and decay, and exorbitant foreign debt and the list goes on.[17]

Algeria is a stark case of a revolution that had fallen short of the revolutionaries' expectations. For almost three decades since independence in 1962, the single party rule of the revolutionary war leaders—the National Liberation Front (FLN)—has led the country into the socio-economic abyss. The FLN's gross mismanagement of a statist economy, its increasingly corrupt and inefficient rule , and the vast enrichment of a favoured political class have finally caught up with the ruling party. The economic riots of October 1988, which spurred initial openings towards reform and democratization, were a turning point in Algeria's history, but history failed to turn. The democratic experiment had to be withheld shortly thereafter by Algeria's military establishment due to fear of a fundamentalist takeover.

Robbed of its election victory in Algeria (1990), the Islamic Salvation Front (FIS) has been banned and suppressed. In January 1992, the then governing High State Council of Algeria cancelled the elections on the eve of victory for the Islamic forces, saying that the radicalists would never allow another election if they won. Since then, fighting between the Algerian authorities and the Islamic Salvation Front has taken more than 1 lakh lives including the assassination of President Boudiaf and President Ali Kafi and other leading leaders and intellectuals. Amid sporadic outbreaks of violence, the security forces took control of the FIS offices since February 1992. It was only in January 25, 1996, that the leadership of the outlawed Islamic Salvation Front sent a letter to the former Algerian elected President Liamine Zeroual proposing dialogue without pre-conditions. The internal leadership of FIS has entirely endorsed the conciliatory dialogue with the Algerian President and expressed its intention to support President Zeroual's call for "Build up Algeria together."[18]

By thronging the polling stations in large numbers and giving a massive mandate to President Liamine Zeroual, the Algerians have thwarted the design of Islamic radicals to turn Algeria into an Islamic theocracy. While the outlawed moderate Islamic Salvation Front (FIS) had given a boycott call, the armed radical Islamic groups had threatened to turn the ballot boxes into coffins.[19] Democracy has, therefore, triumphed over religious fundamentalism.

Islam's appeal

Islam's appeal in Algeria has grown because of economic hardship, political failure, social unrest—a combination of all the three that Algeria underwent after independence. The urban riots of October 1988 were a spontaneous reaction to the deprivations of economic reforms, rising unemployment among the youth and the shattering of social and political expectations. Unemployment rose up to 30 per cent of working population in 1993. Inflation rose from 9.9 per cent in 1990 to 16.5 per cent in 1991. The per capita income declined from $ 2,752 in 1987 to $ 1,607 in 1991. Now Algeria has to import 60 per cent of its foodstuffs to meet the domestic needs. The foreign borrowings escalated the debt ratio to 83 per cent in 1993. The 1994 administrative budget envisaged a deficit of 139.600 m. dinars. Algeria's total external debt at the end of 1992 amounted to US $ 26,349 m., of which $ 24,762 m. was longterm public debt. The cost of debt-servicing represented 83 per cent of export earnings (goods and services) in 1993. The annual rate of inflation averaged 12.7 per cent in 1980-92, 31.7 per cent in 1992, and 20.5 per cent in 1993. Consumer prices increased by 25.1 per cent in May 1994.[20]

The principal aim of the Algerian government's 1990-94 development plan was to liberalise the economy, allowing a greater measure of private investment and encouraging foreign enterprise.[21] By 1994, however, the government had failed to arrest Algeria's economic crisis, and the debt ridden country is faced with the prospect of bankruptcy. The stagnant economic growth which brought misery gave an upperhand to the fundamentalist outfits to weaken the state system.

The atrocities and violence which have rocked the country are not only the outcome of the clandestine groups acting in the name of Islam, Evidence has emerged of torture inflicted by the security forces on communities known to harbour Islamist sympathisers. Besides, there are also people at the helm of the state who have an interest in keeping the war on the boil and postponing the moment of reckoning—which would reveal how they had misappropriated state funds.[22] The masses were looking for new certainties in post-independence era but what they found were old ones, reminders that Islam is in essence a revolt of the poor. The strength of the fundamentalist appeal in Algeria owes much to the French colonial legacy which in itself was the source of number of unsolved tensions and independent Algeria's authoritarian Arab-Islamic socialism. It undermined the traditional Islamic structures of the country, in particular the Sufi orders, and distorted the threads of continuity linking Islam today with its past.

Many leading observers also trace the origin of Algerian extremism to the decade-and-a-half long Afghan civil war where the American CIA and the Pakistani ISI assembled a large number of motivated volunteers to fight in Afghanistan.[23] The veteran Egyptian intellectual Hassanein Heikal attributes the extremism of such type to the extremely narrow interpretation of the Holy Quran by the Pakistan Ulema. In his view the Holy Quran could not be properly interpreted without the knowledge of Arabic and Arab history. In turn these extremist teachings found a fertile ground among the young minds of oil exporting Islamic countries where wide socio-economic gaps developed in society as a result of sudden influx of enormous oil wealth and its skewed distribution.[24] Algeria was one of the countries which gained from the oil boom. The hardened veterans of the Afghan war who went back, formed the core of the militants in Algeria. Since the botched election, Algeria had been in a state of low intensity civil war between the FIS, and the security forces. Scores have been killed on both sides. "It is simply for Algerians to say what kind of society they want; said Malik Ait-Aoudia, an official of the Assembly for Culture and Democracy, a deeply secularist political party. "The Islamists and their political programme don't represent merely an insurrection. Islamism is an assault on Algerian society, with its shock troops in the past three years busy killing women, intellectuals, artists, pupils and professors, journalists and artisans", Mr. Ait-Aoudia said.

The fundamentalists have singularly failed to ignite a popular revolution like late Ayatollah Khomeini's against the Shah of Iran. This is largely because notable blocks of Algerian's, although not supportive of the military or the FLN, are adamantly opposed to a fundamentalist takeover. They include professional and business groups; a large number of intellectuals, academics and journalists; civil administrators; women's organizations; the Algerian trade union movement, Leftist syndicates; and the various socialist-secularist parties. Besides this, the newly elected Algerian President Abdelaziz Bouteflika's plan for peace and civilian accord which received a massive endorsement in a recent referendum (September 1999) provides a limited amnesty to Islamic radicals who give up the armed struggle. Algeria released 2,300 non-violent Islamic militants as part of this Presidential pardon.

The Algerian crisis embodies several long-term issues at stake in the Arab-African world and raises deeper questions about political, economic and social systems and their future prospects. Social, economic and political reforms which allow for a degree of transparency and accountability to the people are critical to the Arab-African region's future economic growth. Algeria will have to sort out its crisis with its own people by adopting viable social, political and economic measures.

Sudan

The only Arab country that has put into effect modern Islamist ideas has been Sudan. It is situated in north-east Africa. It is the largest African country with an area covering 8.3% of the continent. It shares common borders with nine African countries, Egypt and Libya in the North, Chad and Central African Republic in the West, Democratic Republic and Congo, Uganda and Kenya in the South, Ethiopia and Eritrea in the east. The Sudanese people are said to be the descendants of various ethnic groups which had settled or migrated to Sudan since historical times and intermingled and created a multifaceted heritage dominant among which are the Arab-African culture. Since its independence in 1956, Sudan has been contributing in its own way to the welfare of Africa as an active member of the Organisation of African Unity. Now, Sudan is doing its best to solve its differences with other African countries through diplomatic and peaceful means. The long war in southern Sudan has now exhausted all logical and reasonable measures for its continuation.

Southern Sudan has been given the right of self-government, through the Khartoum Peace Agreement of 21 April, 1997.[25]

The Southern problem, which is a 'political' problem inherited from the colonial administration since 1955, has its roots in the Western colonial policy of divide and rule and in the uneven economic development. The above mentioned Khartoum peace accord articulates a comprehensive settlement plan based on citizenship as a yardstick to rights and obligations, irrespective of any religious or cultural affiliations; fair distribution of wealth and power through a federal system; the right of states to choose their own legislation expression of diversities and their protection. The provisions of the "Khartoum peace accord", have already been embodied in the country's constitution, says Abdalmahmood Abdalhalim Mohammed, Sudanese Ambassador to India. Besides this, the Sudanese Constitution governs and gives due regard to social justice, political equality, economic opportunity along with freedom of speech and religion of the Sudanese people, the Ambassador said.

Islam is the religion of majority people in Sudan while there are Christians and other Pagan minorities particularly in the Southern states. The story of the evolution of modern Sudanese politics in an Islamist direction goes back to history. During the 19th century, Sudan was the cradle of the nationalist revolt of Ahmed al-Mahdi from 1881 to 1885, which resulted in the establishment of an independent Islamic state under Al-Mahdi's successor, the Khalifa Abdullahi, which survived until it was overthrown by the Anglo-Egyptian army at the Battle of Omdurman in 1898. There was a high level of popular participation in the Mahadist movement led by prominent local teachers and notables. These notables were the leaders of large ethnic and tribal groups and of major nationalist Islamic associations. As the socio-economic changes of the modern era undermined the autonomy of tribes in many areas, the "Islamic notables" gained increasingly important roles in the day-today politics and society. This trend continued throughout the twentieth century. For majority people in Sudan, there was no contradiction between Islam and democracy as their country achieved independence. Major Islamic leaders and organizations which advocated the establishment of a democratic and Islamic Republic in Sudan were at the core of multi-party and democratic politics in modern Sudan.

Sudan's Islamisation programme since 1980s should be viewed as a response to the broader socio-economic and political context. Sudan in the 1980s faced mounting socio-economic problems. Since 1983, an estimated 1.4 million people have died as a result of natural disasters and political conflict. Like most of the Arab-African world, Sudan also experienced a religious resurgence, whose effects were observable among youth, professionals, students, and some conservative old leaders. At that time the regime of Jaffar Nimeri which had been in power since 1969, had become thoroughly discredited on account of its corruption, incompetence and the failure of its plans for economic development, and seeking a way of rallying support, it hit on the idea of adopting certain aspects of Shariat Law. In September 1983, President Nimeri announced the banning of alcohol, which was accompanied by the conspicuous pouring of large number of bottles of whisky into the Nile river and more seriously, the introduction of the capital and corporal punishments of Islamic Shariah. In April 1985, 18 months after beginning his experiment with Shariah, Nimeri was overthrown by the commander-in-chief of the armed forces, who a year later organised elections and handed power to a civilian Islamic government of new Prime Minister Sadiq Al-Mahdi. In 1988, a border coalition cabinet was formed (National Islamic Front). This was supposed to be a means of promoting national unity as a step towards tackling corruption, severe drought, famine, refugees, administrative chaos and the country's other appalling socio-economic and political problems. The present efforts at establishing an Islamic state in Sudan are identified with Dr Hassan al-Turabi the head of the National Islamic Front and the Sudanese Muslim Brotherhood. Dr. Hasan al-Turabi is a theorist of Islamic revival and is an influential figure among the Arab-African Muslims. With impressive credentials in Western education, as former dean of Khartoum university's law faculty and as a leader in Sudan's political and religious life, Turabi skillfully articulates a moderate Islamist posture. He insists that Sudan's Islamic model will be more akin to the liberal tradition than present-day governments in western Europe.

The present elected Government of Sudan under President, Mr. Omar El-Bashir has incurred (according to the Western scholars) Western and American hostility for its lack of liberal democracy and respect for human rights. On 19 August 1993, the US State Department went to the extent of putting Sudan on its list of countries supporting terrorism.

So far as the developments of the last two years are concerned, Sudan itself was a victim of terrorism as manifested by the US bombing of Al-Shifa Pharmaceutical Factory. Sudan feels that, during the Cold War era itself, anti-colonial and anti-apartheid forces were themselves labelled as terrorists by the very circles who were the backbone of apartheid and current distributors of certificates of good conduct. At home and abroad, realities of Sudanese situation speak for themselves. The country is guided by the principles of cooperation with neighbours, mutual realization of interests, good neighbourliness, non-interference in the internal affairs of others and respect for their sovereignty and territorial integrity. It is living in peace and harmony with its neighbours who are now convinced more than ever that all accusations levelled against its government were well-architectured designs aimed at discrediting Sudan as a punishment for its determined and independent efforts to take its destiny in its own hands, and not to heed or succumb to dictates from abroad. Even the die-hard enemies of Sudan have failed to establish any link, whatsoever, between the Sudanese government and the well known cultural traditions of its people, and terrorism. The western media has been the target of attacks by the Arab-African leaders for allegedly perpetuating ethnocentric misconceptions about their region by reporting only coups, civil wars, refugees, brutalities and corruption—ignoring the "positive" events that occur daily in the Arab-African continent.

Throughout the Afro-Arab region, political Islam has provided hope of fulfilment and change for a generation blighted by socio-economic decline and political degradation. It has channelled frustration, disillusionment and alienation into a political cause and a new morality. But at the same time, the Islamic alternative has singularly failed to provide the public with a realistic, humane and authentically Islamic programme to remove the causes of frustration which it has so effectively exploited. It is interesting to see how the radicals can take vaguely worded verses from the Quran and then erect on it, in details, the vast structure of the Islamic state. Religious fundamentalism does the opposite. It is a return journey to primitive priest-ridden past. It was a progressive doctrine at the time of its inception in its rejection of priesthood and in elevating the status of women. Islam should not be confused with the practise of enveloping the women in veils and issuing death sentences against irrelevant writers. Theocratic terrorism and *Jehad* are not the answers to the problems of the world today.

The challenge is to build up national economies and strive for political and social justice for the people. A stable government, consensus politics and an enlightened democracy can achieve more for the people than violence and sabre ratling in the name of religion. In areas which are subjected to historic injustice based on ethnicity and cultural diversions, the governments have to bend over backwards to help the socially and economically oppressed sections. Inculcation of faith in a shared nationality can be a potent force against tensions arising in a society marked by diversities. The ideas that inspire Indian democracy are relevant in every set-up to promote a common nationhood and values. The responsibility of the majority is always greater than those of minorities to foster a feeling of unity in diversity.

REFERENCES

1 Michael Field, *Inside the Arab World* (London, John Murray Publishers) 1994, p. 3.

2 Quoted in *The Hindu* and *Asian Age* (Delhi) 22 March, 2000.

3 To Faraq, the duty of *Jehad* is regarded as a sixth pillar in Islam and should be reactivated. Faraq was implicated in the assassination of Egyptian President late Anwar Sadat in 1981 and executed.

4 *The Hindu* (Delhi, Madras) 22 November, 1995.

5 *The Asian Age* (Delhi and London) 25 January, 1996.

6 Mahmoud A. Faksh, *The Future of Islam in the Middle East: Fundamentalism in Egypt, Algeria, and Saudi Arabia* (West Port, Connecticut and London: Praeger, 1997), p. 44.

7 Alan R. Taylor, *The Islamic Question in Middle East Politics* (Boulder and London : Westview Press, 1988), p. 54.

8 Richard D. Mitchell, *The Society of Muslim Brothers* (London: Oxford University Press, 1969), p. 7.

9 Sayyid Qutb, *Milestones* cedar Rapids, (Lawa: Unity Publishing Co., 1981) pp. 62, 70, quoted in Alan R. Taylor.

10 *Ibid*, p. 82.

11 For details see Oliver Roy, "*The Failure of Political Islam* (Cambridge: Harvard University Press, 1994).

12 George M. Guiss, *The Politics of United States Foreign Aid*, (London, Sydney: Croom Helm, 1987), pp. 222-225. Also Tim Mitchell, "America's Egypt: Discourse of the Development Industry", *Middle East Report* March-April 1991, pp. 18-36.

13 Jagdish P. Sharma, "Green peril or Islamic Radicalism in Arab-Islamic World", in Chopra, V.D. (ed.) *Religious Fundamentalism in Asia* (Delhi: Gyan Publishers, 1993), p. 207.

14 *The Asian Age* (London) Delhi 10, November 1995.

15 Mahmud A. Faksh, *The Future of Islam in the Middle East: Fundamentalism in Egypt, Algeria, and Saudi Arabia* (West Port and London : Praeger publishers, 1997), pp. 56-57.

16 Sabri Sarayi, "Politicalization of Islamic Re-traditionalism : Some preliminary notes" in Heper, M and Israeli, Raphael (ed); *Islam and Politics in the Modern Middle East* (London, Sydney: Croom Helm, 1984), p. 121.

17 Mahmud A. Faksh, *The Future of Islam in the Middle East: Fundamentalism in Egypt, Algeria, and Saudi Arabia (1997), pp. 66-69.*

18 *BBC World Service* (London) January 25, 1996, also see President Zeroual's address to nation in *News from Algeria,* January. 16, 1996.

19 *Guardian Weekly*, November 26, 1995.

20 *Europa year Book*, Europa Publications (London) 1995, p. 330.

21 For details see *Algeria: Economic Guide* External Bank of Algeria, 1992.

22 *Jordan Times* March 28, 1995.

23 Interview with His Excellency Ahmad Mansour, Former Charge de affairs, Arab Republic of Syria.

24 Mohammed Hassanein Heikal, *Illusion of Triumph: An Arab view of the Gulf War*, (London: Harper Collins, 1993), pp. 71-72.

25 For details see the text of *The Sudan Peace Agreement* Khartoum: The Republic Palace, 21 April, 1997. Also see the text published in *National Herald* (New Delhi), July 3, 1997.

CHAPTER 16

Pakistan and Taliban Role in Chechnya Conflict

Vinod Anand

The current Russia Chechen conflict continues to simmer and there appears to be no signs of its moving towards a long-term solution. The Russian forces are still battling the Chechen rebels in the southern mountains of Chechnya. Russians have used air strikes, helicopter gunships and artillery strikes to subdue the Chechens but there is a continued resistance from the Chechen fighters holed up in the southern mountainous region. During the last week of May 2000, there were reports of Russia considering the possibility of strikes against some terrorist camps based in Afghanistan, which are providing training to Chechens and other Mujahideens for fighting against Russian forces. Sergey Yastrzhembsbiy, a presidential aide to the Russian President mentioned that 'preventive strikes may be made on the rebel bases in Afghanistan'. According to Russian sources, a whole settlement of hundreds of Chechens has grown up near Taliban controlled town of Mazar-e-Sherif in Afghanistan., A camp near the settlement has been imparting guerrilla training to the Chechens. There had been a meeting in Pakistan at Peshawar, between various Chechen, Uzbek, Tazik and Uygur rebels in April this year to make joint plans and efforts to send fresh Mujahideens to Chechnya. However, the Russia-Chechen conflict has had a long history and an insight into circumstances leading to the present impasse would give a clearer picture of the current scene.

It was towards the latter half of seventh century that Islam came to the North Caucasus region through Arab conquests. However, it was only during late Seventeenth and early Nineteenth century when the present day Daghestan and Chechnya were largely converted to Islam with some proportion of Chechen population accepting Islam as late as 1895. This was largely due to efforts of Arab and Caucasian Sufi missionaries and the two predominant orders were Naqshbandiya and Quadriya brotherhoods. The last two hundred years have witnessed first, the effort of Tsarist Russia to keep Chechens under control and thereafter Bolsheviks following suit. During World War II, Stalin deported large population of Chechen and Inguish people to Siberia and Kazakhistan. And now after collapse of Soviet Union, the Russia-Chechen conflict has carried on.

After the disintegration of the Soviet Union, Chechnya declared independence from Russia on September 6, 1999 under the leadership of Dzokhar Dudayev. He was able to sieze all important assets and established control over the region. The Russian state could only organise a concerted effort to overthrow Dudayev in November 1994 when the first major military offensive to remove him from power was launched. However, it was only in August 1996 that this violent Russia-Chechen conflict came to an end albeit temporarily with a peace agreement.[1] The Presidents of Russia and Chechnya signed a pact that rejected use of force and visualised a final agreement on political status of Chechnya after 2001. However, the peace was shattered when Chechens launched a violent incursion into Daghestan in August 1999 followed by explosions in Moscow and two other cities in September killing over 300 people. These explosions were supposedly the handiwork of Chechen militia.

It was some time in 1993 that Dudayev gave the call for *Jihad* (holy war). There were some reports that Dudayev's call was answered by many Pakistani, Afghan and Iranian volunteers. It is also believed that Inter Services Intelligence of Pakistan trained Chechen fighters in the training camps of Afghanistan and Pakistan on the same line as they had trained Afghans against the Soviet Union. During the first Chechen war of 1994-1996, Pakistan along with some other Muslim countries was in the forefront of criticising the Russian military intervention in Chechnya. Pakistan rejected the claims that its citizens were in Chechnya as mercenaries but made the usual remark that 'there is sympathy and concern for the people of Chechnya in Pakistan and other Islamic countries.[2]

In August 1999, Afghan, Pakistani and Arab militants, trained in training camps set-up by militant organizations of various hues and persuasions in Pakistan and Afghanistan are understood to have participated along with Chechen commander Shamil Basayer and Jordanian fighter Khattab when they stormed some areas of Daghestan in Russia.[3] This led to the second military intervention by Russia in Chechnya. These Islamic militants saw themselves as "warriors of Allah" performing their divine duty to carry out the will of God. Ultimately, the Russian forces threw them out from Daghestan and their actions were more akin to those of Islamic terrorists rather than the 'liberators' of Daghestan. Some of these militants, after returning from Chechnya participated in a campaign led by the Farghana-based Islamic Movement of Uzbekistan to capture more than 20 villages in Kyrgyzstan.[4] Thus, such Islamic groups are exploiting weak political structures and law and order situation in the regions of North Caucasus and Central Asian countries.

Shamil Basayev has been coordinating military, political and religious fundamentalist activity against the Russian forces. In the third week of May this year he chaired a meeting with *Ulema* of Tajikistan and designated himself as the 'amir' of the Majlis of the Shura of Muslims of Ichkeria and Daghestan. His agenda was coordination of hostilities against Russians and seeking support from the Taliban. Even, the elected President Aslan Maskhadov of Chechnya had joined the side of rebels. It is believed that he had sent representatives to meet Osama Bin Laden and others for extending support in terms of manpower, weapons and ammunition for Chechnya insurgency.

Pakistan is home to approximately 6,000 religious seminaries that churn out as many as 500,000 students, among them Pakistani, Arabs, Central Asians and even from North Caucasus and the Far East. According to Pakistani sources, as many as 1500 of such schools preach Jihad and are instrumental in giving military training to the students.[5] Before Pakistani Prime Minister Nawaz Sharif was overthrown on 12 October 1999, he had acknowledged Taliban's links with Pakistan's sectarian terrorists, saying "we have made it clear to the Taliban that this is not acceptable". However, Musharraf with an eye on increasing the pressure on India has looked the other way and does not want to antagonise the Deobhandi Islamic militants who are useful for Pakistan's Kashmir policy.

There are a number of religious militant groups and organizations with their headquarters either in Pakistan or in Taliban ruled Afghanistan which are spawning holy warriors for Islamic Ummah' to carry out Jihad in distant lands like Chechnya. Some of the prominent groups/ organisations are:

(a) Harkut-ul-Mujahideen, a successor of Harkat-ul-Ansar which was declared as a terrorist organisation by the USA after kidnapping of four Western tourists in the Kashmir Valley. Jamait-ul-Ulema-lslam and Sipahe Sahaba Pakistan also influence it.

(b) Hizbul Mujahideen, a military arm of the politico-religious party Jamaat-I-lslami (JI). It has been quite active in collecting funds for Jihad in Chechnya.

(c) Al Badr (a militant organization backed by Jamaat-I-lslami).

(d) Sipahe Sahaba Pakistan. A fundamentalist sectarian Wahabi-Sunni group.

(e) Osama Bin Laden's Al-Quaida organization and International Islamic Front.

(f) Lashkar-e-Toiba, the militant wing of Markaz Dawat Wal Irshad, preaching Jihad.

Jihadi commanders aver that the short-term objectives of these training camps is to provide trained and motivated manpower for the struggle in Kashmir and for Taliban's fight against the Northern Alliance forces. However, the long-term objective of these camps is to export this Taliban and Islamic model to North Caucasus, Central Asia, Balkans, Philippines and the Middle East and Xinjiang province of China.

One such training camp that has become infamous is at Akora Khattak in Pakistan, near Afghan border. It is also a religious school housed along with well-known Haqqaniya Mosque. Here, some Chechen militants were given a year of Koranic teaching and thereafter were sent to face Russians in Chechnya. The *madrassa* has state-of -the art hi-tech facilities and has a website, e-mail, computer and other communication paraphernalia. 'And it has boarding hostel for 3000 students.[6] Eventhough Pakistan's rulers deny that any help or incentive is being given to such organizations/institutions, Pakistani police has provided armed guards to the seminary.

The funding for the institution comes not only from the government but through various invisible sources like individuals settled abroad and some friendly Arab countries. The main aim and purpose of this school is to produce 'holy warriors' and bring about an Islamic revolution.

During first week of February 2000, Vice Chairman of the Council of Ministers of Taliban government, Mohammed Rabbani, visited Pakistan. One of the main highlights of Mr. Rabbani's (the second in command in Taliban hierarchy) visit was his speech at Darul Uloom Haqqaniya in Akora Khattak. Some of the 18 members of his delegation had studied at the same *madrassa*. He gave a call for Muslim unity and denounced anti-Islam powers. He further emphasised that Osama Bin Laden, is a guest in Afghanistan.

Lashkar-e-Toiba has become one of the biggest private armies of Islamic militants in Pakistan that is not only engaged in *jihad* in Kashmir but has also set its sights on the ongoing conflict in Chechnya and Central Asia. So far, it has trained over 100,000 'Mujahideens' in military craft in a number of military training camps located in Pakistan and Afghanistan. It has got a vast network in Pakistan with over 2000 unit offices.[7] It follows the Ahle Hadith or Wahabi sect of Islamic beliefs. With Saudi Arabia, and Pakistan's recognition of Taliban, there has been a convergence of anti-Shiite -Deobandi -Wahabi Sunni fundamentalism. And if one adds a dash of Naqshbandiya philosophy to this recipe, then it raises the ire of Russians and Central Asian regimes besides Iran and various Shia sects. A large portion of Muslims inhabited areas of North Caucasian region in Russia follow the shrine -worshipping mystical order of the Naqshbandiya. The conflict in Chechnya and Arab influence has turned the Naqshbandi followers to more strict orthodoxy of Saudi based Wahabi order .

Shamil Basayev and Khattab, as mentioned earlier conducted the raid on Daghestan, in August 1999. Shamil had visited Afghanistan in March 1994 via Baku in Azerbaizan and Pakistan. He had visited guerrilla-training facilities in Khost province of southern Afghanistan.[8] In May, the same year he had returned with first group of volunteers to be trained for 'Jihad' against Russians. These were the same training camps which were struck by US Cruise missiles in August 1998. Khattab is sometimes referred to as Russia's Osama Bin Laden. Besides taking part in the August 1999 raid, he is alleged to have engineered explosions in Moscow and Volgodonsk. He is believed to have trained along with other Arab volunteers in Afghanistan in mid-eighties and in 1992 took part in Islamic militant operations against Tajikstan. In 1995, he moved to Chechnya along with a contingent of Arab volunteers and started imparting training to Chechen militants.[9]

It is believed that Afghan veterans to a large extent support Chechen insurgency. According to Pakistani sources, a large number of Chechens along with other foreign nationals continue to receive training in military camps in Afghanistan like camp named Kargha-1, about 12 km North of Kabul.[10] There were reports in second week of February this year that 70 militants from Pakistan and Arab countries had been dispatched to reinforce militant groups fighting in southern mountains of Chechnya. They had gone through special training camps in Afghanistan and had planned to use the route through Turkmenistan, Azerbaizan and Turkey.[11]

One of the active politico-religious parties which is supporting the cause of Chechnya militancy is Jamat-i-Islami with its headquarters based at Mansoorah near Lahore. On 14 November last year, Naib Ameer (second-in-command) Professor Ghafoor Ahmed gave a call in Karachi for contribution to Jihad against Russians in Chechnya. In his public speech he asked for donations and established a "Sheshan Jihad Fund" meant for Chechnya.[12] He also organized a demonstration to express solidarity with Chechens and waxed eloquent on valour of Chechen people, predicting that Chechnya will prove to be a graveyard of Russian troops. He considered the struggle in Chechnya to be a continuation of Afghan struggle that had resulted in disintegration of the former Soviet Union. He exhorted CEO, Gen Pervez Musharraf to openly announce support to Chechen Muslims. Again on January 27, this year Jamaat-e - Islami Ameer (Chief) Qazi Hussain Ahmed appealed to Pakistanis to help and support Chechen Muslims in Grozny with arms, food and medicines.[13] He urged Pakistanis to donate generously and stated that Muslim Ummah had always looked towards Pakistan for help in need. On February 9, 2000 Qazi urged Musharraf to bring an end to anti-Islamic practices. He also demanded that Pakistani government should recognize Chechnya. Earlier in October, Qazi had stated that Kemalism or secularism would not be tolerated in Pakistan; and added only an Islamic system can work here'. He went on to state that "if somebody has an obsession with Kemalism or any other system, he should clear his mind of all such thoughts. The people and the armed forces of Pakistan will not tolerate any such system. They will rather resist such condemnable ideas."[14] This was a direct rebuff to remarks of Gen Pervez Musharraf who had stated earlier that he was impressed by Kemal Ataturk. This was a pointer towards the hard-line stance of militant and politico-religious organizations as far as efforts or reforms to control their activities by the military junta are concerned. Qazi believed that overthrow of Nawaz Sharif government was not the result of the coup by a few individuals. Instead, it was the outcome of all the collective well-thoughtout mass movement against Sharif government.

In February this year, Zelimkhan Yandarbayev, a former President of Chechnya visited Pakistan on his way to Afghanistan. He was granted visa by Pakistani government. He carried out an extensive tour of Pakistan to garner support for Chechen militants. Qazi Hussain Ahmed of Jamaat-i-Islami was instrumental in contributing about $200,000 to Zelimkhan.[15] The former Chechen President visited many mosques and met militant leaders of numerous factions and organizations and raised unspecified amounts for Chechen war effort. It was all accomplished under the benevolent eye of the present Pakistan government. The militant groups and organizations headquartered in Pakistan and Taliban-controlled areas were quite receptive to Zelimkhan's visit. On various occasions since 1992, such groups have exported arms, mercenaries and trained militants of various nationalities to Chechnya. The route used for such exports has been from Pakistan to Afghanistan, through Tazikistan and thereafter straight to Caspian sea and then cutting across Daghestan to Chechnya. Harkat-i-Jihadi Islam a militant groups is believed to have used this route to dispatch about a platoon worth of holy warriors to Chechnya to fight against the Russians in the current Russia-Chechen conflict.[16] It is also believed that one Maulana Dadullah had taken a Taliban contingent to Chechnya as reinforcements for jihad against the Russians. Apparently, the activities of extremists have been spurred by the visit of Zelimkhan. Taliban's Foreign Minister Wakil Ahmed Muttawakil said that, "It is Muslim world's shame that it does not support Chechens. They are my brothers. They are Muslims. The only solution is to help Chechens." He went on to state that they were not terrorists and they were fighting for freedom and independence from Russia.[17]

Al Badr is also one such group that has organized fund raising activity for Chechen war effort. Even Sipah-e-Sahaba, the militant Sunni fundamentalist group joined the bandwagon to support Yandarbayev's effort.[18] All these groups exhorted the government to declare Jihad against Russia so that they could legitimately send militants to North Caucasus. Zelimkhan in an interview during his visit to Pakistan stated "I have seen and studied all systems, nothing will work but the Islamic system". He believed, like any other radical Muslim that Shariat and *jehad* were answer to all problems and ills of a society and the nation. Jihad was the best course of action against injustice and the terror of powerful.

In January this year Taliban government recognised Chechen Republic of Ichkeria as a separate country and Zelimkhan Yandarbayev was appointed as envoy to Taliban. Russia has not only raised objections to visit of the Chechen-to-Pakistan but had also protested regarding Islamabad's failure to oppose the recognition of Chechnya by the Taliban.[19] Pakistan's official stance is to regard Chechnya as an integral part of the Russian federation and not to interfere in their internal affairs. However, covertly, it does not discourage any inimical activities being carried out on its soil against Russia. In fact, Pakistani state is a willing facilitator for extending moral and material support to Chechen insurgency. This can be easily judged from the activities of politico - religious parties and militant groups which are openly supporting the Chechen cause.

Taliban leader Mulla Mohammed Omar had decided to support the separatist government headed by President Aslan Maskhadov after having met a delegation from Chechnya in second week of January 2000. Russia has asserted that recognition of Chechnya by Taliban regime was legally void as the regime itself is not recognised by the UN and it is the Government of Burhauddin Rabbani which is recognised by the UN as the legitimate regime of Afghanistan. The UN Security Council resolution on introducing international anti-terrorist sanctions against the Taliban movement from November 14, 1999 also contains provisions for applying additional and more severe measures, if required. Thus, Taliban's open support for terrorists, operating from areas under Taliban control gives adequate reasons for toughening of UN sanctions against the Taliban movement.

During his sojourn of Pakistan, Zelimkhan had proposed formation of an international army of Islamic states to prepare themselves against Russian aggression and challenge by others to the entire Islamic Ummah. He even went on to suggest that Pakistan, Afghanistan and Chechnya form a confederation with common armed forces to counter the onslaught of anti-Islamic forces.[20] He expressed his satisfaction at negotiations conducted with some Pakistani officials. Though he did not divulge the names or appointment of such officials. He was asked to leave by Pakistani authorities after a three-week visit in view of the impending visit of President Clinton in March and due to fierce objections by Russians to his fund-raising and rabble-rousing activities. Though Pakistani authorities maintained that he was their guest but he had been asked to leave since his visa had expired.

Some Pakistanis find a reflection of their own society's ethos (which has evolved since 1947) in Chechen way of behaviour, especially during times of danger. Brigadier Syed Tirmazi, a Pakistani author in his book, *Chechnya; Tragedy and Triumphs'* mentions that "traditionally, Chechnya is a society of military democracy. In times of danger and when threatened by aggression, Chechens, elect a military leader and obey his commands."[21] Pakistan has had mostly military dictators ruling it and apparently India has been the only ever present danger throughout Pakistan's existence. Pakistan has always endeavoured to become a leader of Islamic Ummah by indulging in questionable activities. When a *de facto* Chechen Republic was established. Pakistanis too solace in the fact that a smaller Chechen nation defeated the 'mighty forces' because of Chechens motivation, faith and ideas of revenge and hatred for Russians. This is precisely what the Pakistani State has been trying to achieve, especially since days of General Zia-ul-Haq and after its defeat in India-Pak war of 1971.

The politico-religious parties in Chechnya and the Taliban exhort their 'Mujahideen' by fostering the doctorine that if the Taliban could defeat the mighty force of Soviet Russia and send its army packing, there is no reason why the Chechen mujahids and Islamic Ummah cannot repeat the same in Chechnya.

Along with the Islamic rhetoric and politics it is the strategic importance of Chechnya itself which compels various actors like USA, NATO nations and other countries to take an active interest in Chechnya imbroglio notwithstanding the much touted human rights violations by Russians in Chechnya. The strategic importance of Chechnya mainly relates to its location in North Caucasus and the part it plays in the oil pipeline politics. It is quite evident that the USA follows a policy of moving the Caspian oil pipelines away from both Russia and Iran to reduce Russia's influence in Central Asia and wherever else possible. If Russians get a firm hold on Chechnya then they would be successful in bringing into fruition two pipeline projects which would carry oil from Kazakhstan and Azerbaizan to Black Sea ports through Chechnya. American alternative is to take Kazakh and Azerbaizan's oil through Georgia and Turkey to the Black Sea. An agreement on this project was signed in November 1999.[22] America also has a complex relationship with the Taliban. On the one hand it is not happy with the Taliban sheltering Osama Bin Laden, on the other hand it needs Taliban's help to achieve its aim and purpose of pipeline politics. To avoid Iran, some of the oil pipelines have to pass through Afghanistan and Pakistan. On February 3, 2000, Pakistan and Taliban agreed to implement Pak-Afghan-Turkmenistan gas pipeline and refinery project in Afghanistan.[23] It is not clear as to how the project will be funded. A similar project of American UNOCAL Corporation has been suspended because of human rights violations by the Taliban and the UN sanctions against the Taliban-led government.

One event which has largely gone unnoticed.is the dispatch of a Pakistani Army officer Major General Anis Bajwa in January 2000 as CMO (Chief Military Officer) of UNOMIG (United Nations Observer Mission in Georgia) to monitor the problem of Abkhazia, a Muslim predominant region of Georgia.[24] The mandate of UNOMIG, which was to expire on January 31 has been recommended to be extended by six months. The mission has 101 UN military observers looking for peaceful solution in Abkhazia. Chechnya and other North Caucasus Muslim republics of Russia share borders with Georgia. Russia has been attempting to seal off Chechnya's southern mountains and fight rebels there. Such an action, as envisaged by President Vladmir Putin, would prevent the rebels from coming down into the plains to attack the Russian positions. It is also believed that Chechens are receiving arms, ammunition and other material aid through porous borders with Georgia. Russo-Georgian border has been the main supply route through which Chechens have been receiving equipment. Because of American, Western Europe's and Pakistani sympathy for Chechens, the posting of a Pakistani General to a sensitive area assumes added significance. It may be remembered that Richard Butler, Chief of the UNSCOM, the UN

Commission in Iraq for monitoring their WMD (Weapons of Mass Destruction) programme, had provided sensitive intelligence to the American and Israeli intelligence agencies. Moreover, Pakistan, which has been suspended from Commonwealth of Nations and is on the way out from NAM (Non- Aligned Movement) because of forcible removal of democracy and its replacement by military dictatorship, should not have been permitted to send a member of its highly Islamised army to Georgia. In fact, because of Pakistan Army's aversion to secular, democratic, progressive and liberal principles it should have been debarred from holding any UN assignment or sending a UN contingent. It is intriguing to note that the USA, the sole superpower with levers of control of the UN has thought it fit not to object to allotment of such significant UN assignment to Pakistan military. The interest of both America and Pakistan lies in converging. As far as Chechnya problem is concerned they are on the same side.

When Zia started his drive in eighties to Islamicize Pakistan, he made large amount of funds available to *madrassas* from the *Zakat fund*. He had also equated the certificates given by *madrassas* to those given by the universities. *Madrassas* offered to the poor and illiterate not only free education but a cause to make one's life more meaningful. And this cause was Jihad. This was an antidote to the disillusionment of common people with political and socio-economic state of affairs in the country. The onslaught of modernism had also threatened the fundamentalist and extremist religious parties as the spread of modernism questioned the very basis of religion. During Soviet-Afghan war, Americans provided the funds and a large arsenal of weapons. But this source dried up after Americans lost interest in the region. The present source of funding is through public collections and donations and contributions from Arab countries. Apparently, this is inadequate to support the ever-burgeoning requirements of funds by the growing factories of terrorism in Pakistan and Afghanistan.

"The most important attraction that Afghanistan holds for fugitive Islamists from around the world is the opportunity to finance their activities through heroin and smuggling of contraband goods. Whatever be Talibans' shortcoming they offer perfect security and protection to its citizens and traders", says a Pakistani analyst. Revenue on poppy crop is the main source of income as the Taliban charge ten per cent 'Ushr' at manufacturing stage. The extremist groups garner funds by facilitating the transportation of drugs through Central Asia, Pakistan, Arab countries, Turkey, Caucasus and Russia. The Chechnya connection therefore, comes in very handy to the militant groups operating in North Caucasus.

Afghanistan, being a land-locked country, all its imports come through Pakistan's ports. Its situation is somewhat similar to that of land-locked Nepal with respect to India. There is a rampant smuggling and trade in contraband item. The militant groups have a share of this trade, the volume of which is estimated to be $1.96 billion a year.[25] The Taliban also makes a considerable sum on goods transiting through its territory and being exported to Central Asian countries.

The conflict, in Chechnya has created another *raison d'être* for jehadi organisations. Pakistan and the Taliban are in the forefront of encouraging and facilitating the existence of such organizations. Gen. Pervez Musharraf has advised all the Jihad organizations and militant groups to come under one banner but apparently, some of the politico-religious parties like Jammat-i-Islami are apprehensive of erosion their power and role if they unite under one umbrella organization. The *jehadi* organizations and militant groups are becoming increasingly powerful and more extremist in their views and assertive in action because of independent sources of funding and increasing disenchantment with the prevailing economic and socio-political conditions in Pakistan. The schisms in Islam religion have given rise to the sectarian violence in Pakistan that is nibbling at the very innards of modern, progressive, liberal and democratic society of Pakistan. Though the activities of such militant groups suite Pakistan's Kashmir policy yet, the activities of these groups has had the effect of isolating Pakistan and Afghanistan from the international community.

Pakistan's support to Chechnya has antagonised Russia, China is also not happy with some of its Muslim rebels from Xinjiang province being trained in militant training camps in Pakistan and Afghanistan. Central Asian states are wary of Islamic resurgence in their countries being fostered by Islamic radicals having connections with Pak and Afghan religious fundamentalists. America is also displeased with the Taliban for harbouring its enemy number one Osama Bin Laden. It is also not happy with Pakistan's inability to influence the Taliban to hand over Laden to the US. Thus, General Musharraf is in an unenviable position; he is riding the tiger of Islamic militancy. During Pakistani tour of Chechnya's former President Zelimkhan Andarbayev, Government of Pervez Musharraf maintained a cautious distance from him. However, allowed him to carry out a fund-collection campaign for cause of Chechen militancy. Zelimkhan was able to establish rapport with the various *jehadi* organizations.

Along with the Kashmiri, Bosnian and Palestinian causes, the Chechnya cause has been added to target enemies of Islam. The jehadi organizations that had become causeless after Soviet withdrawal from Afghanistan were provided a fresh impetus by Kashmir insurgency in the nineties and now they have been given additional momentum by Chechnya insurgency. Pakistan being a theocratic state, whether ruled by civilians or military junta has looked on benevolently and with an approving eye on the activities of religious radicals. For the Taliban, it is business as usual since intolerance, terrorism and fanaticism and profiteering therefore seem to be its principle goals. In fact, Pakistan and the Taliban ruled Afghanistan have become focal areas from where holy terror is being exported. The Taliban has the dubious distinction of being the only entity in the world to have recognised Chechnya as a separate republic. The Taliban ruled Afghanistan is itself recognised only by three countries, Pakistan, Saudi Arabia and United Arab Emirates. Thus, equation on who is aiding whom is quite clear. The Chechnya conflict seems to be nowhere near a peaceful resolution even though Russians have claimed that they have gained control over Chechnya. If one looks back to the past results of Russia-Chechen conflicts, the present conflict is more likely to be a long drawn-out affair. The Taliban and Pakistan support to Chechens has only added fuel to the fire and is unlikely to mitigate the travails and tribulations of the Chechen people. It is only through a Russo-Chechen dialogue that a mutually acceptable solution to the present imbroglio can be found.

General Pervez Musharraf continues to be dominated by the Islamist politico- religious organizations as is evident from his failed attempts to amend blasphemy laws. He draws fine distinctions between jihad and terrorism. On the other hand, the Taliban suffers from no such dilemmas. The Taliban thrives on *jihad* and its export in any form to all the troublespots of Islamic Ummah. Pakistan's ambitions of becoming the leader of Islamic world are well known and with its newly demonstrated nuclear capability it believes that it has acquired a new status. It is unlikely that Pakistan and the Taliban would curtail their support to the ongoing Chechnya insurgency in the near future.

REFERENCES

1. Sergei Kovalev, "Putin's War", *The New York Review of Books,* February 10, 2000.
2. Brigadier Syed A.I, Tirmazi; (Retired), *Chechnya Tragedies and Triumphs,* Fiction House, Lahore, 1999.
3. See n.l. Also see Ismail Khan in *Newsline,* February 2000 and "Comments; Chechen Rebels Getting Training in Pakistan", *POT* (Pakistani Series) Vol. 28, No. 83, April 8, 2000.
4. See M. Ilyas Khan in *Herald,* January 2000. He spent 40 days touring in Afghanistan. Also see "Islamic Extremism—Afghan Connection", *POT* (Afghanistan Series) Vol. 25, No.4, February 2000.
5. *Ibid.*
6. Robert Fisk, "A Taliban Factory in Pak", *The Hindustan Times,* April 14, 2000.
7. See Arif Jamal in *News,* February 20, 2000 and "Comments: The Biggest Private Army of Islamists in Pakistan", *POT (*Pakistan Series), Vol. 28. No. 23, March 3, 2000.
8. Ismail Khan and Stevè LeVine, "The Rebel Connection". *Newsweek,* March 13, 2000. Also see n.3 for detailed report on activities of Chechen commanders Shamil Basayev and Khattab.
9. n.3.
10. *Ibid.*
11. Dadan Upadhyay, "70 Pak, Arab militants head for Chechnya", *The Indian Express,* February 13, 2000.
12. See website of Jamaat-I-Islami on the Internet, address http://www.jamaat.org.
13. *lbid.*
14. *lbid.*
15. The *Newsweek* report at n.8 above mentions an amount of $185,000. Another report appearing in *Dawn* mentions a collection by Zelimkhan of rupees 0.2 million from one mosque only of Jamiat

Able Hadith. Earlier on February 8, local Jamaat-I-Islami (JI) Ameer, a Karachi advocate Naimullah Khan, handed over Rs. 5.8 million to Zelimkhan. The total collections could be much more since Zelimkhan visited many mosques and seminaries.

16. See n. 8.
17. *Frontier Post,* February 1,2000. Also see, " Taliban Troops to Support Chechen Fighters", *POT* (Afghan Series), Vol. 25, No.7 of February 24, 2000.
18. See n. 8.
19. *Dawn,* January 28, 2000.
20. *News,* February 11, 2000.
21. See n. 2.
22. See n. 4.
23. *News,* February 4, 2000.
24. *Pakistan Times,* January 26, 2000.
25. See n. 4.

CHAPTER 17

Chechnya: Background and Prospects

Ravi M. Bakaya

Background

To understand the problem of Chechnya a brief look at its location and historical background is essential. Chechnya is a tiny republic situated in the north Caucasus. Until the break-up of the USSR it was part of the Chechen-Ingush ASSR within the Russian Federation. Other north Caucasian ASSRs were Daghestan, Kabardino-Balkaria and north Ossetia, and the autonomous region of Karacheyevo-Cherkassia. Like in other parts of the former USSR, the population of all these republics constituted mixed ethnic groups. In 1986, the population of the Chechen-Ingush ASSR was 12,22,000. According to the 1979 Soviet Census there were 7,56,000 Chechens and just 1,86,000 Ingushes in the entire USSR. Traditionally the north Caucasian peoples are Muslims, following in the past a tolerant Sufi variant of Islam. Ethnically, the Chechens and Ingushes belong to the Turkish group. In 1944, Stalin issued the barbaric order to deport the entire Muslim population of Chechens and Ingushes to far-off regions of Kazakhistan for supposedly not cooperating adequately with the Red Army. However, after the 20th Congress of the CPSU they were allowed to return to their homelands and, in fact, two regions of the Stavropol Krai were added to the Chechen-Ingush ASSR. Grozny, the capital of Chechnya, grew into a modern city of almost 400,000 with a mixed population. Under Soviet rule considerable investments were made for oil exploration and laying the pipeline from Baku in Azerbaijan to Grozny to Novorossisk in the RSFSR.

Like other nationalities in Soviet times, many Chechens received their higher education in Moscow, Leningrad, Rostov, Kharkov and other metropolitan cities.

In 1990-91 an open conflict had already begun developing between Gorbachev and Yeltsin as the most prominent leaders of the USSR and RSFSR. On 29 May, 1990 Yeltsin was elected parliamentary leader of the Russian Federation and on July 12 he resigned from the CPSU. On 17 March, 1991 Soviet citizens voted in a referendum in favour of Gorbachev's Union Treaty. On June 21, Yeltsin was elected to the newly-created presidency of the Russian Federation. The Russian parliament passed a resolution affirming the sovereignty of the Russian constitution in the RSFSR territory. Then came the ill-fated and short-lived coup against Gorbachev on August 18-21, 1991 which, though defeated, sealed Gorbachev's fate. He had to resign as head of the CPSU on August 24 and on August 29 the USSR Supreme Soviet outlawed the activities of the Communist Party. On December 1, 1991 the Ukrainians voted for independence and a week later on December 8, Yeltsin met the leaders of Byelorussia and Ukraine in Minsk to declare the dissolution of the USSR and the formation of the CIS. Gorbachev resigned on 25th December 1991 formally as President of the USSR and the Soviet Union ceased to exist.

During this entire period Yeltsin kept on urging various constituents of the Union to seize as much independence as possible. A feeling was cultivated that Russia was subsidising the economies of other republics at its own expense and without them would be in a better condition to build a market economy. But after the break-up of the USSR, the vast Russian Federation with its 16 autonomous republics, 5 autonomous regions and 10 autonomous areas began facing problems. There was an exodus of Russians (and others) not only from many of the erstwhile Soviet Republics, but also from several regions within the Russian Federation itself where they now felt unsafe as a minority.

Chechnya Declares Independence

It was in such a situation that the Chechen leader Dzhokhar Dudayev declared the independence of Chechnya sometime in the autumn of 1991 (Ingushetia did not Join Dudayev). A product of the Chechen elite of Soviet times, Dudayev was a charismatic personality, a general of the air force and commander of a division stationed in Tartu in Estonia. Alexander Solzhenitsyn (who otherwise supported Chechnya's secession as he thought it was a liability for Russia) had this to say in an article in 1997:

"In the autumn of 1991, Dudayev declared the independence of Chechnya, but withdrew it within three days. And then for three whole years the Russian government took no decisive steps at all. An unprecedented scene— a part of the state with its own strong army and light and heavy armaments (all of them left behind with cynical disregard by the Centre itself declares its independence. Mass expropriation of non-Chechen population (at that time amounting to nearly half a million) began in the Chechen republic... While their forced expulsion, murders, kidnapping of women and rapes were going on, the Central authorities did not come to the rescue of the victims.... The explanation lies in the fact that certain important and influential people were interested in a secret deal with Dudayev for dividing up the income from the oil which came from Tyumen (Siberia) into Grozny oil refinery and most of which later disappeared altogether.... With the same lack of explanation why for three years no action was taken, and later military action was suddenly launched in. December 1994.... After suffering extremely heavy losses and causing mass destruction, the Federal forces were finally able to occupy the greater part of Chechnya by the summer of 1995..."

Grozny had been destroyed by heavy bombing in which thousands of innocent civilians were killed. The war in Chechnya was most unpopular in Russia and the Russians were violently criticised abroad for violation of human rights. World media in an attempt to destroy what was left of a great power, shut its eyes to the terroristic attacks on civilians kidnappings and killings by Chechen terrorists, showed the Russians as aggressors and the Chechens as fighters for freedom. Liberal opinion in Russia was also outraged by the stories of mass cruelty perpetrated by their own government and human rights groups from Russia travelled to Chechnya's war-torn regions and their reports did grave damage to the reputation of the Russian government. Young freshly mobilized lads were sent to the front to fight against determined Chechen fighters and thousands lost their lives in a war which no one understood why it was being fought.

Sometime in May 1996 it became known that Dudayev had been killed, though the mystery of how, where and when remained unsolved. The fighting in Chechnya had in the meantime been intensified and acts of terrorism, kidnapping, extortion and murder became rampant under the leaders who followed him. Zelimkhan Yandarbiyev had become Chechnya's acting President. The Russian organized "Elections" and the Zavgeyev government installed by them were never accepted by most of the Chechens. General Grachev, who had boasted he would bring Chechnya to heel in a matter of hours, completely failed to subdue the rebellious Chechens. With the death of Dudayev, who was a strong and modern leader, the leadership passed into the hands of fanatical leaders who began mobilising the Chechens under the banner of militant Islam.

Boris Yeltsin was re-elected President of the Russian Federation in June 1996 after a tough fight. He was then very ill and was growing more and more unpopular. General Alexander Lebed, a Cossack leader, was amongst his strongest opponents after the communist Zyuganov. After the election Yeltsin fell even more seriously ill and he had to undergo a complicated heart operation and there was talk of another presidential election becoming imminent. Yeltsin then appointed Lebed as the Secretary of Russia's Security Council soon after the presidential election.

Lebed brings Chechen war to an end

On the 6th August 1996, the Chechen separatists captured Grozny once again in a sudden attack and overthrew the unpopular Russian-supported Zavgayev government. Aslan Maskhadov became acting President. On 22nd August 1996, Lebed had two days of fruitful negotiations with Maskhadov and returned to Moscow to get approval from Yeltsin and Chernomyrdin (then prime minister). After several visits to Chechnya, Lebed was able to sign an agreement with the Chechen leaders in the presence of observers from the Organisation for Security and Cooperation in Europe (OSCE). Under this agreement a treaty on mutual relations between the Russian Federation and the Chechen Republic was to be signed in five years time (before 31 December 2001). A joint commission was to be formed before 1st October 1996, to oversee the decree of the Russian President of 25th June 1996 for framing proposals for a withdrawal of troops and for taking steps to fight against crime, terrorism and those fanning national and religious hatred, to frame proposals to restore currency and financial relations and to reconstruct war-ravaged Chechnya and supply food and medicines to the population.

It was also agreed that the constitution of the Chechen republic would be based on observing human rights, the right of people to self-determination, principles of equality of peoples, restoration of civil peace and security for all residents of Chechnya irrespective of nationality, religion and other differences. The joint commission was to finalise its work in accordance with an agreed schedule.

On 27th January 1997, elections of the Chechen parliament and President were held with international observers from OSCE and others present. Aslan Maskhadov was elected President, securing about 69 per cent of the votes cast. Maskhadov later met Yeltsin in Moscow and his government was recognized, Zavgayev being shown the door.

However, conditions in Russia started deteriorating and Yeltsin's popularity took a nosedive. He sacked Lebed as Secretary of the Russian Security Council. (Lebed is now governor of the huge Krasnoyarsk territory, having been elected to the post.) In Chechnya too Aslan Maskhadov failed to establish a viable government. Local warlords made their living by kidnapping, smuggling and stealing oil from the Black Sea pipeline. The Russian government took no fresh initiative to stem the rot.

Second Chechen War Begins

In August 1999, one of the top Chechen warlords Shamil Basayev, invaded neighbouring Daghestan. The Russian weekly *Obshchaya Gazeta* on 12-18 August reported under the headline "Shariat Comes at Night, Armed to the Teeth":

> According to reliable information about 1500 militants entered Daghestan from Chechnya .... Eyewitnesses say the Islamic detachments represent a real 'international' force. Apart from Chechens and Daghestanis there are amongst them Arabs, persons from the Baltic, Albanians, Russians, Ukrainians, Uzbeks, Tajiks and even Blacks. Military sources say that the war is being financed by the International terrorist Osama Bin Laden. The amount paid for establishing 'Shariat rule' in Daghestan is also mentioned—25 million dollars.

On 9th August Yeltsin nominated 46-year old Vladimir Putin, a hitherto unknown personality, as the third prime minister of Russia within a year. He also nominated him as his own successor to presidentship in the election due the following year.

In Russia Duma elections were due in December 1999, to be followed by election of the President a few months later. Unlike the last Chechen war which was extremely unpopular even amongst most Russians, the attack on Daghestan was almost unanimously denounced by one and all. Public opinion was outraged at the acts of the terrorists and their international connections. In early October 1999, the Russian military invaded Chechnya in an 'anti-terrorists' operation that soon turned into a full-fledged effort to refight the previous war. Masood Ali Khan, writing in *Mainstream* from Moscow, wrote in an article published in the 9th October 1999 issue of the journal:

> At the present the war is going on there on the borders of Chechnya and Daghestan in the high mountains. Hundreds of armed men who call themselves 'fighters for Islam' attack border villages to 'liberate' the people and establish 'real' and 'pure' Islam (as opposed to the traditional Sufi variety of Tariqat Islam the people have been following in the region which the invaders call 'heresy') and want to proclaim a puritan 'Shariat rule' *a la* Taliban. Here these people are popularly known as Wahabites. They belong to an international wing of fanatic, fundamentalist and extremist religious movement which originated in Arabia in the 18th century....

In an article published in a Moscow weekly, Grigory Yavlinsky who had earlier denounced strongly Russia's war in Chechnya, called for stopping the mass bombing of the territory of Chechnya and calling off ground operations. He called for conducting negotiations with Aslan Maskhadov, the legally elected President of Chechnya, on his acceptance of six conditions: 1. All hostages should be freed, new kidnappings and slave trade should stop; 2. Minimum conditions should be created for a civic law-based state; 3. Terrorists named in international search-lists should be handed over to Russian authorities, or those charged with terrorism should be deported from Chechnya; 4. All non-governmental armed formations on the territory of Chechnya should be disarmed; 5. All militarised repressive organs should be ended; 6. Chechnya should refuse shelter to persons charged with international terrorism on its territory.

The 'Memorial'—an organization which has been working for the rehabilitation of victims of Stalin's repression adopted a document on 9 December, 1999 saying among other things: "The 'Memorial' Society is of the opinion that the question about granting the Chechen Republic of Ichkeria the status of an independent state for the present cannot be on the agenda of negotiations at any level, because the power structures of the Republic of Ichkeria have demonstrated their inability to stop robberies, plundering, kidnapping of people by illegal armed formations based in Chechnya and adjoining territories. As a result, the territory of Chechnya has been converted into a source of threat to the neighbouring Russian regions." (Yelena Bonner, Andrel Sakharov's widow and member of 'Memorial' differed on the question of independence for Chechnya in a letter next day. But the 'Memorial' committee stood by its position).

In a report from Moscow dated 31 March, 2000 *The Hindu* said that the Russian authorities presented a former Indian medical student in Daghestan, S. Mishra of Orissa, to newsmen. Mishra had fallen into Russian hands when a group of 10 rebels surrendered to Russian forces in, Chechnya. Mishra had spent 17 months with the Chechen militants. In 1997 he had gone with some acquaintances to Chechnya from Makhachkala, where he was studying. He was detained by militants and spent a few months in jail. Later he was converted to Islam and made to join the militant groups. Later reports say that Mishra was captured and was cooperating with Russian authorities as he was forced to join the militants.

Postscript

Satyanarain Mishra has since returned to India on May 16. In an interview to *The Hindu* correspondent in Delhi on May 17 he related how he was handed over by his "friend" Rasool to the Barayev gang of militants while they were both walking along the streets. Mishra said, "They kept me in a lock-up and physically tortured me. Food was given once in two or three days and that too was inadequate. After they found no response from the Indian Embassy (to their demand for a huge ransom amount—*RMB*) they began using me for menial work. ...My day would begin with morning *namaz* which I was forced to do... And then the daily chores of filling water, sweeping, cleaning... For all this I would get horse meat for food. That too once a day."

After 17 months of mental and physical suffering Satyanarain Mishra managed to escape when they came under heavy shelling in late February in which many of the gang members were killed. The rest decided to surrender to the Russians.

The Russian security organization found Mishra to be a genuine victim and released him, after which he was allowed to return to India.

The December Duma elections returned a parliament less inimical to the President. President Yeltsin surprised his compatriots and the world by announcing on New Year eve his resignation and preponing the elections. Putin became the acting President and as we know he was later elected President in the first round itself. Though Putin's role as a strong, young man played a part in the elections and in this way the war in Chechnya was useful to him, amongst most Russians this time there was no division on the question of fighting the second Chechen war.

What of the future?

The positive factor is that Russian society is united now on the question of fighting international terrorism . However, large sections are greatly dissatisfied with the excesses committed by the Russian side, the denunciation of almost all Chechens as terrorists and suspects, the bombing of Grozny and the 'filtration camps' where Chechens were forced to live after being asked to leave Grozny. It is too early to say how Putin will shape as a leader. Youth and good health are on his side and at present he has the sympathy of many Russians. He has been travelling a lot within the country and has been to Chechnya. He met intellectuals to discuss various ways to settle the problem of Chechnya and now international terrorism. As Fred Weir said in a despatch from Moscow last year: "... The Soviet order is gone, and North Caucasus is today the poorest, most conflict-ridden and socially restless region of Russia. Nearly three-quarters of Daghestan's 2.2. million people live below the official poverty line, and unemployment is estimated at 80 per cent." The Chechens are a proud people. Today they feel hurt by the remorseless bombing to which they were subjected. But sympathy for the militants is reported to be far less than five years ago as their rule has disillusioned most people and the entry of foreigners has alienated them, no matter how much the likes of Basayev talk about Islam.

Ultimately, a political solution has to be found. This will depend on how the Russian government handles the situation not only in

Chechnya and in the north Caucasus, but also how it tackled the Mafia at home.

Much has been written about Putin's secret service career. In Russia it has not always been a disadvantage. After all, Gorbachev's mentor was Andropov, the head of the KGB. Primakov, one of the most popular prime ministers of the Yeltsin period, was also for a time in charge of the secret service. Putin was in the past a career secret service man; he then joined Sobchak, one of the prime reformers of post-Soviet period and a former Mayor of St. Petersburg. The Russians (they are not alone in this!) have always believed in a strong leader, a "firm hand" as they say in Russian. Putin does not have the advantage of previous popularity as a leader that Gorbachev and Yeltsin had. Those who see in him as a Pinochet perhaps do not know that Russian society today is very different and will not tolerate dictatorship. In any case, it takes many years (even Stalin took more than 10 years) to become a dictator.

The secretary of the Russian Council Security Sergei Ivanov, has visited India. An extradition treaty has been signed already between India and Russia. The fight against international terrorism must be fought by the combined efforts of many countries. Our own intellectuals and academics can make their contribution by making a thorough and painstaking study in detail of each region and function as think-tanks for the official bodies. There are many similarities as also important differences in the terrorist movements in various countries. Gandhi's India can make a unique contribution in tackling the problem both on the political and the human plane not forgetting how Khan Abdul Ghaffar Khan, the "Frontier Gandhi" had turned thousands of militant Pukhtoons into non-violent Khudai Khidmatgars.

Acknowledgement

For factual material used in this paper the author wishes to express his special gratitude to *Mainstream* (specially articles by Fred Weir and Masood Ali Khan, sent from Moscow), *The Hindu* and its regular columnist from Moscow Vladimir Raduhin, and to two Russian language weeklies—*Obshchaya Gazeta* of Moscow and *Russkaya Mysl* which is published from Paris.

CHAPTER 18

The Yugoslav Tragedy

O.N. Mehrotra

It is an irony of history that Yugoslavia was disintegrated on ethnic lines in spite of the two million mixed marriages in the total population of twenty-three million. No doubt the Serbs had primarily been blamed for the foremost perpetrators of ethnic hatreds and "ethnic cleansing" in Yugoslavia, especially in Bosnia and Herzegovina, Croatia and Kosovo, but in reality Croatian, Bosnian and Albanian: Muslims were equally responsible for the tragedy. The four years of ethnic civil war in Bosnia -Herzegovina, unending civil war in Kosovo and "ethnic cleansing", in Krajina and Slavonia of Croatia left more than 2,00,000 people dead or missing. Many more were forced to flee to safer places as many cities and villages were either badly damaged or totally destroyed. In many cases, once inhabitants left their dwellings for safer places, they were never allowed to return and resettle.

This paper does not dwell on the details of distintegration of Yugoslavia, the reactions of major concerned countries and the resolutions adopted by the United Nations Security Council or European Union (EU) or Organisation for Security and Cooperation in Europe (OSCE) or North Atlantic Treaty Organisation (NATO) or Organisation for Islamic Conference (OIC). Nor does it chronicle the day-to-day twists and turns of ethnic crises in the former Yugoslavia. It seeks, instead, to highlight and explain the general perception about the crises, the real problems and the solutions sought to resolve those crises.

All nations have their self-servicing myths. But they have generally been challenged by public leaders and intellectuals. In Yugoslavia, "The pervasive culture of ethno-centric myths are unchallenged even by intellectuals."[1] There was hardly any dissident literature like Samizdat in Russia. Yugoslavia had neither a labour movement like Solidarity in Poland nor a historian like Adam Michnik who advocated the doctrine of civil society. It also failed to produce dissident novelists, playwrights and intellectuals like Vaclav Havel and Milan Kundera in the former Czechoslovakia.

The oral tradition of past history had always been prevalent in Yugoslavia, especially in rural areas. The Serbs had widely suffered from the nihilistic view that the history had never rewarded them for their noble idealism. Though they fought against Ottoman Turks and Nazi Germans, yet their "non-Serbian Yugoslavs have conspired against them from the beginning, undermining Yugoslavia's unity, often at Serb's expense."[2] In fact Croats and Slovenes never reconciled to the federation of the Slavs of the south—the literal meaning of Yugoslavia. They had their own nationalism and folklore. The major dividing line amongst the Serbs, Croats and Slovenes was that while the former were orthodox Christians, the latter two were Roman Catholics. The latter believed that they were more cultured and prosperous Europeans than the Serbs who were oriental, having lived for generations under the Ottoman Empire. But the Serbs believed that they were great warriors who fought and won independence from the Ottoman Empire and could fight bloody war for years.

The foundations of Yugoslavia was laid on a weak ground. On 4 December 1918, the Kingdom of Serbs, Croats and Slovenes was proclaimed. Prince Alexander accepted the regency of the new state, becoming king in August 1921. He assumed dictatorial power in January 1929 and formally changed the country's name to Yugoslavia in October. He was assassinated by Croation extremist in October 1934 in France. He was succeeded by his brother, Prince Paul, who granted internal autonomy to Croatia in 1939.

During the World War II an "Independent state of Croatia," incorporating Bosnia -Herzegovina was established under Axis protection. The newly independent state was administered by the cruel Ustasha, who, under Ante Pavelic, persecuted and killed Jews, Serbs, Gypsies and Croation opponents of the regime. After the conclusion of the war, Yugoslavia was reunited under the leadership of Marshal Josip Broz Tito, a Croat himself. In reprisals against Croats, Serb partisan units persecuted and killed many supporters of the Axis rule.

In January 1946, a federation of six republics—Serbia, Montenegro, Croatia, Slovenia, Macedonia and Bosnia and Herzegovina—with two autonomous regions—Kosovo and Vojvodina, was established. Aware of inter- ethnic rivalries and apprehensive of clash for leadership in Yugoslavia after his death, President Tito introduced a collective leadership and regular rotation of personnel between posts in July 1971. It was an attempt to unify various nationalities in the country. Consequently a collective state presidency was established, which was led by Tito until' his death in 1980. His responsibilities were transferred to the collective state presidency and to the presidium of the League of Communist of Yugoslavia (LCY). In the meantime, a new constitution was introduced in February 1974 which gave the republics a controversial right of secession from the federation.

The former Yugoslavia was a unique multi-ethnic country with the least homogeneity as a nation state. The common unifying denominator was that its inhabitants were Slaves of the south. The major common dividing factor was religion which was largely contained during the communist regime. There were six officially recognised "Nations of Yugoslavia": Croats, Macedonians, Montenegrins, Muslims, Serbs and Slovenes. Apart from the nationalities, there were 18 ethnic minorities, the largest being the Albanians and the Hungarians, concentrated in two autonomous provinces of Serbia-Kosovo and Vojvodina ' respectively. The other ethnic groups, were Bulgarians, Czechs, Gypsies, Italians, Hungarians, Romanians, Ruthenians, Slovaks and Turks. The remaining ethnic groups were classified as "Other Nationalities and Ethnic Groups": Austrians, Greeks, Jews, Germans Poles, Russians, Ukrainians, Vlachs and others including those who preferred to classify themselves as Yugoslavs.

In a multi-ethnic state, like Yugoslavia where centrifugal forces are much more stronger than those of centripetal forces, it is always difficult to maintain unity and integrity. If the prominent single largest ethnic group is considered as the ruler by other smaller ethnic groups, then any move of strengthening the federation may be considered by other ethnic groups as erosion of their rights and domination of the former. In certain cases it may be possible that the combined population of smaller ethnic groups is more than the single largest group. But the smaller groups invariably perceives themselves as minorities and may complain about their suppression by the largest group. Such a perception persisted in the former Yugoslavia where Serbs were merely 36 per cent of the total population of the country but were generally regarded as rulers of the country and thus the exploiters of other ethnic or national groups. In other words, it was widely believed that the Croats and Slovenes usually felt that the central political authority was vested with the Serbs who could use the state power to suppress the aspirations of other ethnic groups. The Serbs possessed the monopoly of legitimate violence in the name of preserving the state and thus not allowing them to secede from the federal Yugoslavia. Their apprehension gained strength when the Serbian nationalist leader Slobodan Milosevic initiated the adoption by the Assembly of the Republic of the constitutional amendments limiting provincial autonomy of Kosovo and Vojvodina.

Whether there was a history of nationalism in an area or not, once the demand for independent sovereign status for that area was raised, the nationalists would generally claim that nationalism was always present in a latent suppressed form. In fact, in such a situation an ethnic or national group would oppose being ruled by the another group. Their relation would be termed as rulers and ruled. Once such an emotion was generated or surcharged, as Lord Acton put it "there began a time when the test simply was, that the nations would not be governed by foreigners. Power legitimately attained and exercised with moderation, was declared invalid."[4]

The end of Cold War led to shifting of boundaries of two East European countries and the former Soviet Union. While the disintegration of the erstwhile Soviet Union and the bifurcation of the former Czechoslovakia were peaceful, the break-up of Yugoslavia was bloody. The disintegration of the former Yugoslavia began when Croatia and Slovenia announced their decisions to secede from the federation in summer of 1991. The decision was indeed constitutional but the process of its implementation was unconstitutional because it should have to be endorsed by the other republics of Yugoslavia. Without giving significance to the constitutionality of the procedure of the right to secede from the federation, the issue was overshadowed by the constitutional right of self-determination for the Croats and Slovenes, and its opposition by the Serbs was largely considered as an undesirable obstruction aimed to perpetuate the Serbs' domination in Yugoslavia. This was propagated by both the republics and endorsed by the international community which committed a fatal mistake in generally accepting their proposition. The United States and some European countries made mild diplomatic appeals against the break-up of Yugoslavia. They had not considered it as a serious crisis and thus they did not make concerted efforts to avoid the disintegration of the country, and if it became unavoidable, to facilitate the process peacefully without undermining the right of self-determination for the minority in a multi-ethnic country.

While most Western countries were yet to emerge from the euphoria of winning the Cold War against the Soviet Communists, Germany, which had just risen as a strong united country from the debris of the Cold War, having strong historical ties with Croatia, aggressively supported the independence of Croatia. In fact, Germany was instrumental in forcing the European community (EC) to grant recognition to Croatia. However many political leaders, experts and commentators warned against the secession of republics from the federation in haste because they rightly feared that bloody ethnic violence would certainly erupt in Croatia because of its history and its leadership headed by an ultra-nationalist President Franjo Tudjman. They were right in their thinking, as he initiated "ethnic cleansing" in the former Yugoslavia. However, the Croatian crisis was overshadowed by the Bosnian crisis.

It was an irony of history that while West European countries were moving towards integration, the same countries sincerely opposed to disintegration of a state failed to make efforts to contain the rise of national hatred. The 1990 elections in Yugoslavia witnessed emergence of strong nationalist parties of various republics and their leaders openly advocated extreme nationalism. Though Milosevic himself was a nationalist leader, yet he propagated for the unity of Yugoslavia. Croatia and Slovenia had proposed transformation of the Yugoslavia federation into a loosen confederation, republics having right to maintain their own armed forces and enter into diplomatic relations with other states. While Serbia and Montenegro were in favour of a centralized federal system, Macedonia and Bosnia advocated a federation of sovereign states, based on the model of the E.C.

Croatia

In the 1990 election campaign, Tudjman made no effort to hide his racial, ethnic and religious intolerance. He categorized the Croats as western - oriented, and the Serbs as Byzantine. The Croats are Roman catholics and the Serbs are orthodox Christians. His political party's name was the Croatian Democratic Union (CDU) which stood for Croatia and for Croats. Of course, his prejudices against Jews, Serbs and Muslims were not out of place with public .sentiments in Croatia. He began discrimination against Serbs in 1990 when his government adopted a new constitution for the republic that declared that Croatia was "the national state of the Croatian nation". The new constitution gave Croatia right to secede from Yugoslavia. At the same time President Tudjman had not hidden his intention of making his country "ethnically clean". He retained in the Croatian national flag the traditional red-and-white checks that the Ustashe used. His government also used some of the same symbols as the wartime Ustashe, like the coat of arms, police uniforms and currency. Moreover, he renamed public places to convey the same kind of appeal. For example, the square for the Victims of Fascism was renamed as the Square of Croatian Greats. In fact, Tudjman wrote a series of books arguing against such facts that the Fascists killed hundreds and thousands of Serbs and other minorities in Croatia. He argued vehemently that the estimate of six million Jewish deaths in the Holocaust was an overstatement.[5]

Virtually every family of Serbs in the Krajina region lived with the memory of relatives butchered during World War II. The Zagreb government that declared independence in 1991 ignored those memories. Instead, demanded that Krajina Serbs should take an oath of loyalty to Croatia and was vague about minority rights. In the meantime a 'Serbs National Council', based at Knin (in Krajina) was formed and organized a referendum on autonomy for the Croatian Serbs. By October 1991 three 'Serbian Autonomous Regions' (SARs) had been established in Croatia: Krajina, eastern Slavonia and western Slavonia. Later the three SARs announced their union as a "Republic of Serbia Krajina (RSK)."

The Serbs acquired control of a third of Croatian territory, covering the area of Krajina and Slavonia, where they were in an overwhelming majority. It may be recalled that the Serbs were first sent to Krajina by the Austro-Hungarian (The Habsburgs) Empire to build a buffer against the Turks. Vojna Krajina means "military frontier" which was defended by Serbs for centuries. They defended the Croats against Turkish aggressors and as a reward they were persecuted by the Croatian Ustashe.

In early 1995, Tudjman declared that he would not allow further extension of UN peace-keeping forces in Croatia after March. He complained that the UN had failed to "liberate" the Serb-held territory of Croatia. He made his intentions clear for the Serbs to come under his autocratic rule. In early 1992, the warring Croats and Serbs agreed to a ceasefire and the UN peace-keeping forces were stationed to protect the Serb-held territory. The UN peace-keeping forces' tenure in Croatia was until the end of March. As a bargain on extending a fresh mandate for the presence of UN peace-keeping forces there, the UN Security Council passed a resolution recognising Croatia's territorial integrity. Zagreb considered the Security Council's decision as a legal mandate for launching an offensive against the Serbs who held a third of Croatia.

In May 1995, Tudjman launched an armed offensive against Western Slavonia, "ethnically cleansing" the land from the Serbs. The stage was set to execute the most planned "ethnic cleansing" in Krajina. On August 4, 1995 the Croatian government troops launched a massive military operation and within five days captured Krajina. In the aftermath of military operations, as many as 2,00,000 Croatian Serbs were forcibly expelled from Krajina. In mid-January 1998 the mandate of UN Transitional Administration for Eastern Salvonia (UNTAES) ended and western Salvonia officially came under the Croatian authority. Thus, Tudjman could achieve his life dream of establishing Croatia for Croats only.

Bosnia

In the post-Cold War period, the Bosnian tragedy of "ethnic cleansing" was surpassed only by the Rwandan ethnic civil war, slaughtering a million people in a short period of two months in summer 1994 while the "civilized world" was a silent spectator to the human carnage. The general perception about the Bosnian crisis is that the Bosnian Serbs were primarily, if not solely, responsible for the bloodbath in the former republic of Yugoslavia and they had been the real stumbling block in the resolution of the problem because they rejected many reasonable proposals offered by the mediators and international organizations until the signing of the Dayton accord in November-December 1995.

A brief reference to the history of Bosnia-Herzegovina may be in order here. The Bosnians were Slavs, like other people of former Yugoslavia, but a large numbers of them called Bogomiles (a heretical sect) who were persecuted by both the Serbs and the Croats. After the conquest of Bosnia by the Turkish Muslims in 1463, a large number of Bosnians, especially Bogomiles, converted to Islam. Many Serbs reportedly looked down on the Muslims for converting themselves for some pecuniary gains. The Bosnian Muslims did not have any historical aspiration to have their own nation state based on ethno-nationalism that gained prominence in the post-Cold War period.[6]

In 1964, the Muslim, earned recognition as the sixth nation of the former Yugoslavia. Thus, the Muslims began to think that Bosnia-Herzegovina was their nation like those of Croatia, Macedonia, Montenegro, Serbia and Slovenia of different national groups in the federation. The 1974 constitution became a departure point for the Bosnian Muslims' national assertiveness because it gave the right to the republics to secede from the federation. The Bosnian Serbs reacted adversely to the concept of an independent Islamic state in their own country. In fact, the Serbs were reduced to a minority in Bosnia because of a large-scale massacre, and many of them migrated to Serbia and other republics. According to the 1961 Census, Serbs accounted for 42.7 per cent of Bosnian population and the Muslims only for 25.5 per cent. But in 1971, the percentage of the Muslims rose to 39.6 of the population as against 37.2 per cent for the Serbs. According to the last Census, in 1981 (in terms of ethnic breakdown), the Muslims accounted for 43.7 per cent of the 4.3 million population in comparison with the Serbs 33.4 per cent and Croat's 17.3 per cent in Bosnia.

The Serbs in Bosnia had deep-rooted suspicion about the Bosnian Muslim leader, Alija Izetbegovic. The suspicion was not altogether unfounded in view of his highly controversial pronouncements and declarations in his book, *The Islamic Declaration*, written in 1970 but not made available to the public at large. However, it was illegally duplicated and circulated among the Muslims, to serve as an ideological roadsign, a manual and a practical Instruction for the Islamic-propagandist —political and organizational work of adversaries of secular non-Islamic order."[7] He was sent to jail for initiating hatred towards other ethnic groups. He along with a group of like-minded people was publicly rehabilitated after the communist renounced power in Yugoslavia. Though he made unsuccessful efforts to project himself as a supporter of the multi-ethnic state of Bosnia, yet he never renounced the declarations and pronouncements he made either in his book or in public speeches.

The nationalist parties swept into power in all the republics of the former Yugoslavia in the first post-Cold War elections in 1990. A coalition government of Muslims, Croats and Serbs was installed in Bosnia. But in 1991, the politics of Bosnia got largely influenced by the Serb-Croat conflict.

In January 1992, the Badinter Arbitration Commission attached to the EC Peace Conference recommended that a referendum take place before any further consideration could be given to extending recognition to Bosnia. The Bosnian Muslim President Izetbegovic, declared the republic's independence after holding a referendum on independence on Bosnia from Yugoslavia on February 29-March 1, 1992. The Bosnian Muslim leadership followed the policy of Croatia, without realizing the repercussions entangled in a decision of declaring independence of the republic against the wishes of the Serbs. The Croats collaborated with the Muslims to realize their own objective of establishing "Greater Croatia".

The referendum was boycotted by the Serbs. The declaration of independence caused tension between the Muslims and the Serbs, leading to civil war in Bosnia in the last week of March. The independent Bosnia was recognized by the EU and the United States in April without taking into account the fact that the government had failed to fulfil the requisite condition that it had sovereign authority on the entire territory of the state. Even the capital Sarajevo of Bosnia was not under the control of the new independent state. The Serbs announced the formation of a 'Serbian Republic of Bosnia-Herzegovina' which comprised Serbia-held areas of the republic (about 65 per cent of the total area). Incidentally, "the Croation Union of Hezeg-Bosna" was also established by Bosnian Croats.

In the 'might is right' situation in Bosnia, the Serbs and Croats acquired more land than they had before the civil war began. During the course of the civil war, on the one hand, the Croats and Serbs joined together and fought against the Muslims and on the other, the Croats and Muslims jointly fought against the Serbs. Washington forced the Muslim and Croat leaders of Bosnia to establish a federation in early 1994. The objective of formation of a new federation was that Serbs would be forced to join it, failing which they would be isolated in the country. The Croats apparently joined the federation because it would facilitate in the establishment of a confederation with Croatia. Incidentally armed conflicts between Croats and Muslims continued even after they established a federation.

A series of cease-fire declarations could not stop civil war. Even the NATO's air strikes on Serbs positions failed to end the civil war. The joint United Nations-European mediators, Cyrus Vance (later he was replaced by Thowold Stolenberg) and Lord Owen, worked out a plan for the division of the country on the ethnic lines but it was not acceptable to all warring groups. The Contact Group (consisting of representatives of the US, Britain, France, Germany and Russia) also met with innumerable problems. Finally, at the initiative of President Bill Clinton, Presidents Izetbegovic, Tudjman and Milosevic (the latter representing both Yugoslavia and the Bosnian Serbs) and representatives of the Contact Group and the EU negotiated a peace accord on Bosnia in Dayton, Ohio in November 1995. On November 21, the three Presidents initiated a definitive accord, dividing Bosnia and Herzegovina between the federation with 51 per cent of the territory, and Serb republic with 49 per cent of the area. On December 14, 1995 the Dayton peace agreement was formally signed by the three Presidents and by President Clinton and a number of European political leaders in Paris, France. The United Nations Protection Force (UNPRFOR) was replaced by an international NATO-commanded 60,000 strong 'Implementation Force' (IFOR). The strength of force has substantially reduced but stable peace has not been established so far.

Kosovo

The Kosovo crisis is a complicated one and cannot be understood in the proper perspective until one knows its background. The Serbs, who belong to the Slav race had come to the Balkans and settled primarily in the present province of Kosovo at the end of the sixth and the beginning of the seventh centuries. For the Serbs, Kosovo is of exceptional importance for the Serbian history and for the cultural civilization identity of Serbia. It is the cradle of Serb civilization. It is emotionally as important for the Serbs as the Wailing Wall is for the Jews. In fact, many Serbian cultural monuments are situated is Kosovo (200 medieval churches, some of them under the protection of UNESCO).

Constitutionally, Kosovo is called Kosovo and Metohija. Kosovo is a Serbian word which means 'land of blackbirds' Metohija is a Greek word that means land (property) of monasteries. It is popularly known as Kosovo as Jammu and Kashmir is called Kashmir in short. Kosovo and Metohija is known as Kosmet like Jammu and Kashmir is called J&K. According to the Serbian sources, 50 per cent of the territory of Kosovo belongs to monasteries though in the recent past, Kosovo Albanians have illegally occupied some of the territory, vandalised monuments and forced priests and nuns out from places in which they have been living for centuries.

For almost 800 years, the Serbs remained the sole inhabitants of Kosovo. The chequered history of Kosovo began with the Battle of Kosovo in 1389 when the Serbs were defeated by the Turks and the Ottoman Empire advanced toward Europe. Consequently, the occupying Turkish forces forcibly settled Muslim Albanians in Kosovo. The Serbs, in large numbers abandoned the region and even moved their churches from Kosovo to north Serbia. In the Serbian national consciousness, the Battle of Kosovo has immense significance because for them it is a symbol of the struggle for freedom and independence. Though Serbia achieved its independence from the Ottoman Empire in 1878, and acquired international recognition as a sovereign nation, Kosovo could be reunited with Serbia only in 1912 after the First Balkan War. Incidentally, for the Albanians, "it was in Kosovo that the Albanian national revival began with the founding of the League of Prizren in 1878".[8] However, Kosovo was never a part of Albania, claim the Serbs. During World War II, Kosovo was occupied by Italy and Germany but it was reunited with Serbia after the conclusion of the war. According to another account, while Serbia was occupied by Germany during the war, Kosovo was annexed by Albania. Be that as it may, Kosovo was legally never a part of Albania except when it was annexed by it during the time of war. Nevertheless, the Serbs have always been apprehensive of annexation of Kosovo by Albania as and when it gets an opportunity because the Albanians are in an overwhelming majority in Kosovo. In this respect, it may be noted that when Yugoslovia began to disintegrate in the early 1990s it was widely feared that Kosovo would be the major bloody flashpoint in the Balkans. Though the Kosovo crisis did not explode then, it had been persisting for long especially since 1981.[9]

The current Kosovo crisis may be traced back to the reconstitution of Yugoslavia by Josip Broz Tito after the conclusion of the World War II. Like the other Communist leaders, Tito also granted separate identity to distinct ethnic groups and nations of Yugoslavia. Perhaps those leaders believed that different nationalism and ethno-nationalism in a multinational and multi-ethnic country could be submerged in a utopian classless and stateless society. In fact, neither in the former Soviet Union nor in the former Yugoslavia, which were multi-ethnic and multinational countries, was nationalism allowed to grow or prosper. The Russians and Serbs considered their affiliation to their countries more than other groups and therefore, they are more remorseful about the disintegration of their former countries than the others. Once these two countries began to collapse, they were divided on different national lines and crudely demarcated in the form of various republics.

In the post-war Yugoslavia, for the first time the Albanians were recognized as a distinct national group as their language was made one of the official languages and they were granted the right to education in their own vernacular. This recognition laid the ground for the growth of Albanian nationalism in Kosovo. Their main grudge which began to emerge was that they were not given the status of a republic while they constituted the largest minority in the country and their population was almost equal to the Slovenes and Macedonians and more than these of Montenegrins who were given their own republic in the new political structure of the country. However, this discontentment generally remained latent for almost two decades.

Since the late 1960s, Kosovo Albanians have been complaining that their gains in the post-war period were undermined by the repressive policies adopted by Alexander Rankovic, a Serb, who was head of the state security police. After his downfall in 1966, the Kosovo Albanians staged large-scale demonstrations calling for granting of republican status to Kosovo province. Such a demand sent a shock wave in Serbia and Macedonia where the Albanians were suspected of harbouring their cherished dream of merging with neighbouring Albania and thus establishing a "Greater Albania", which has also been opposed by both Serbia and Macedonia. The Albanians constitute more than 20 per cent of the population of Macedonia.[10]

Without taking into account the apprehensions of the Serbs and others as well as subsequent repercussions in the fractured and volatile region, the Yugoslov Constitution of 1974 granted autonomous status to Kosovo province within the Serbian republic. Kosovo was given many of the powers of a republic within the Yugoslav Federation. It has its own Constitution like the other republics and its consent in the decision-making procedure at the federal level became significant where the principle of consensus was followed. It had a right to enter into bilateral cooperation agreements with other countries. Consequently, Kosovo developed close relations with Albania, and the Kosovo Albanians' aspirations to join Albania gained confidence and strength. It is appropriately observed elsewhere that the "1974 Constitution had established decentralisation and so provided the framework for nationalist activity once the restraint of Tito's power was removed." The granting of autonomy to Kosovo and the Serbs' claim of control over Kosovo because it was their province emerged as a major cause of nationalist conflict between the Albanians and Serbs in the 1980's.

At the same time, the Serbs' abject fear was growing rapidly because of the declining ratio of population of the Serbs in Kosovo. It may be recalled that before World War II, the Serbs and Montenegrins constituted 61 per cent of the population of Kosovo. During the occupation of Kosovo between 1941 and 1945, the Serbs and Montenegrins were forced to leave Kosovo and the Albanians were reportedly settled in their living places. After the war, the new Yugoslav socialist regime banned the return of the Serbs and Montenegrins to Kosovo in order to strengthen the confidence of the Albanian national minority in the new political dispensation. Though Kosovo is rich in natural resources, it was the least developed region in Yugoslavia. In the post-war period, the region was economically developed but the Serbs and Montenegrins continued to migrate to Serbia and Montenegro for better employment opportunities and due to the growing Albanian nationalist aggressiveness. In 1961, the Serbs were reduced to 23.6 per cent of the population of Kosovo, which declined further to 13.2 per cent in 1981. The Kosovo Albanian's ratio of the population was growing not only because of the migration of the Serbs from Kosovo but also because of the high rate of birth of the Albanians.

The Serbian fear of Kosovo Albanians' motive to secede from the Yugoslav Federation increased after the death of Tito as Kosovo Albanian representatives gained equal rights in the ruling collective Presidency of Yugoslavia. At the same time, Kosovo Albanian nationalism was gaining strength because of growing acute unemployment amongst the intelligentsia in Kosovo. In certain quarters, it was believed that this situation was exacerbated because of the establishment of an Albanian university in Pristine, the capital of Kosovo, in 1968. The Kosovo Albanian nationalist discontentment exploded in 1981, with massive demonstrations calling for granting of republican status to Kosovo autonomous province. Though the demonstrations were controlled with the help of federal armed forces, 300 people reportedly died and several hundred were wounded. At the same time, as many as 7,000 Albanians, mostly young men, were arrested and many of them received prison sentences because of their nationalist/disruptive activities. These incidents further widened ethnic relations in Kosovo and strengthened the nationalist aspiration amongst the Albanians. The Serbs as well as Montenegrins continued to emigrate from Kosovo complaining of systematic harassment involving rape, murder and attacks on their property by members of the Albanian population.[11]

In the media, time and again, it has been highlighted that the Serbian nationalist leader Milosevic has taken away the autonomy of Kosovo. No doubt, the Kosovo autonomy was curtailed in 1989 but nowhere was it noted that such a step was taken because of the deteriorating law and order situation in Kosovo, due to the Kosovo Albanians' nationalist and separatist activities. In fact, on March 1, the two Chambers of the Federal Assembly held an emergency joint sitting to discuss the situation in the province. In the keynote speech, Lazar Mojsov, the member for Macedonia of Yugoslavia's Collective State Presidency, blamed the Albanian intelligence service for helping nationalist and separatist activities in Kosovo with the objective of making the province an integral part of a "Greater Albania".[12] In short, though the Serbian nationalist leadership has recently been blamed for its repressive measures against Kosovo Albanians, yet Albanians' unconstitutional demand for independence and their indulgence in terrorist activities in Kosovo have hardly been taken note of. Moreover, reference is rarely made to the Albanians' non-cooperative and agitational activities in Macedonia, and harsher measures have been taken by the Macedonian government to count them. In fact, the Macedonian government has even objected to Albanian nationalist names and at times forced the Albanians to change their names. In retrospect in the former republics of Yugoslavia, the Albanian minorities with active assistance from Albania had been engaged in disruptive activities, and in Kosovo, the constitutional authority of the Serbian government was challenged.

Before Milosevic became the leader of Serbia, the Kosovo Albanians had already declared their intention to separate themselves from the Republic of Serbia and establish their own republic. That could not be possible without amending the Constitution for which the consent of Serbia was required. For the Serbs, the Kosovo Albanians could raise their demand of becoming a republic because their province was granted autonomy in the 1974 Constitution. Thus, if the autonomy of Kosovo was to be taken away, then the Kosovo Albanians' movement could easily be controlled, the Serbs felt. But that proved counter-productive because the Kosovo Albanians movement has gradually become strong and violent.

After the former four republics—Croatia, Slovenia, Macedonia and Bosnia—declared independence from Yugoslavia, Serbia (including the provinces of Kosovo and Vojvodina) and Montenegro brought into being a new federal Republic of Yugoslavia by adopting a new Constitution on April 27,1992. While the Kosovo Albanians boycotted the federal elections in May 1992, they elected their own 130-member Assembly, which was declared illegal by the Serbian Assembly. But Ibrahim Rugova was elected "President" of the self-proclaimed "Republic of Kosovo." He held talks in Geneva with Lord Owen and Cyrus Vance (peace negotiators in Yugoslavia) in September, during which he reiterated his position that Kosovo should be treated as a part of the former Yugoslavia, and not as a province of Serbia. In reality, it meant that Kosovo would become a republic of Yugoslavia with the right to secede from the federation. The Kosovo Albanian leaders rejected a proposal by the federal Prime Minister, Milan Panic that talks should be held in Belgrade on the Kosovo question. Instead, they insisted that any talks between them and the Serbs should be held under international auspicies.[13]

The Kosovo crisis was heightened in early 1998. The militant Kosovo Liberation Army (KLA) had established its stronghold in a part of the Kosovo province. The KLA was unknown before 1998 though it has been set up in 1994 and declared its existence in 1996. The Serbian government declared the KLA a terrorist group. Its terrorist activities assumed serious proportions not only because it was engaged in guerilla warfare but because it also drove some Kosovo Serbs out of their villages and interfered in the functioning of workers in the mines. In the last week of February, the Serbian special police units launched an offensive against rebel strongholds. In an anti-terrorist operation, some civilian casualties are bound to occur. The Western media immediately stressed on the civilian casualties and fleeing refugees. It blamed the Serb forces for committing atrocities. It failed to refer to the Kosovo Albanians' aggressiveness and the decline in the percentage of Serb population from 23.6 per cent in 1961 to 10 per cent in about three decades.

The KLA was the fastest growing guerrilla force. In March 1998, Western diplomats estimated that the tiny KLA had only 1500 to 2000 trained fighters, who were hopelessly outgunned by heavily armed Serb paramilitary police.[14] But within three months, the KLA claimed to have 50,000 men under arms. This claim was considered exaggerated by a factor of two or three.[15] The KLA had reportedly received training in many camps in Albania. The main source of its income was reportedly based in Switzerland where the Kosovo Popular Movement had been collecting money from ethnic Albanians. They were also active in Germany. Like many other terrorist outfits, the KLA has also been engaged in large-scale drug trafficking and reportedly controls the largest drug mafia in Europe.

The Clinton Administration threatened to take military action against the Serb's forces if they failed to stop their policy of atrocities against Kosovo Albanians in May 1998. In the same month, Milosevic met Rugova and agreed to have regular meetings and work together to defuse the tense situation in Kosovo. However, they failed to keep the promises as Rugova could not come to Belgrade for the next meeting. In the same month, President Clinton met Rugova and Prime Minister Bujar Bukoshi of the self-proclaimed republic's government, and Veton Surroi, a Kosovo negotiator and spokesman. In a related development, the US Agency for International Development announced an increase in its assistance to Kosovo by $6 million.

Even in 1998, President Clinton insisted on military action by the North Atlantic Treaty Organisation (NATO) against Serb forces in Kosovo, though he could not secure the consent of some NATO members. He maintained that NATO did not need sanction from the UN Security Council for any military action in the Balkans but the leaders of many other countries did not approve of his contention. The Kosovo crisis was further heightened in early 1999. There were reports of mass migration of Kosovo Albanians. The rejection of so-called Rambouillet Accords by Serbia and migration of Kosovo Albanians prompted the NATO bombing campaign against Yugoslavia on March 24, 1999 which continued for 76 days. Though the Yugoslavia armed forces withdrew from Kosovo and the NATO—led international peace force was deployed there, ethno-religious violence has not completely ended so far.

REFERENCES

1. Cvjects Job, "Yugoslavia ethinic furies" *Foreign Policy*, No.92, Fall 1993, p. 64.
2. Alaska Djilas, "A profile of Slobdan Milosevic," *Foreign Affairs*, Vol. 72, No. 3, Summer 1993, p. 93.
3. See Minority Right Group (ed), *World Directory of Minorities* Essex, Longman, pp. 132-140.
4. Quoted in *Nationalism, its Meaning and History*, Princeton, 1955, pp. 122-123.
5. Bruce Nelan, "Tudjman seeking revenge after four years," *Time*, August 14, 1995, p. 23.
6. See Qi Degang, "The Bosnian Civil War: Retrospect and Prospect," *Contemporary International Relations*, Beijing, Vol. 4, No 8, August 1994, p. 2.
7. Alija Izetbegoyic, *Islamic Declaration: A Programme for the Islamisation of Muslims and the Muslims Peoples*, Sarjevo, 1990, p.1.
8. World Directory of Miniorities, N.3, p. 137.
9. "Kosovo and Metohija—an Integral Part of the Republic of Serbia and F R Yugoslavia", *Review of International Affairs*, Belgrade, No. 1037 , October 15, 1995, p.11.
10. Ivo H. Daalder, "Fear and Loathing in the Former Yugoslavia", in Michael E. Brown (ed) *The International Dimensions of Internal Conflict*, Massachusetts, 1996, p. 40
11. Jame G.Kellas, *The Politics of Nationalism and Ethnicity*, London Macmillan, 1991, p.114.

12. *A Short History of the Yugoslavia Peoples,* Washington, Library of Congress, as quoted in *Times of India* New Delhi, July 24, 1998.
13. *Keesing's Record of World Events* Vol. 34, No. 3, March 1988, p.36514.
14. *Newsweek*, March 23, 1998, p. 28.
15. *Economist,* June 20, 1998, p. 58.

CHAPTER 19

Nature and Genesis of Terrorism and Ethnic Conflicts in Indonesia

Udai Bhanu Singh

As the Cold War ended and the "end of history" was predicted it was widely believed that international tensions would be reduced and stability restored. However, these hopes were belied as ethnic conflicts came to ravage different parts of the globe. In Europe, the end of the Cold War has seen the outbreak of ethnic conflicts. The Asia Pacific is an anthropological cauldron of ethnic diversity. Ethnic, religious and cultural diversities in the Asia Pacific hold immense potential for tremendous turmoil. And as has been rightly said, the time to make peace is when there is peace. The economic crisis in East Asia, not surprisingly, has been accompanied by ethnic strife. Ethnic tensions have erupted in Indonesia threatening to tear apart the socio-political fabric of the nation. Past experience has shown that any disturbance in any one of the South-East Asian countries is capable of sparking off conflicts in neighboring areas and creating regional instability. Indonesia stands out as an important case study of how ethnic differences when they are accompanied by economic turmoil and unfulfilled political aspirations, can bring even strong pluralistic states down on their knees.

The Chinese community in each of these countries who are often traders have become the internal enemies and are frequently demonised. Indonesia witnessed the worst kind of mob violence against some communities. To tackle the problem of ethnic conflict so that it does not pose a security threat requires the political will and the willingness to take up sensitive issues in the ARF.

There is a view that by allowing East Timor to slip away from its grasp the Indonesian government has unwittingly encouraged separatist movements in other parts. It will have profound short and long term domestic political, social, economic and cultural, implications for Indonesia. In a widely dispersed nation with a multi-ethnic, heterogenous society. Shutting the gates after the horse has bolted, the Indonesian Home Minister Surjadi Sudirdja has said Jakarta will consistently reject all demands for separation. He said that the legislation on wide-ranging regional autonomy (Law No. 22/1999) was the best the Centre could offer for regions to become self-sufficient. Meanwhile, the debate on federal vs unitary State continues in Indonesia.[1] Jakarta's concern has to be seen in the context of the deeper question of the relevance of ethnicity. Can each and every ethnic or sub-ethnic group aspire for statehood and to what extent is this in the best interest of international relations?

Ethnic Identity

The Javanese constitute about 60 per cent of lndonesia's population, but there are other ethnic communities including Malays and Madurese. It was widely feared that in an archipelagic State with such diversity in terms of its ethnic, linguistic, religious composition, granting of autonomy to one part would spell trouble in another (Irian Jaya, Aceh, Riau, Ambon).

TABLE 1

Indonesia: Religions *(percentage)*

Muslims	86.9
Christians	9.6
Hindus	1.9
Buddhists	1.0
Tribal religions	0.6

Source: The Far East and Australasia 2000 (London: Europa Publications Ltd. 1999).

It is not enough to say that the majority in Indonesia are Muslims because the Muslim of Sumatra will be as different from the Muslim of Java as a Punjabi Sikh is from a Tamil Sikh. Both Hinduism and Islam were introduced in Indonesia from India. But the animist tradition among the Balinese Hindus is still strong.

Other Asian States with multi-ethnic societies are similarly confronted with separatist movements (often with support from across the border accompanied by proliferation of small arms).[2] While in opposition, Megawati Sukarnoputri of PDI-Struggle (Indonesian Democratic Party-Struggle) had objected to relinquishing hold over East Timor on grounds that it was too much of a burden on Indonesia and maintained that whatever happens East Timor is part of lndonesia.[3] There are others who argue that East Timor was a case *sui generis* in as much as East Timor had been a Portuguese colony whereas Indonesia is made up of the former Dutch East Indies. But the Indonesian military definitely regarded it as setting a wrong trend which could lead to the disintegration of the country.

Geographical Configuration

Indonesia enjoys the distinction of being the world's most fragmented major state. It is no wonder that Sukarno once said that his greatest achievement was that Indonesia existed—occupying a privileged position in terms of size, population and location. It is an archipelagic state consisting of about 17,500 islands of which only about 6,000 are inhabited. Besides having strategically located islands, it commands a number of important straits. Indonesia is the fourth most populous nation in the world with a population in 1999 at 200 million. Indonesian islands are like "stepping stones" between the Indian Ocean and the Pacific Ocean. The relatively narrow straits hold commercial and strategic importance. These are: Malacca, Lombok, Sunda and Ombai-Wetar. The Malacca Strait is a potential chokepoint for the seaborne traffic between Japan and the Persian Gulf.

Some islands like Java, Madura and Bali which comprise only one-thirteenth of the total area of Indonesia, contain as much as about two-thirds of its population. Java itself has less than 7 per cent of Indonesia's total area but has about 60 per cent of its population. The over population has led to acute social turmoil.

TABLE 2
Indonesian Islands: Size and Population

Islands	*Size (sq. km.)*	*Population*
Kalimantan	547,891	10,807,900
Samatera (Sumatra)	482,393	41,840,700
Irian Jaya	421,981	2,020,900
Sulawesi (Celebes)	191,800	14,019,800
Java and Madura	127,499	116,379,200
Maluku (Moluccas) group	77,871	2,141,700
Nusa Tenggara group	67,502	7,348,600
Bali	5,633	2,924,400
Indonesia	1,922,570	197,483,200
East Timor	14,609	859,700

Source: The Far East and Australasia 2000.

Geographical factors have imbued certain areas with considerable importance. The northern coastal plains of Java acquired importance not only because of its large population but also because of the Straits (Sunda, Bali, and Lombok). Sumatra and Kalimantan became major industrial and economic centres.

Internal Threats

Internal security has vied for time and attention of policy makers in Indonesia.

Democratic Threat

The increasing globalization of the economy and the globalization (esp. in the field of information technology) in other spheres is beginning to have its impact on South-East Asia including Indonesia. There is growing demand for a more open and pluralistic system in which non-governmental organizations (esp. relating to environment) can have a major role. Many think-tanks have proliferated in Indonesia.

Secessionist Threat

Fissiparous Tendencies (Separatist Movements)

Three notoriously famous secessionist threats to Indonesian security have been in Aceh, West Irian and East Timor. The official pejorative for them is *Gerombolan Pengacau Keamanan* (GPK, or Security Disturbance Bandit Groups).

Aceh

President Wahid's off hand declaration that Aceh would be permitted to have a referendum on its future (if East Timor could have one) raised hopes. He retracted his statement later (perhaps under pressure from the military and others) when he subsequently said that any referendum would be about autonomy and the imposition of Islamic law for Aceh, not independence.[4] Threat of break-up of Indonesia equally caused concern to the ASEAN leaders who at an informal summit spoke out in support of Indonesia's territorial integrity even as Wahid reassured them. The Indonesian Armed Forces Chief, Admiral Widodo spoke of pursuing a political solution, something that had never been tried in East Timor.

This province on the western tip of Indonesia was an independent sultanate until the late nineteenth century when it was conquered by the Dutch. Indonesia took it over at the time of declaration of its independence in 1945. According to Alagappa, though this province initially supported the Republic of Indonesia, it was political mishandling by Jakarta which led to its alienation.[5] It became known for its radical Islamic tradition and for being fiercely independent-minded. The 'Free Aceh' movement was crushed with the help of the army and the imposition of martial law in 1989.

There are a number of religious, and socio-economic causes for the Aceh movement. At the religious level, the radical Acehnese look down upon the tolerant Islam being practised by the Javanese. An important economic grievance is that though Aceh has Indonesia's largest LNG plant, the fruits of this natural resource have not accrued to the province but to the Central government. Aceh' s oil and gas fields have served as an important source of revenue for Jakarta.

Irian Jaya

Historical factors have made the Irian Jaya problem more difficult for Indonesia than Aceh. The western part of New Guinea island had been a part of the Netherland East Indies but could not be integrated. The Dutch delayed the handing over of West Irian to Indonesia till 1962.' They took advantage of West Papuan's ethnic differences (who are Melanesians) with rest of Indonesia (dominated mostly by Malays). The Dutch had encouraged growth of nationalism in West lrian in order to thwart Indonesian takeover of West lrian. Indonesia initially named it Irian Barat (West Irian) and later in 1972 it came to be called Irian Jaya (Victorious lrian). Under the terms of the UN agreement, an "Act of Free Choice" was to be conducted and Indonesia carried it out in a way that imposed Indonesian rule on them. The cause for resentment among the locals was that they feared demographic changes were taking place to their detriment and they were losing their jobs to better educated and qualified people who came and settled there. In 1965, a rebellion by the *Organisasi Papua Merdeka* (OPM, Free Papua Movement) erupted and in 1971 a Republic of West Papua was proclaimed under Gen. Seth J. Rumkorem and the unrest has discontinued.

The majority of West lrians are Melanesians and their religion is animistic or Christian, as compared to the Indonesian majority of Malays and Muslims. However, the unrest in West lrian does not really have ethnic but rather socio-economic roots which are related to the Central government's policy of settling outsiders on the island and its economic exploitation.

East Timor

Jakarta for the first time raised the possibility of independence for East Timor in January 1999. President B.J. Habibie categorically stated on February 11, 1999: "We do not want to be burdened by the problem of East Timor as of 1 January, 2000."[6] East Timor (or Loro Sae province), an island 300 miles north of Australia, covers an area of about 14,874 sq km and a population of 830,000. Smaller in population and size than Hawaii, it is a tiny Catholic enclave. Roman Catholics constitute more than 60 per cent of its population. Since 1988, Bishop Belo reports directly to the Vatican and not to the national Conference of Bishops. So he enjoys a greater degree of independence in religious matters than other Catholic representatives of Indonesia. The people of East Timor comprise of mixed Papuan, Malay, and European origin. They are physically very different in appearance from each other, say, the Javanese. Their language is Tetum (Tatum) which is a West Indonesian language with a Portuguese admixture. Muslim and other non-Timorese settlers since 1975 now constitute over 20 per cent of the population.

The Portuguese colonized East Timor in 1586. During the four centuries of colonial rule there was total neglect of East Timor. Though Indonesia did make substantial investment in infrastructure and schools, there was heavy immigration from neighbouring islands of Java, Bali and Sulawesi. This curtailed the employment opportunities for the youth and important posts came to be occupied by 'outsiders'. The western-half of Timor island formed part of the Dutch East Indies which became part of Indonesia in 1949. The General Assembly placed East Timor on the list of Non-Self Governing Territories in 1960. In 1974, the announcement by Portugal acknowledging East Timor's right to self-determination, was followed by civil war between *Frente Revolucionaria de Timor Leste Independente* (FRETILIN) and two smaller parties—*Uniao Democratica Timorense* (UDT) and the *Associacao Popular Democratica de Timor* (APODETI). In August 1975, FRETILIN managed to get control of the colony formally and on November 28, 1975 it unilaterally declared the independence of the territory. The remaining parties proclaimed their integration with Indonesia. Various factors had inhibited Indonesia from taking a proactive approach. It had earlier declared that its territorial claims were coterminous with the former Dutch Empire in South-East Asia and therefore did not extend to Portuguese ruled East Timor. Moreover, Indonesia did not wish to be a source of anxiety for any of its neighbours. What Jakarta secretly did hope for was that one of the East Timor groups would overthrow the Portuguese rule and appeal for merger with Indonesia.[7]

Certain new developments provided just such an opportunity and on 7 December, 1975 Indonesian troops landed in East Timor. In July 1976 it was formally integrated as the 27th province of Indonesia. Indonesia's action in East Timor was cited as another instance of authoritarianism. Portugal reported this to the United Nations Security Council.

So, what went wrong in East Timor? Though Jakarta invested millions of dollars to build up East Timor's infrastructure and education what got highlighted was the army excesses which accompanied it and what was perceived by its inhabitants as a centre-periphery kind of relationship. Since the Church articulated the aspirations of the people it gained in legitimacy and strength. Though Jakarta sought to appear even-handed the underlying motivation was read differently by the East Timorese. The occupation of East Timor was cited as an example of brutal repression—200,000 Timorese or approximately one-third of the population were said to have been killed in the process of integration.[8] It has often been censured by human rights organizations like Amnesty International. For instance, in November 1991, Indonesian troops shot and killed 273 independence demonstrators outside the Santa Cruz cemetery in Dili. The UN never officially recognized East Timor as a part of Indonesia and several UN resolutions condemned the plight of the people of East Timor and demanded withdrawal of troops so that an act of self-determination under UN supervision could take place.

The referendum finally took place on August 30, 1999 in which about 98.5 per cent of the population participated and in which the East Timorese by an overwhelming vote rejected the autonomy proposal of Jakarta. As chaos followed the results, the peacekeeping troops, the International Force for East Timor (INTERFET) landed in the territory on Sept. 20, 1999. By the end of the year, the last of the Indonesian soldiers had left the territory and the process of reconstructing a new future had begun.

East Timor has been the greatest diplomatic and political embarrassment for Indonesia. The threat it poses relates not only to the dismemberment of the country but to the very foundations on which it had hitherto been functioning. It has brought into question many ideas and institutions on which the Government had been functioning. Jakarta claims that it is committed to bring to book those responsible for human rights abuses in East Timor.[9] The Indonesia Commission Investigating Human Rights Violations in East Timor (dubbed as KPP-HAM) submitted a report covering the period starting from January 1999 and a draft law on the establishment of a human rights court is being finalised. Some hope for future was expressed in the visit of Xanana Gusmao to Jakarta in November 1999 and the visit of President Abdurrahman Wahid in February 2000 to the territory when an important agreement was reached concerning the establishment of an Indonesia-UNTAET Joint Commission to promote cooperation between the peoples of Indonesia and East Timor .

Economic Turmoil

Indonesia's success as a developmental model was largely hailed before the economic crisis overtook the country in 1997. This was visible in indicators such as GDP growth rate (see Tables 3-5), infrastructure development, decline in poverty and population. Suharto's New Order regime had been responsible for pulling Indonesia out of economic doldrums and making it a power to be reckoned with. He brought down inflation, opened up the economy to Western aid and investment. He relied on Chinese businessmen with international business connections rather than indigenous businessmen. The Indonesian government gained from the oil price hike in the 1970s. In the 1980s, when the oil prices fell it encouraged technocrats to build up an efficient non-oil sector. Before he was overthrown, Suharto presented a very unrealistic budget. Later Habibie also did not demonstrate the ability to take tough decisions after him.

Growth under Suharto had however, not been able to bridge the yawning gap between the rich and the poor. The impact of the crisis was felt in rising unemployment, rising prices (to meet IMF requirements) and rising poverty. Buying up stocks and shares became easier in South-East Asia because of the hike in the rate of the dollars. Those with dollars could buy up companies sold for cheap price. Countries like Indonesia which have been avowedly pro-West could be compelled to reconsider their options if international financial and lending institutions like IMF and World Bank did not make their policies more flexible and suited to the needs of their creditors. Critics in fact point out that the bail out of the debtor countries is actually a bail-out of the lenders to the country.

Indonesia's State Minister for Human Rights Dr. Hasballah M. Saad speaking before the 56th session of the UN Commission on Human Rights in Geneva on March 30 admitted that while the financial crisis would be held mainly responsible, there were other contributing factors like lack of accountability and malpractices such as corruption, collusion and nepotism, in both public and in private institutions in our country. The economic crisis demonstrated that several domestic factor—social, economic and political have a bearing on a country's security policy. Many constraints were placed on Indonesia's security policy as a result of the financial turmoil. This particularly had its impact on arms acquisitions. Besides, any kind of social conflict could have long-term adverse impact on security .

Anti-Chinese feelings are common. The Chinese community tended to be demonised causing them to flee. When rioting broke out and Chinese shops became targets, then President Habibie openly stated that he would be happy to see them replaced by indigenous traders. Demands were raised to redress the balance in favour of the indigenous Indonesians by instituting positive discrimination (as achieved in Malaysia). Habibie relied heavily on Muslim support and alienated Chinese support. This delayed normalisation as the indigenous Indonesian businessmen were denied access to Chinese money to restart their business.

The Indonesian economy appears to be stabilizing. Following Mr. Wahid's assurances to foreign financial institutions that corruption will be severely dealt with, World Bank and IMF agreed to negotiate on the next loan package that had been withheld because of bank scandal and dispute over East Timor. Indonesia's net foreign exchange reserves in the third week of November 1999 increased to 16.5 bn US dollars: the increase was attributed to an increase in the proceeds from oil sales.[10]

In the meantime, gross foreign exchange reserves also increased by 210.8 m to 27.42 bn dollars.

TABLE 3

Economic Forecast for Indonesia: Real GDP/GNP

	1997 Actual	*1998*	*1999*	*2000*
PECC Forecast	4.7	-14.0	-2.5	2.0
OECD Forecast	4.7	-15.5	-3.0	3.0

Source: Based on PECC and OECD figures in *Regional Outlook: South East Asia* 1999-2000.

TABLE 4

Recapitalization Needs of Indonesia's Banking Sectors, 1998 Estimates

(Percentages)

NPLs/Total Loans	*Capital-Asset Ratio (CAR)*	*CAR after NPL write-off*	*Recapitalization Needs (% of GDP)*
30-40	8-10	-17	19

Source: Ramkishen S. Rajan, *The Currency and Financial Crisis in South East Asia: A case of "Sudden Death"" or "Death Foretold"?* IPS Working Papers No.1 (Singapore Institute of Policy Studies, 1998).

TABLE 5

GDP: Growth Rate (per cent)

1980-89 Average	*1990*	*1991*	*1992*	*1993*	*1994*	*1995*	*1996*	*1997*	*1998*	*1999*	*2000*
5.3	9.0	8.9	7.2	7.3	7.5	8.2	7.8	4.9	-13.7	0.0	2.0

Sources: *Asian Development Outlook* 1999, 1998, *World Economic Outlook*

May 1998 (IMP), *Regional Outlook: South East Asia* 1999-2000; and *Regional Outlook: South East Asia* 1998-99.

TABLE 6

Indonesia: Inflation Rate (Consumer Price Index) *(per cent)*

1980-89 Average	*1990*	*1991*	*1992*	*1993*	*1994*	*1995*	***1996***	***1997***	***1998***	***1999***	***2000***
9.6	7.8	9.4	7.5	9.7	8.5	9.4	**7.9**	**6.6**	**58.2**	**17.0**	**9.5**

Sources: World Economic Outlook May 1998 (IMF)
Asian Development Outlook 1999 (in bold)
Asian Development Outlook 1998.

TABLE 7

Indonesia: Exchange Rate to the Dollar

Currency	*1993*	*1994*	*1995*	*1996*	*1997*	*1998*
Rupiah	2,102.6	2,180.9	2,275.8	2,363.6	4,666.9	10,147.5

Source: Asian Development Outlook 1999.

TABLE 8

Indonesia: External Debt Outstanding ($milion)

1993	*1994*	*1995*	*1996*	*1997*	*1998*
83,299	**101,278**	**106,455**	**113,143**	**138,018**	—

Source: The Far East and Australasia 2000.

TABLE 9

Indonesia: Foreign Direct Investment ($milion)

1992	*1993*	*1994*	*1995*	*1996*	*1997*
1,777	2,004	2,109	4,348	6,194	5,350

Source: The Far East and Australasia 2000.

South-East Asia had seen substantial arms build up with the emphasis on air and maritime defence.[11] But the economic crisis in Indonesia succeeded in achieving what the arms control advocates were unable to accomplish. Second, lack of financial constraints has led Indonesian companies to look for collaborative ventures. The economic crisis contributed to the political turmoil. But the political turmoil was not solely the creation of the economic crisis. It had been developing over a period of time because of a number of factors.

Political Threat

This has manifested itself at both the ideological and institutional planes. The political system is a product of the ideas and institutions in vogue at any point of time. Indonesia is presently passing through a period of political turmoil. This political churning coincides with the period of economic crisis, which has hit Indonesia along with the rest of East Asia. The first phase of the crisis ended when President Suharto resigned in May 1998 (after 32 years of rule) and Habibie (who was perceived to be part of the same elite) took over. The second phase began when the ghost of the unfulfilled political aspirations of the people came to haunt the ruling elite of Indonesia yet again with the people of Indonesia demanding radical changes in the economic policy, the centre-province relations, the role of the armed forces in governance. They desired radical changes to the system that Suharto had so carefully built over the years. The world's third largest democracy, Indonesia, held its first free elections in 44 years on June 7, 1999. As many as 48 parties contested. President Suharto had kept political aspirations bottled up and in the changed circumstances if new demands from various ethnic groups and outlying regions begin to emerge, it will be difficult for the political parties to remain unaffected. If this amounts to political turmoil, then the armed forces may be tempted to intervene.

Political activity in Indonesia was substantially controlled. The Suharto regime had provided tangible material advancement that was widely noticed. What got neglected were the due process of law and a semblance of fair play. The people of Indonesia are now demanding what they missed during the 32 years of Suharto's rule. The people's struggle is not likely to subside until some radical changes are brought about. According to some, Habibie was really a chip off the old block and so many of those entrusted with the task of making massive changes under Habibie belonged to the Suharto era. Nonetheless, Habibie was the man of the hour and he was instrumental in bringing about some important political changes.

Yet the demand for *reformasi* resounded once again as the opposition regrouped yet again. Thus began the third and the current phase which has Abdurrahman Wahid as President and Megawati Sukarnoputri as Vice President. This change was brought about by a vocal leadership. This includes Amien Rais, who took over as Speaker of the People's Consultative Assembly (MPR) in October 1999. Besides, being an academic he headed the Muhamadiyah movement (a Muslim welfare organization). Abdurrahman Wahid is the leader of Nahdlatul Ulema, Indonesia's largest Muslim organization with 30 million members.

The UN Norms on Self-Determination, Secessionism and Terrorism

The concept of 'self determination' has been dynamically interpreted over the ages. Originally the term referred to the right of the people to choose their own government or form of government.[12] " As a general term, it is an expression of the aspiration to rule oneself and not be ruled by others.."[13] It is the right of a group (based on some shared sentiment or racial identity associated with common territory, language or religion) to shape its own economic, political and cultural destiny. The idea of self-determination, closely linked with the idea of the nation state and popular sovereignty can be traced to the American (1775) and the French (1789) Revolutions. It is embodied both in the American Declaration of Independence (1776) and in the French Declaration of the Rights of Man (1793). Based on this postulate that the state must reflect the national group, self-determination in its extremely exaggerated form includes the right of a national group to secede from a multinational state in order to merge with another state or form an independent state. It was used by the Allied Powers for propoganda purposes during World War I and II. The virtues of national self-determination were glorified by the League of Nations and the United Nations. Woodrow Wilson's 'Fourteen Points' accorded recognition to this aspiration following the disintegration of the Austro-Hungarian Empire. The great multinational Empires of Europe were disintegrating as the forces of separatist nationalism led to a resurgence of small nation states. Woodrow Wilson and the scheme of League of Nations only reflected the ideals of nineteenth century liberalism which called for both external and internal democracy. The League was based on the Wilsonian assumption that the nation is the natural and proper unit of world politics. "Just as the people had a right to govern themselves within the national system, so the nations had the right to govern themselves within the global system... Sovereignty was not a naughty word for the League; it was a symbol of liberty in international relations, comparable to democracy as a symbol of domestic freedom."[14] It was believed that if political units were formed on the basis of nationality these units would serve to make international relations more harmonious and remove fiction from world affairs. This was Wilsonian idealism which got its inspiration from the ideas of John Locke rather than from Thomas Hobbes.[15] The importance accorded to self-determination in the present century can be traced back to the Lockean dictum that the ultimate basis of political obligation is the consent of the governed. From this derives ultimately the right to rebellion by the people against the ruler. While this rule of consent advocated by Locke was used to justify the Glorious Revolution of 1688 in England, the American Revolution in later years, and the French Revolution still later when the people decided that with the withdrawal of their consent the right of their rulers to rule over them had ceased. Similarly, it also became the rallying cry of the nationalists against colonialism and imperialism.

This idea is a double-edged weapon. While it has performed a very positive and constructive role in bringing about social justice it has also contributed unwittingly to the growth of civil strife, transnational conflicts and terrorism. The Indonesian Minister speaking at Geneva recently drew attention to Article 3 paragaraph 1 of the Charter of the United Nations which states the need to achieve international co-operation in promoting and protecting human rights. While he voiced his country's commitment to these principles he was also critical of double standards which reduce confidence in the dialogue on human rights.

Intra-state Conflicts in Indonesia and Conflict Resolution Theory Building

Though intra-state conflicts have proliferated theory-building on the subject, especially ethnic conflict, has remained a neglected field of inquiry. The magnitude of the problem becomes even greater in pluralistic societies like Indonesia. The social sciences discipline has looked at conflict from a variety of angles. Issues of conflict have been examined from the standpoint of psychology, sociology, anthropology. This only reflects the heterogenous and pluralistic nature of societies.[16]

Marxist theorists have generally failed to take into account the pluralistic nature of societies and the importance of different ethnic groups. Ethnicity is merely interpreted as "false consciousness" and religion dubbed the "opium of the masses". It is unable to visualize the threat posed by religious fundamentalism as a source of conflict. It also has its limitations in explaining the role of nationalism.[17] Liberal theory on the other hand, with its emphasis on the individual underestimates the importance of group affiliations.[18] Theorists also overemphasise the role of the State as an actor and neglect the role of non-state actors in conflicts. Intra-state conflicts and their linkages with low-intensity conflicts, spread of small arms and spread of drugs, and their transformation into inter-state conflicts have to be studied under a new theoretical framework. Social conflicts are seen to coincide with economic conflict and absence of adequate political and structural safeguards at times.

Conflict Resolution and Role of External Powers in intra-state Conflict.

The world is increasingly becoming a global village and events in one part of the globe intimately affect developments in another part. This often brings up the dilemma of state sovereignty versus international intervention on grounds of human rights and democracy. Where does State sovereignty end and the right of the international community to intervene begin?[19] When intra-state conflict spills over into the international arena or there is an attempt by various forces to intervene. At times a State witnessing ethnic conflict may attract international sanctions. This may receive monetary and moral support of non-resident nationals of that state. Second, in the case of an ethnic conflict, if the same ethnic community resides in a neighbouring State, there is a possibility of destabilization there as well in case members of that community are mobilised. eg. The Chinese community in SEA.

Intra-state conflicts and consequently conflict resolution mechanisms acquires an added significance in countries which have a pluralistic society. Theory-building in the context of intra-state conflict needs to be encouraged and nurtured. Indonesia (like many other SEA States) is faced with the practical problem of dealing with issues relating to economics, democracy and security. This has put existing institutions under pressure. For instance, within ASEAN there was a demand for breaking away with the traditional ASEAN-way of non-interference in the internal affairs of member-states. In order for Indonesia to face up to the security challenges in the new millenium it may have to evolve a new theoretical framework and innovative new methods and techniques of conflict resolution enabling its people to address both issues of domestic and international security.

A Change for the Better?

Indonesia enjoyed a federal state structure for about a year till a transition to a unitary structure took place in 1950 with the enactment of its Constitution. Whether it was the 'guided democracy of President Sukarno or the 'new order' of President Suharto, there is a continuity in the manner in which Indonesia's ruling elite has struggled to hold on to the reins of power. There has been uneven development of Indonesia's region. This is seen in the case of Java. Java happens to be the centre of power and dominates over the rest of the country. Here 60 per cent of the population occupies only 7 per cent of the land. The other regions which possess considerable natural resources and contribute substantially to the revenues collected by the Centre are demanding a greater share in the revenue collections and a greater role in managing their own affairs. While the Centre has promised to increase provincial powers it would appear that a loosening of control and a federal structure may not be easy to grant because of deeply entrenched economic and political interests. In the struggle which ensues, the concern for human rights gets compromised at times which in turn leads to a hardening of position on either side. This has led to accusations that Dutch colonialism was replaced by Javanese rule. The leadership has often cautioned against human rights excesses.[20]

Indonesia's State Minister for Human Rights Dr. Hasballah M. Saad speaking before the 56th session of the UN Commission on Human Rights in Geneva on March 30 said: "Overemphasis on stability for the sake of economic growth has resulted in neglect or even the suppression of certain civil and political rights of citizens. This has led to the disability of citizens to have any control over the Government".[21]

REFERENCES

1. *BBC/SWB/FE/3716, B/2,* December 12, 1999.
2. See Montserrat Guibernau and John Rex,ed, *The Ethnicity Reader: Nationalism, Multiculturalism and Migration,* Polity Press, Cambridge, 1997.

3. *Ibid.* She blamed those in power (including the legislature, the executive, and the judiciary) for turning it into a burden.
4. *Intenational Herald Tribune,* November 11, 1999.
5. Muthiah Alagappa, ed, *Asian Security Practice: Material and Ideational Influences* Stanford University Press, Stanford, 1998.
6. *New Straits Times,* Kuala Lumpur, February 12, 1999.
7. D.R. SarDesai, *South East Asia: Past & Present*, Boulder: Westview Press, 1994, Third edition.
8. According to one writer, "..not even Pol Pot succeeded in killing proportionately, as many Cambodians, as the Indonesian generals have killed East Timorese". See John Pilger, "Horror behind the West's big wink", *Guardian Weekly*, Paris, February 27, 1994. The figure of 200,000 was first estimated by East Timor's church while an Australian parliamentary committee referred to "at least 200,000" killed in a report in January 1994.
9. For details refer: Udai Bhanu Singh, " Indonesia's Security Perspectives", *Strategic Analysis,* March 2000, Vol. 23, No. 12. Also see "East Timor: Pebble in Indonesia's Shoe", *Strategic Analysis,* September 1996.
10. *BBC/SWB/FEW/0617, WB/1,* December 1, 1999.
11. See for details, Udai Bhanu Singh, "Growth of Military Power in South East Asia", "in *Asian Strategic Review 1994-95,* IDSA: New Delhi, 1995.
12. Alan Bullock and Oliver Stallybrass, eds, *The Fontana Dictionary of Modern Thought,* London, Fontana/Collins, 1986. Also see, Roger Scruton, *A Dicitionary of Political thought,* London, The Pan Books Ltd, 1983 and M.B Khopkar, *A Dictionary of Political Terminology,* Bombay: Jaico Publishing House, 1970.
13. R.S. Saini, "Right to Self-Detemination/Secede and International Terrorism: What are the United Nations Norms and Practice?", in Abdulrahim P. Vijapur and Kumar Suresh, eds, *Perspectives on Human Rights,* Manak Publications, 1999.
14. Inis L. Claude, Jr., *Swords into Plowshares: The Problems and Progress of International Organization,* New York: Random House, 1984.
15. *Ibid.*

16. *International Encyclopaedia of the Social Sciences,* Vol. 3 and 4, 1968, Macmillan.
17. Kumar Rupesinghe, "Theories of Conflict Resolution and Their Applicability to Protracted Ethnic Conflicts", in Kumar Rupesinghe, ed, *Ethnic Conflict and Human Rights,* Norwegian University Press, Oslo, 1988.
18. *Ibid.*
19. RS Saini, "Is the right to self-determination relevant to Jammu & Kashmir?", *Indian Journal of International Law,* Vol. 38, No. 2, April, 1998, pp. 157-181.
20. For instance, (the then) President Habibie on the occasion of the TNI's 54th anniversary celebrations called upon the military establishment to uphold security in a fashion consistent with the protection of human rights. *See Hindu* October 6, 1999.
21. Easttimor@igc.apc.org.

CHAPTER 20

Ethnic Issues and Insurgency in Xinjiang

K.N. Ramachandran

Introduction

Formerly known as Chinese Turkistan, Xinjiang is situated in the north-western part of China, bordering Mongolia to the north, Central Asia to the west, Afghanistan and Pakistan occupied Kashmir (PoK) in the south-west and Tibet to the south.

After the establishment of Peoples' Republic of China (PRC) in 1949 when the Chinese Communist Party (CCP) overwhelmed the Nationalists (KMT) in the civil war, China came under centralized control and the country was reorganized. Xinjiang became an autonomous region of China in 1955. In terms of area, it is bigger than other autonomous regions such as Zhuang, Nei Mongol, Ningxia Hui and Tibet. Covering an area of 1.6 million sq. km., Xinjiang is over 16.7 per cent of Chinese total land area of 9.57 million sq. km.

The Uighurs, Muslims of Turki origin, constitute the dominant ethnic group in this region. Besides the Uighurs, Xinjiang has other minority people such as Kazakhs, Hui Mongols, Tajiks, Kirghiz and Silo (Tungusic). The region has also a sizeable Han population. This issue will be discussed subsequently.

Historical Background

China made its presence felt in this region in the second century B.C. during the Han dynasty. The subsequent history is one of ebb and flow of Chinese power resulting from either weakness or the strength of 'Son of Heaven' who presided over the fortunes of the Chinese empire. In the latter part of the nineteenth century, the area which was called 'new territories' or Xinjiang became a full-fledged province of Chinese empire. In the twentieth century, Xinjiang was formally governed by the Central Government after the Revolution of 1911 that overthrew the Manehu dynasty. This control, however, was tenuous and the Chinese governor enjoyed virtual independence. This situation continued during the 1930s and 40s during the period of power struggle between the CCP and the KMT— a grave political crisis which was further worsened by the Japanese invasion of China and the Second World War.

One may also take into account the fact that this region has had a tradition of ethnic Muslim rebellion under Chinese rule down the centuries. Complicating the factor was the political and economic stakes that the Czars of Russia, and later the Commissars of the Soviet Union, sought to create in this area which was at the borders of Soviet Central Asia and prone to instability. Moreover, the large degree of autonomy enjoyed by the province and political turbulence helped further close linkages with Moscow. The Muslim rebellions during 1930-34 led by a Tunghan General was crushed by the local authority with Soviet assistance. Further, Soviet assistance during the Muslim rebellion of 1937 strengthened these bonds. In 1943, the Chinese Central Government reasserted its control over Xinjiang as the local government swore allegiance to the Nationalist-led centre and the Soivet privileges and influence in the economic sphere were curtailed. In 1944, the Muslims again revolted and proclaimed "Eastern Turkistan Republic". The situation led to a compromise under which provincial autonomy was granted and a Provincial Council dominated by Muslims was created. This compromise was short lived.[1] It was only after the Communist seizure of power in China, consolidation of central control over Xinjiang and negotiations with Moscow under new political realities that regional stability came into being.

Developments since 1950

Since the 1950s, the ethno-cultural and ethno-religious landscape of Xinjiang dominated by Muslim Uighurs underwent dramatic change as a result of government-supported migration of Han people to this area. These migrants were of four categories: (1) Demobilised soldiers and officers of the Peoples Liberation Army (PLA) settled with a programme of military land reclamation; (2) Educated youth cadre sent to assist in frontier construction; (3) Semi-organised and unorganised migrants who went to participate in economic construction activities including cultivation of land; and (4) Officials and party functionaries. As a result of this migration, Han population in Xinjiang increased dramatically and changed the demographic profile.[2] In 1949, for instance, the Han people constituted 6.7 per cent of the population numbering 300,000 people. In 1996, the Han group was 38 per cent of population. The proportion of native people Uighurs and other small minorities who constituted 93.3 per cent of the population in 1949 dropped to 62.5 per cent in early nineties. Further, owing to the liberal migration policy, other ethnic minorities settling down in Xianjiang also increased. According to 1990 Census, there were 49 ethnic groups in Xinjiang as compared to 13 in early fifties. This demographic change has in no small way contributed to sharpen Han-Uighur ethnic contradictions.

The economic aspects of the demographic factor is equally significant. A distinct economic pattern, has emerged since the fifties consolidating the earlier trends. In northern Xinjiang, the Urumqi-Shihezi-Karamay area came to be developed in both the industrial and agricultural spheres. In this part, the Han nationality is the dominant group. In the southern part of Kashi-Hetian-Kizilsu, the Uighurs are the dominant group and it is less developed and backward. The northern sector is well connected in terms of transport and communications, whereas in the southern sector a comprehensive infrastructure is not in place.[3] This factor has also provided conditions for the assertion of ethnic nationalism and identity.

The situation also became more complex because of China's relations with the erstwhile Soviet Union and its radical internal experiments. The deterioration in Sino-Soviet relations during the sixties heightened China's suspicions of a continuing Soviet role in this frontier region. Beijing accused Moscow of encouraging "separatism" in Xinjiang by providing safe haven and sanctuaries for the ethnic militants in the adjoining Central Asian States. Whatever the truth behind these accusations and Soviet counter accusations that followed, this period contributed to some tensions on this border.

The Great Leap Forward (GLF) launched by the late Chairman Mao in late fifties to catapult China into modern age turned out to be an unmitigated disaster with severe economic consequences. This had its impact on Xinjiang too as central resources were in a disarray. However, the Great Proletarian Cultural Revolution (GPCR) launched by Mao in

1966 took an extreme radical course and the rampaging revolutionaries caused considerable damage to the culture, tradition, and way of life in minority areas such as Xinjiang and Tibet. These events sharpened the discontent in these regions and the fact that the Han population also suffered during this phase of radicalism did not offer any consolation either to the aggrieved ethnic minorities.

It was only after the end of Cultural Revolution in 1976 and the beginnings of post-Mao liberalization in China since the early eighties, the ethnic minority issue came to be viewed from a fresh perspective and the revolutionary wrongs of earlier years came to be righted. Further, the reform and opening up policy had a beneficial impact on China in general and minority regions such as Xinjiang. Moreover, the beginnings of Sino-Soviet normalization in the eighties helped confidence-building in border regions and initiation of border trade.

Economic development since eighties with increased central assistance and promotions of individual and cooperative enterprises has indeed produced results, but this has not abated the assertive search for identity among the Uighurs. Moreover, the new economic policy helped to develop the backward South dominated by Uighurs, it was the industrial North dominated by the Hans that witnessed appreciable increase in economic wealth.

There were other major causes too for the rise of militancy, religious fundamentalism, and quest for independent identity in Xinjiang. The rise of fundamentalism in Pakistan and Afghanistan in the eighties, the trends towards break-up of Soviet Union and the assertion of national identity by Central Asian States—three of them bordering Xinjiang—contributed to raise the hopes and aspirations of Uighurs who sought independent nationhood. In the current phase, religious zeal, terrorism, and assertion of identity are interlinked in this area.

The undoing of the effects of Cultural Revolution and the lop-sided benefits of reform programme and the factors noted above led to a Islamic revival. This was clearly seen in the building of new Mosques, Islamic colleges, Koranic teaching and even efforts to revive Islamic architecture. Moreover, the reform framework of China also led to external funding for Islamic causes from Saudi Arabia, Gulf States and pan-Arab Organizations such as World Islamic League and its sister organization, the World Council of Mosques. In a phase of armed struggle in

Afghanistan and militant activities in West Asia, the Islamic linkages also included the concept of *jihad* against the infidels. In the context of Xinjiang, it meant war against Chinese regime. The development of contacts also led young people from Xinjiang to go across Pakistan or Afghanistan to receive fundamentalist education and training for war. Many of them joined the Afghan Mujahideens and fought along with them around Khost, with its main base at Zhawar, close to Xinjiang borders. These militants developed widespread links with Palestinian outfits, "Islamic Warriors" of Pakistan, Kabul's Hizbul-e-Islam and other militant outfits of the region.[4] Arms and ammunition of various kinds followed and confrontation with Chinese authorities came about in both political and military terms.

A survey of these clashes and protests against Chinese authorities in the last one decade suggests that resentment against Chinese authorities has grown in the relative sense. The following are some of the reports that had reached the outside world. In May 1989, a major riot occurred in Urumqi as a protest against the publication of a book on the sexual mores of the Muslims which was perceived as derogatory. The book was eventually withdrawn.

An uprising in Baren, near Kashgar occurred in late March-early April 1990. An official report said that this "counter-revolutionary armed rebellion" by a "small number of ruffians" who acted under the "cloak of religion" was put down. Western reports added that Oasis towns of Kashgar, Khotan, and Aksu were closed to foreigners because of troop movements. In the same month, a Xinjiang television report noted that "national splitism is the main threat to Xinjiang's stability".[5]

On March 6, 1992, Tomur Dowamat, Chairman of Xinjiang autonomous regional government admitted that there has been an increase in Uighur 'separatist' activity. "A handful of national splitists in Xinjiang, colluding with national splitists outside have stepped up their splitting activity". He also reflected the Chinese concern and apprehension that the dismantling of Soviet Union would have an impact on China's minorities such as the Uighurs of Xinjiang.[6]

On May 18, 1996, officials in Xinjiang ordered the suppression of the activities of a Islamic group called *Talipu* and its sympathisers in the regional communist party for having organized a series of bombings, riots and other terrorist acts. Among other things, it was said that on 29 April a Vice-chairman of the regional Peoples Political Conference was killed. It added that since February at least six to seven police personnel and officials have been killed in Urumqi and it included Akenmu Sidike a pro-government cleric.[7]

A major disturbance occurred at Yining, close to Xinjiang's border with Kazakhstan on 11 February, 1997 when the Uighur nationalists and Chinese government forces clashed. In an interview to *The Independent* (London), Yusubek Mukhlisi exiled Chief of United National Liberation Front of East Turkistan said from his base in Almaty, Kazakhstan that 30 militants were publically executed in early February. The militant attack was carried out to mark the fifth anniversary of the decision jointly made by some separatist groups to employ violence to secure freedom for Xinjiang.[8] The joint decision was obviously deliberated and made in 1992 in the context of the break-up of the Soviet Union and increasing linkages with Islamic militants elsewhere. The French News Agency (AFP) reported on 13 February that more than 100 freedom fighters were killed. Perhaps as a response, the Uighurs exploded three bombs in buses in Urumqi killing nine people and injuring fifty others.[9] A similar bomb explosion occurred on 7 March in Beijing and an exiled Uighur organization for Turkistan freedom claimed responsibility for the action.[10] The Uighur militants responsible for earlier attack were rounded up and Xinhua reported on May 29 that nine were executed for the earlier bomb attacks.[11]

Further, on 3 October, the Hongkong paper *Tung Fang Jih Pao* disclosed that in September a "comparatively large scale armed rebellion" had led to the death of nine officials and Peoples' Congress Deputies. The report added that the 'rebellion' was put down and several militants were taken into custody.[12]

In the following year (1998), Xinhua reported on 16 February that a bomb exploded in a bus in Wuhan two days earlier killing 16 people. Wuhan was the third Chinese city to be targeted in a period of one year and as on previous occasions, the suspects were Uighur separatists or their sympathisers who had taken up residence in many of China's major cities.[13]

On 12 January 1998, a court official in Urumqi announced the execution of 16 militants on December 29, 1997, for their role in the riots of February that year in north-western Xinjiang.[14] There were also a few reports in 1999 on the activities of the Uighur militants and the Chinese response. As a follow up to the Chinese action against militant activity in Yining capital of Yili region, it was announced than on 28 January, two leading Muslim separatists Yibulaying Simayi and Abdurreyimu Aisha were found guilty for Yining riots and put to death.[15]

This perhaps led to further clashes between Uighurs and Chinese authorities. The Hongkong based organisation *Information Centre for Human Rights and Democratic Movement* in China noted that at least 100 youth clamouring for independence were arrested and at least five were wounded in a clash in mid-February 1999.[16]

A more serious incident reportedly involved an attack on a guided missile base, 10 km from the city of Korla in Central Xinjiang by unidentified persons in early 1999. The PLA had kept the attack under wraps, but the people of the area had spread the news, according to Eastern Turkistan National Centre based in Istanbul.[17]

A cumulative report released by the *Amnesty* on 20 April 1999 accused China of "gross and systematic human right violations" and "routine arrest torture and execution" of Uighurs in Xinjiang.[18]

Incidents of violence and counter measures continued in the current year. Notwithstanding, severe measures by Chinese military and public security organs, armed Uighur militants and security forces clashed in January in the town of Aksu in north-western Xinjiang. It was reported in Beijing that a major attack was launched by the Chinese authorities with helicopters to rescue five police officers who had been kidnapped. The *Xinjiang Daily* added that five militants were sentenced to death.[19]

It was also reported that the Ministry of State Security has issued a circular to its cadres to be vigilant against any move to infiltrate into China by fundamentalist fighters from "Saudi Arabia, Gulf states, Turkey and India". The reference to India may essentially be seen in the context of mujahideens—largely of foreign origin—moving from Kashmir to Xinjiang. The circular also demanded a close watch on movements of weapons into China and expose plans of attack on "Chinese facilities".[20]

The brief and sketchy survey of the militancy in Xinjiang culled from the scanty information available to the outside world provides the broad contours of ethnic nationalism, fundamentalism, and violence in the region which has become more frequent and widespread since the late 80s as a result of combination of external and internal factors. The external factors noted earlier had provided the necessary stimuli.

We had briefly noted the Chinese responses to deal with this issue in the earlier sections. These are: increased central assistance for the development of this region to alleviate economic discontent and efforts to integrate the people politically and socially. The latter aspect involved training of minority cadres to take position of responsibility in the administrative and economic structures of the province. Since the trained and qualified personnel are not aplenty, the progress in this sphere has been modest, although in terms of both numbers and percentage the participation of local cadres has been growing. However, ethnic and religious factors have also played a major role in recent years despite progress in other areas. Hence, Beijing's major thrust is to contain and eliminate them by political, military, and other means.

The spread of religious fervour was made possible by a proliferation of mosques, Islamic schools, and Koranic classes at the village levels. The external factors contributing to it, as noted elsewhere, were the liberal funding from Islamic countries and organizations. In many of these Islamic colleges and schools, fanatical clerics presided over although clerics in general needed the approval of the region's religious body controlled by Beijing. Alarmed by the rise of these religious structures, Beijing has banned construction of new mosques without Government approval and has closed unregistered mosques. Further, under the liberal package of post-Mao era, many Muslims who have become prosperous began to undertake pilgrimage to Mecca. This provides them with new contacts in the Islamic world. In Beijing's view, many such pilgrims are fundamentalists and hence it has stipulated that only those who are over 50 years of age could go on the Haj. This is a better version of the highly-controlled official pilgrimage of earlier years. The other measures adopted include selective purging of clerics suspected of promoting fundamentalism, ban on sale and publication of religious materials, audio tapes, etc., which do not have the approval of Religious Affairs Bureau and closure of unregistered village Koranic schools and classes.[21] Thus, one may say that internally Beijing's approach is a blend of economic incentives with careful, political and religious control. These measures are in place since early nineties.

It may be relevant in this context to analyse China's attitude to religious freedom. A White Paper on Religious Freedom was issued on October 16, 1997 by China's State Council.[22] It is an authoritative document listing the legal guarantees and achievements by China in promoting freedom of religion. The document has basically highlighted the religious freedom enjoyed by the Christians and Buddhists—presumably because the external world has been specifically critical of China's treatment of the adherents to Christianity and Buddhism. The concluding part of the paper has listed its guarantees to the followers of Islam and its achievement in promoting its cause. It says: "The Chinese Government also respects and protects the Muslims' freedom of religious belief as well as the folk customs". The achievements listed are as follows: (1) Provision of special pilgrimage related services; (2) Enactment of regulation for the production of Halal meat; and (3) Opening of special cemeteries for Muslims. It added that since the eighties more than 40,000 pilgrims have gone to Mecca. With special reference to Xinjiang it noted: As of 1997, there are 23,000 mosques and 29,000 clerics to meet the religious needs of the people. However, it warned: "The Chinese government resolutely opposes attempts to split the country along ethnic lines and any use of religious fanaticism to divide the people, split the country, or harm unity among all ethnic groups, engage in illegal activities and terrorist actions under the signboard of religion".[23] In sum, the document reiterated that assertion of independent identity is illegal.

Beijing has also taken into account the external aspects of ethnic nationalism. It is widely known that many militants went to Afghanistan and Pakistan for training with fundamentalist outfits and had returned to Xinjiang. It was reported in the media that during 1998-99 Beijing had made a request for the repatriation from Pakistan of a list of militants and Pindi obliged without any hassle. This is also indicative of the fact that Beijing has developed yet another channel of consultation with Pindi and the latter has been cooperating in the overall interests of what has often been described as "all weather friendship" between the two countries. Similarly, while most nations do not recognise the Taliban government in Afghanistan on 10 December, 1998 Beijing and Kabul signed a military accord. The full details of the accord are not available but it was revealed that among other things Beijing has agreed to train

Kabul's Air Force pilots.[24] Speculations have been rife that Kabul has also agreed to let Chinese specialists examine the unexpected US Cruise Missiles on its territory. Whatever the truth, one cannot ignore the fact that Beijing seeks some kind of presence in Kabul to track militants going over there for training, etc., and eventually seek a *modus vivendi* with Kabul for denying access to militants there.

This pattern of political, diplomatic and other linkages to deny Uighurs sanctuaries has vividly been demonstrated by the agreements that Beijing has reached with three Central Asian neighbours and Russia. The signing of border accords, promotion of trade and military confidence building measures on the borders constituted the core of accords. The five countries, namely China, Russia, Kazakhstan, Tajikstan and Kirghistan, often called the "Shanghai five" have held regular summit meetings since 1996 when the first summit was held in Shanghai. At the fourth summit held on August 25, 1999 at Bishkek, the Kirghiz capital, mutual cooperation to combat separatism and religious extremism were discussed in a comprehensive manner.[25] It was revealed subsequently that the five countries have created an institutional structure to meet the challenges posed by ethnic nationalism and its various manifestations.[26] In sum, it appears, that China has secured a consensus on this festering issue from its neighbours.

Conclusions

To sum up, the adoption of Marxism-Leninism as the exclusive and inclusive ideological and political framework of Peoples' Republic of China led gradually to the recognition of various ethnic groups as "nationalities". The definition of "nationalities" originally followed the Stalinist model in theory but in practical terms the differences between Han and others came to be defined in a flexible manner suiting Chinese conditions. The leadership usually exhorted its Han cadres serving in minority areas to abjure "Han Chauvinism" but it was not observed satisfactorily in many minority areas. More significantly, the Han-minority linkages were gravely disrupted by the Great Proletarian Cultural Revolution (1966-76) when the rampaging Red Guard and radicals violated every rule in the book on minority right and culture. They insulted minority culture, including religion. In Xinjiang, as in Tibet, they destroyed symbols such as mosques or Buddhist temples and sought to implement a semi-mystical radical form of social change which was at sharp variance with the realities on the ground. These realities are born of particularities of various nationalities, the extent of their political socialization and the specificities of their economic conditions. The radicalism of the cultural revolution fortified the traditional minority perception of Han hegemony and fuelled ethno-religious nationalism among the dominant nationalities such as Uighurs and Tibetans. It took more than a decade for the Chinese leadership to undo the harm and the policy of reform and opening up had its impact on the process.

The surviving trauma of cultural revolution and the assertion of ethnic identities in the dying years of Cold War provided a new lease of life to a search for national identities in Xinjiang. In this context, a comparison between Tibet and Xinjiang is relevant because they are among the major nationality areas of China.

Tibet acquired over a period of time an 'international personality' thanks to the dynamic role of its spiritual leader his Holiness the Dalai Lama, who had taken asylum in India in 1959 in the wake of China's crackdown in Tibet to end Tibetan assertion of identity and consolidate its hold over the region. While the Tibetan cause was ignored to a large extent—by the West during the early years of the Cold War—the US made a modest commitment to its cause in the late fifties by providing various kinds of assistance to the Khampa rebels. The rebellion itself was crushed by China and the US too abandoned the cause as prospects of Sino-US normalisation came into focus since late sixties. However, Dalai Lama's diplomacy in the West won him several admirers in various countries, including the US. This has helped keep the Tibetan cause, if not for total independence, at least for genuine autonomy alive.

On the other hand, the Uighurs of Xinjiang, notwithstanding some support from Turkey and some Central Asian Republics of the then USSR, could not muster support in the West even during the Cold War years. Whether this was due to the absence of a dynamic leader like the Dalai Lama among the Uighurs or general lack of interest in this remote region is unclear. Perhaps it is a combination of both factors although many Uighurs believe that it is the absence of a high profile leader like the Dalai Lama which is the critical factor. Even today, in the period of post-Cold War and post-Soviet world, in which the neighbouring Central Asian Republics have emerged as independent nations, the Uighurs of Xinjiang are not in focus. There is a modernized and more sophisticated version of the "great game" of nineteenth century which is being played today in Central Asia for economic and political presence by the West but this game does not include Xinjiang even as a minor participant. In short, the struggle of the Uighurs has almost been forgotten and is confined to the opaque margins of a contemporary politics. However, some Uighur intellectuals and students to whom this writer had talked to in London during 1995 are intensely nationalistic and believe that their cause is not dead, though it may not be in the upswing in the current phase. They described themselves as people from Chinese-controlled "Eastern Turkistan" building their movement gradually and spreading awareness of it in the West so that their cause may gain a major spotlight. Whatever their hopes and aspirations, as of today it is not a movement with major implications.

This does not mean that Beijing has no problem on hand, for any minority discontent in a strategic area produced by a multiplicity of factors could become a potent mix that can cause grave societal and security problems. For instance, if the present moderate regimes in the three Central Asian Republics bordering Xinjiang autonomous region are replaced by fundamentalist regimes, the Uighurs will get a shot in the arm and Beijing's concerns will grow. As of today, the carrot and stick approach of Beijing is seen by its leadership as a viable measure to contain and eventually eliminate sources of discontent and ensure prosperity and wellbeing of the ethnic nationalities. Some scholars, however, are of the view that "extensive liberalization linked to democratization" will produce optimum results in this sphere. Thomas Heberer has observed, "Without true liberalization, the party leadership will continue to reach with pressure and force to every attempt by the minorities to gain more independence. In the long run, such a hard line and its effects may be the ultimate block to the unity of the country".[28] In some ways, Beijing's strategy of managing minority self-assertion, is somewhat similar to the ones adopted by many multicultural and multiethnic nations in the developing world. It needs to be noted, however, there are many dissimilarities too and these arise out of the nature of the political system in a given nation-state.

REFERENCES

1. See for details: K.N. Ramachandran and S.K. Ghosh, *Power and Ideology: Sino-Soviet Dispute—An Overview*, New Delhi, Young Asia Publications, 1977, pp. 42-46.

2. See for details: David Wong, 'Han Migration and Social Change in Xinjiang, in *Issuess Studies* (Taipeh) Vol. 34, No. 7, July 1998, pp. 48-50.

3. *Ibid.*

4. See Anthony Davis, 'Xinjiang Learns to live with resurgent Islam', *Janex Intelligence Review* (London) September 1996, pp. 418-19.

5. Keesings Record of World Events (Cambridge, UK) April 1990, p. 37373 (Hereafter noted as *Keesings*)

6. *Keesings*, March 1992, p. 38814.

7. *Keesings*, May 1996, p. 41098.

8. *Keesings*, February 1997, p. 41492-93.

9. *Keesings, Ibid.*

10. *Keesings*, March 1997, p. 41541.

11. *Xinhua* (Beijing) 29 May, 1997.

12. *Keesings* October 1997, p. 41860.

13. *Keesings*, February 1998, p. 42065.

14. *Keesings*, January 1998, p. 42011.

15. *Keesings*, January 1999, p. 41492-93.

16. *Ibid.*

17. *Keesings*, February 1999, p. 42891.

18. *Keesings*, April 1999, p. 42891.

19. See *International Herald Tribune*, (Bangkok), 28 January, 2000.

20. *Ibid.*

21. See the summary in Anthonoy Davis, n. 4.

22. See full text of the White Paper on Religious Freedom, Xinhua (Beijing), 16 October, 1997.

23. *Ibid.*

24. See *Keesings,* December 1998, p. 42674.

25. See *Keesings,* August 1999, p. 43100.

26. This was disclosed by Mr. Leonid P Mosseyev, a visiting Russian Foreign Ministry official in New Delhi, at a discussion on 27 March, 2000 in the Institute for Chinese Studies, New Delhi.

27. A brief summary of author's private discussion with a group of Uighur intellectuals and students during an International Conference on Minorities held in London in 1995.

28. See for details, Thomas Herberer, *China and Its National Minorities: Autonomy on Assimilation?* New York, M.E. Sharpe Inc. 1989, pp. 127-31.

CHAPTER 21

Ethnic Cauldron in Sri Lanka

V. Suryanarayan

Last night
I had a dream
Lord Buddha was shot dead
by the police—
guardians of the law.
His body lay drenched in blood
on the step
of the Jaffna Library.

Under cover of darkness
came the Ministers
Their name—not in our lists
Why did you kill him ?
they ask in anger.

'No, Sirs, no!
There was no mistake.
Without bumping him off
it was impossible
to harm even a fly
Therefore...; they stammered.

'Okay, Okay!
Hide the corpse,
The Ministers vanish.

The men in civvies
dragged the corpse
Into the library.
They heaped the books,
rare and valuable
ninety thousand in all.
They lit the pyre
With the
*Chikalokavada Sutta**

Thus the remains
Of the Compassionate One
were burned to ashes
along with the
*Dhammapada***

M.A. Nuhman

** Title of the Buddhist Text.

*** Collection of the teachings of Buddha.

In his, book, *Ceylon: Dilemmas of a New Nation,* Howard Wriggins dealt with group attitudes in the island. He referred to a study made by T.L. Green, formerly of the University of Ceylon. Seventy Sinhalese children were asked to characterise themselves and the Tamils Sinhalese self-perception included terms like "kind, clever, rich, brave, jealous, proud, good, religious, courageous, lazy and honest." Their characterization of the Tamils was equally interesting: "cruel, clever, poor, diligent, cunning, rich, thrifty , ugly, arrogant, business minded and proud."[2] Not even one Sinhala student attributed 'bravery' as a quality of the Tamils!

How times have changed! *Serendib* (Arab name for Ceylon, which means island of happy fortune) has become one of the notorious killing fields of the world. Torn by internal dissensions, Sri Lanka is a fractured island today. The 'docile' Tamils have taken to the cult of the bomb and the bullet and those who support the Liberation Tigers of Tamil Eelam (LTTE) are convinced that only a separate state can provide security and safety to the Tamils. But violence in Sri Lanka is not confined to the Tamil areas alone. During 1988-90, aptly characterized as *Bhisana Samaya* (massive repression) *"Kelani Ganga* and *Kalu Garlga,* Sri Lankan rivers of exquisite beauty...were clogged with bodies and foamed with blood."[3] And violence in Sri Lanka, as Prof. Valentine Daniel has pointed out, "is no longer inter-ethnic, but intra-ethnic, with more Tamils killing Tamils and Sinhalas killing Sinhalas, with the Lankan state killing the most, Tamils and Sinhalas."[4] Bishop Reginald Heber, with prophetic vision, wrote in the 19th century:

What though the spicy breezes
Blow soft o'er Ceylon's isle
Though every prospect pleases
And only man is vile.[5]

Janata Vimukti Peramuna (JVP)

It is necessary to highlight the fact that the first major challenge to the Sri Lankan political system did not come from the Tamils, but from the Sinhalese. In April 1971, the *Janata Vimukti Peramuna* (JVP), reflecting the disenchantment and frustration of the Sinhalese educated and the under-privileged raised the banner of armed revolt.[6] This revolt of youth was the first instance of "tension between generations breaking out into military conflict on a national scale. The creed of generational war was linked to eradicating the colonial status which had ended two decades previously, but was presumed to be still in existence".[7] The revolt was crushed with external assistance, but it had farreaching repercussions as far as the Sri Lankan political system was concerned. Emergency was proclaimed in April 1971, which continued without a break until February 1977. Thousands of Sinhalese youth were detained without trial. The armed forces had their first major experience in tackling a violent revolt.

Sri Lankan Governments could not find a lasting solution to the increasing dichotomy between the revolution of rising expectations of youth, whose outmoded system of education was at variance with stagnating economic opportunities. After remaining dormant for a few years, the JVP rose like a phoenix following the India-Sri Lanka Accord, 1987. The JVP leaders realized that they could spread their influence far and wide, if they could successfully mobilize anti-Indian sentiments. The Party, therefore, shifted its slogan from 'socialism through class struggle' to 'liberation through patriotic struggle'[8]. Capitalizing on the Sinhala backlash, the JVP became the champion of Sinhala extremism, spread its own brand of violence and following the dictum of 'punishing the traitors' systematically assassinated political opponents. As a Sri Lankan writer has put it, the period saw "Ruhuna (rightly or wrongly) once more rising up to its traditional role as the "protector" of the Sinhala-Buddhist identity."[9] For a few months there were doubts regarding Colombo's capacity to tackle the deepening political crisis. Due to a variety of factors, the JVP could not attain its objectives; the army gradually got the upper hand and systematically decimated Sinhala youth.

After the killing of Rohana Wijeweera, Ranjan Wijeratne, then Defence Minister, boasted that the 'match is over'. Perhaps from a long term perspective it is too early to write the obituary of the JVP. Unless the basic issues confronting the Sinhala youth chauvinist traditions going back to the Dutugemunu period, combined with severe economic hardships are not resolved, the reservoir from which the JVP draws its strength will remain intact. In other words, the Sinhalese society is bound to live in social and political ferment for years to come.

It is interesting to note that a few JVP .cadres and some Tamil militants also established their contact in jails, where they were detained by the Sri Lanka Freedom Party (SLFP) Government. Certain parallel features of the movements deserve mention. The Tamil militants and the JVP represented generational revolts; they revolted against the *status quo* politics of the Tamil United Liberation Front (TULF) led by the Vellalas and the UNP-SLFP politics dominated by the Goigamas. Prabhakaran was born in the Karaya caste and Wijeweera belonged to the Karavas. The two groups .subscribed to the path of armed struggle. The JVP at present is following the parliamentary path, but if the crisis in the South further deepens, the possibility of the JVP taking to armed struggle cannot be ruled out. And, for tactical reasons, will the JVP and the LTTE come together? (If President Premadasa and Prabhakaran can come together, why not the JVP and the LTTE?). A dismal scenario, but Sri Lanka watchers will not rule out the possibility.

Dynamics of Ethnic Politics

Sri Lanka is a fascinating laboratory for studying the dynamics of inter-ethnic relations. From a South Asian perspective, it is interesting to note that in the era of decolonization, Ceylon was generally referred to as a 'model colony'. The transition to independence was smooth; there was no prolonged and bitter anti-colonial struggle as in India, Indonesia and Vietnam. On the eve of independence, it was relatively a peaceful country, compared to the orgy of violence that accompanied the birth of its northern neighbours, India and Pakistan. D.S. Senanayake, the first Prime Minister, was not only the leader of the majority Sinhala community, he also had the tacit support of other minority groups. Most commentators felt that the newborn state would be politically stable and that the major ethnic groups would be integrated into one nation. The state was also committed to the ideals of democracy and promotion of social justice through welfare programmes.

Five decades and two years later, the political system has undergone a fundamental transformation. The common links and aspirations which united the elites among the Sinhalese and the Tamils have disappeared; what is more tragic, Sri Lanka has degenerated into one of the most notorious 'killing fields' of the world. In a Message to the Nation, on the fiftieth anniversary of Sri Lankan independence President Chandrika

Kumaratunga underlined the failures of political leadership in building a united nation. To quote Kumaratunga:

> We have failed to forge together the diverse communities of our peoples into one coherent and strong Sri Lankan nation. We have faltered along for 50 years, permitting the differences to emerge and dominate our social fabric, rather then nurture the commonalties."[10]

Two important strands in the Sri Lankan scene should be highlighted in the beginning itself. During the 1950's and 1960's , Sri Lanka undoubtedly was the most vibrant democracy in Asia. The governments changed at regular intervals through free and fair elections. All the essentials of a dynamic democracy — free press, independence of the judiciary, rule of law, free and fair polls, strong trade unions and active student unions—were in evidence. All these welcome features have become relics of the past. Mrs Sirimavo Bandaranaike promulgated an emergency, following the outbreak of the JVP revolt in 1971, which continued up to 1977. Northern and eastern parts of Sri Lanka have been under a continuous emergency since July 1983. The Constitutions have been tampered with and democratic institutions have been subverted. Political assassinations have become common and the militant groups, especially the Tigers, are armed to the teeth. Chandrika Kumaratunga and the Peoples Alliance, which came to power in 1994 on the slogans of peace and democracy, are also resorting to authoritarian methods. The Presidential election of December 1999, was held under the backdrop of an abortive attempt on the life of the President and the killing of several activists belonging to the two major political parties. The laws of reason and persuasion have given way to the cult of the bomb and the bullet.

Equally noteworthy was the high PQLI—Physical quality of life which made Sri Lanka the envy of Third World countries. Successive governments—UNP and SLFP—invested considerable amount in education, health and infrastructure; as a result, the quality of life in the island was compared favourably with developed Scandinavia countries. However, the fuelling of the war machine during recent years has resulted in diversion of funds to defence. Even then, Sri Lanka still ranks high in South Asia in terms of human development.

Falsification of History

To look at the past through the prism of the present is falsification of history. The projection of Sinhalese and Tamils as two antagonistic entities at war with one another for several centuries by Sinhalese/Tamil chauvinist writers (two sides of the same coin) is an illustration of the well-known axiom that truth and objectivity are the first casualties in times of conflict. As Eric Hobsbawm has pointed out "History is the raw material for nationalist or ethnic or fundamentalist ideologies, as poppies are the raw material for heroin addiction. Prof. Stanley Tambiah, after years of painstaking research, has come to the conclusion that Sinhalese and Tamils share many parallel features of "traditional caste, kinship, popular religious cult, customs and so on. But they have come to be divided by their mythic characters and tendentious historical understanding of the past."[12] He has also exploded the myth of racial divide, i.e., "Sinhalese are (fair) Aryans and the Tamils are (dark) Dravidians."[13] Quoting Gananath Obeyesekere, Tambiah adds "if it were possible to trace the present day Sinhalese population's ancestry far enough, all lines would in major part lead to South India. According to Obeysekere, "Biologically speaking, those whom we call Sinhala are in fact racially inter-mixed with South Indian peoples and with aboriginal groups like the Vedda; and the Tamils, who live in the north and the east, are also similarly biologically mixed."[15]

Prof. K. S. Singh, in his monumental study of the *People of India,* has remarked that several communities can be classified as having more than one religion. It is interesting to note that Sinhalese religious practices also point to the same direction. The Hindu Bhakti cult has influenced Theravada Buddhism and there are images of Hindu Gods in Buddhist temples. The deity of Skanda (Muruga) in Kataragama, located near the Yala sanctuary in the north east of the island, continues to be the major "institutional intersection of several religious faiths. Hindus, Buddhist, Christians and Muslims—all go to Kataragama, where the atmosphere is one of tolerance and goodwill.[17] During our recent visit to the temple, we found Buddhist pilgrims far outnumbering Hindus. The Sinhalese carry the *Kavadi* with great devotion and fervour.

According to *Mahavamsa,* the Buddhist sacred text, the founding father of the first Sinhala kingdom was Prince Vijaya, a Prince from North India, who came to Sri Lanka with 700 followers and decided to settle in the island. They did not have any women with them and therefore they brought women from the Pandyan kingdom in Tamil Nadu; Vijaya himself married the Pandyan king's daughter. In other words, even according to Buddhist texts, from the very beginning the Sinhala nation was a product of assimilation between the Sinhalese and the Tamils

Few Sri Lankan scholars want to subscribe to the objective truth that Buddhism was a virile religion in South India (from first century AD to seventh century AD) and that the spread and efflorescence of classical Buddhism in the Anuradhapura and Pollanaruwa periods had much to do with their contacts with Buddhist centres of learning in South India. Recent research in linguistics also reveals several communities. According to Gunawardenet " in grammatical structure Sinhalese was Dravidian (i.e., South Indian, though its vocabulary was mainly Aryan (north Indian)."[19]

Despite the cultural commonalties, the chauvinists among the Sinhalese and the Tamils propagate the falsehood of age-old animosities between the two communities. These tendentious arguments remind us of the famous statement of Voltaire "if you will believe in absurdities you will commit atrocities.[20] It is our submission that the Sinhalese-Tamil conflict is a product of post-independence politics an offshoot on the one hand, of the nation-building experiment, where the Sinhalese leaders wanted to build the nation on the basis of the Sinhalese language and the Buddhist religion to the exclusion of minority claims and on the other, to the politics of ethnic mobilization resorted to by chauvinist Sinhalese and Tamil leaders.

What is of relevance, however, for our analysis is the subjective belief of the Sinhalese and the Tamils that they are unique and separate communities. And as Gananath Obeysekere points out in crucial moments of ethnic identity formation, the "identity is influenced more by myths of the past than the actual occurences."[21]

Competing Nationalist Narratives

An analysis of the ideological constructs and a review of significant Sinhalese writings provide fascinating insights into the majority communities concept of nation-building, which had been the main stumbling block to the emergence of a tolerant multi-ethnic society in Sri Lanka. The concept of *Sinha Dipa* (land of the Sinhalese) and

Dhamma Dipa (land of Buddhist Dharma) were exploited to portray the Tamils and the Muslims as non-native intruders, who had to subordinate to the 'sons of the soil'. The popular Sinhalese formulation was that the Sinhalese have only Sri Lanka., while the Tamils can go back to Tamil Nadu and the Muslims to Arabia.

The educational system also helped perpetuate these dangerous myths. The Council for Communal Harmony, which undertook a study of the contents of Sinhalese and Tamil textbooks, came to the following conclusions. While the Tamil books "do seek to create an understanding of and respect for the way of life and culture of non-Tamil and non-Hindu linguistic and religious groups, and do attempt to project a sense of common national identity, the Sinhala books are exclusively non-cultural in their content i.e., the way of life they present is not only solely Sinhala, but also solely Sinhala.-Buddhist... The Tamils are identified throughout the books as traditional adversary ..."[22]

The nationalist narrative authored by President Jayewardene is also replete with such falsehoods. *Golden Threads*[23] was published in May 1984 by the Sri Lankan Government. The book claims to be a 'sketch of the story of our land' and dedicated "for the youth of Sri Lanka...to whom the torch must pass." As Sankaran Krishna has pointed out, the text begins by "locating the narrator and his audience, the narrator is some one who has, in an Olympian metaphor, led the charge, carried the torch of the national journey and is preparing to bestow the responsibility on his young wards."[24]

Jayewardene's view of Sri Lankan history should be highlighted because it throws light on the man and his mission. The book is divided into three parts. Part I deals with post-544 BC to 1815 AD. According to *Mahavamsa,* Prince Vijaya came to the island in 544 BC and the Kandyan kings surrendered their sovereignty to the British in 1815 AD. By beginning Sri Lanka's history with the arrival of Prince Vijaya, Jayewardene completely blacksout the earlier rich history of the country; he also "pushes to the margins the Tamils and other ethnic and religious communities, who have no comparable mythic charter of their presence."[25] Nor does Jayewardene consider 1948, the year in which Ceylon was granted independence, as a landmark. More interestingly, the third part begins with the UNP coming to power and Jayewardene becoming the Prime Minister in 1977.

Throughout the book, Sri Lanka and the Sinhala nation are used to convey the same idea. In a seminar organized by the Centre for South and South East Asian Studies, University of Madras, a few years ago, Jayadeva Uyangoda made the telling comment that in the Sinhalese language the term used for nation-building is *Jathiya Goḍanegema.* It means the making of the Sinhalese nation and not the Sri Lankan nation. Jayewardene projects the Sri Lankan Tamils as intruders who (disturbed the peace and harmony in the island. The book records: "In the first quarter of the thirteenth century from South India came the *Magha* the Tiger. The wasteland that he created became the kingdom of malaria, the domain of the anopheles, breeding prodigiously in the dark stagnant waters of the great irrigation works."[26]

Jayewardene did not display even an iota of sympathy for the minority groups, who became victims of regular communal riots in the post-independence era. He referred to terrorism as—"A world phenomenon raised its ugly head in the North and the East and some Tamils joined them to press for separation. In 1980 these activities increased and the killing of the Sinhala security forces in the North in 1983 was followed by Sinhala-Tamil riots throughout the island."[27] By equating the Tamil grievances and resultant violence with terrorism, Jayewardene clearly proved that he was not a neutral non-sectarian Head of State. When the communal holocaust took place in July 1983 — "dark night of the collective soul" as Jonathan Spencer rightly described it[28] - Jayewardene not only failed to express any sympathy for the victims, he also failed to condemn the lumpen sections of the Sinhalese population, who ran amok in the Tamil areas of Colombo. As Paul Sieghart, the distinguished jurist, remarked:

> ...The President did not see fit to utter one single word of sympathy for the victims of violence and the destruction which he lamented. If his concern was to re-establish communal harmony in the island, whose national unity he was so anxious to preserve by law, that was a misjudgment of monumental proportions....[29]

The communal riots and the resultant trauma were the major factors behind the refugee phenomenon. Within Colombo alone, nearly 100,000 Tamils, more than half the Tamil population in the city, were displaced. There was hardly any Tamil family that escaped death, destruction or displacement. A Tamil woman, who was a victim of repeated cycles of violence, exclaimed, 'To be a Tamil is to live in fear'.[30] The agony and anguish of the Tamil population was expressed by R.R. Sivalingam, Indian Tamil political activist., as follows :

> The Tamils in Sri Lanka are in anguish.
> We are searching ourselves. Is it a crime
> to be a Tamil in this country? Our
> convictions have all been shattered.
> Generations of effort to build a base of
> life have all been shattered to smithereens
> in a matter of few hours. How long! Oh!
> How long will it take for us to feel as brothers
> and sons of the soil.[31]

The Sinhalese — a majority community with a minority complex — were consistently opposed to devolution and federalism. They believed that federalism would be the first step towards the creation of a separate state. The three Constitutions and their underlying ideologies contributed to the exacerbation of ethnic conflict, distortion of liberal democracy and emergence of authoritarianism.[32] The first Constitution of Sri Lanka, the Soulbury Constitution of 1947, promulgated by Britain one year before independence, enshrined majoritarian democracy in a unitary state. Provision was made for protection of minority rights under Section 29 (2) of the Constitution, which prescribed limitations on legislative sovereignty. The 1972 Constitution marked a distinct departure from the past. The United Front Government, led by Mrs. Sirimavo Bandaranaike, equated its overwhelming majority in Parliament with consensus. The Tamil demand, for federalism and protection of minority rights was ignored. On the other hand, the Constitution gave Buddhism an elevated position within the country and made Sinhala the official language. The role of the judiciary was eroded. As Dr. Radhika Coomaraswamy pointed out: "Not one case on fundamental rights was decided by the courts during the tenure of the Constitution.[33]

The Second Republican Constitution of 1978 introduced the system of Executive Presidency. The main objective of the Constitution makers was to provide political stability with a strong executive head, free from the whims and fancies of Parliament. The 'mighty executive' coupled with a 'devalued Parliament' hastened the downfall of democracy and paved the way for authoritarianism. A free press and regular elections became memories of the past. Centralization of power, whether through Parliament as in the 1972 Constitution or through the President as in the 1978 Constitution did not contribute to political stability. The period witnessed two JVP uprisings and also intensification of ethnic conflict. As Regi Siriwardena aptly put it, "centralisation begot not order, but disorder."[34]

The Indo-Sri Lanka Accord of 1987 and the Thirteenth Amendment to the Constitution were significant steps in introducing devolution of powers. In sum, it aimed at sharing of powers between the majority and minority communities and between the Centre and the Provincial Councils. Unfortunately, in the perception of large number of Sinhalese, the whole exercise was an imposition by India. While one section of the Government led by President Jayewardene supported the idea, another equally powerful section, led by Prime Minister Premadasa, attempted to sabotage it. Without a Sinhala consensus and Tamil participation, the accord itself became a source of discord in Sri Lanka.

Given the Sinhalese ideology , which subscribes to centralization of state power and close identification of the nation state with the Sinhalese community, it was inevitable that the Provincial Council System got mired in serious difficulties, The Provincial Council of the North East had only a short life of 17 months — November 1988 to March 1990. It lacked financial resources and through some disingenuous mechanisms, central dominance was re-established in many areas like agriculture and transport. In his inaugural address to the India-Sri Lanka Consultation on Devolution, Prof. G.L. Peiris admitted: "In fact, we have no devolution at all decentralization yes, devolution no."[35]

Sri Lankan Tamil Politics—An Overview

The early Tamil nationalists like Ponnambalam Ramanathan and G.G. Ponnambalam viewed Ceylon as a single political unit transcending ethnic, religious and linguistic differences. Their successors got disillusioned with the political system with the passage of the 'Sinhala, Only Act, in 1956. Further, the irreconcilable perceptions of injustice and relative deprivation by Sri Lankan Tamils and the Sinhalese — the former being an 'achieving minority' and the latter being a majority community felt 'historically deprived'[36] further widened the schism between the two.

We would like to submit two propositions which can be considered as the yardstick for the success of nation-building in multi-ethnic societies in South Asia. First, the political system should provide sufficient space for minorities so that they can preserve, promote and foster their identities, while being part of a united country. Second, a federal polity with entrenched provisions for sharing powers between the Centre and the States, can lead to the softening of secessionist demands and pave the way for eventual political integration. Two illustrations, one a success, story from India and second, a tragic narrative from Sri Lanka, both relating to Tamil minority groups, are given below. What is interesting to note are the differing political developments and contrasting responses on the issue of nation-building.

In Sri Lanka, the Tamil political leaders drifted-from collaboration with the Sinhalese elite and eventually began to demand a separate state of Tamil Eelam. The Dravidian movement in India followed a diametrically opposite course. The scholars working on the Dravidian movement are unanimous in pointing out the important milestones—the formation of the Justice Party and the non-Brahmin movement from 1917; Periyar E.V. Ramaswamy Naicker's Self-Respect Movement and anti-Hindi agitation; the formation of the Dravida Kazhagam in the mid-1940s and its advocacy of the separate state of Dratudanadu; the formation of the Dravida Munnetra Kazhagam (DMK) under C.N. Annadurai in 1949; the coming into power of the DMK following the 1967 elections; and the domination of the DMK and its offshoot All India Anna Dravida Munnetra Kazhagam (AIADMK), formed in 1972, in the politics of Tamil Nadu. The DMK got gradually domesticated, because the Indian political system provided sufficient political space within which Tamil identity and regional autonomy could be protected and fostered. What is more, the domestication of the DMK was evident even before Annadurai formally renounced secessionism in 1962 (after the Sino- Indian conflict) and the 16th Amendment to the Constitution (which prescribed secessionism and required from all candidates seeking political office an oath upholding the Constitution) was passed. The DMK/AIADMK stakes in the unity of the country got further strengthened, when these parties started sharing power at the Centre. The AIADMK joined the Charan Singh Government in the 1970s and the DMK joined the V.P. Singh Government in the 1980s.

On the contrary, an overview of the Sri Lankan Tamil politics since independence clearly shows that the Tamils had been mainly 'reactive' to Sinhalese politics. Since Sinhalese-dominated governments never fulfilled their hopes and aspirations, frustrations became intense, demands became more radical, finally culminating in the demand for a separate state of Tamil Eelam in Vaddukodai in 1976. The politics of Tamil opposition started with the demand for balanced representation and responsive co-operation, which spanned the period from 1948 to 1956; the demand progressed to federal state and non-cooperation during 1957-1972; escalated to separatist slogans during 1973-1976; and ended with the demand for a separate state in 1976. But while the demands changed, the mainstream of the Tamil political leadership confused its strategies to peaceful agitation, parliamentary and non- parliamentary alike. From 1979, militancy began to creep into Tamil politics. To Tamil youth, majoritarian democracy meant the rule of the brute Sinhalese majority. They were not enamoured either with earlier forms of peaceful struggle.

By the mid-1970s, the Sri Lankan Tamils, who were to begin with reluctant secessionists began to define themselves as a separate nation, entitled to self-determination and a separate state. Discriminatory legislative enactments and governmental policies in the areas of language, education, land colonization, religion and employment opportunities; the abrogation of the Bandaranaike-Chelvanayakam Pact (1956) and the Senanayake-Chelvanayakam Pact (1965) , which conferred limited autonomy to the Tamil areas; the competitive Sinhala politics which marginalized the Tamils; and above all, the practice of brutal military repression, convinced the Tamils that their legitimate rights could be guaranteed only by a separate state.

Tamils: No Homogeneity

It is necessary to highlight the fact that despite their adherence to a common language, the Tamils in Sri Lanka are not a homogenous group. The Sri Lankan Tamils are subdivided into three categories — the Jaffna Tamils, the Batticaloa Tamils and the Colombo Tamils. The Jaffna Tamil society is dominated by the Vellalas, the eastern region by the Mukkuvars. There are also differences in kinship—in Jaffna, kinship is traced bilaterally while in the eastern region, the matrilineal system still survives.

Jaffna is in a state of social ferment; the sidelining of the Tamil United Liberation Front (TULF) not only represented the fading away of the moderates, it also sounded the death knell of Vellala domination of Tamil politics. The current phase of struggle is in many ways a leveller of Tamil society, which explains how Prabhakaran belonging to the fisher man-merchant community of *Karaiyar* could become the leader of the major Tamil militant group. Support to Tamil militancy is relatively less in the East, where the Tamils have been coexisting with the Sinhalese and the Muslims. Some eastern Tamils also express concern that in a state dominated by Jaffna Tamils, they may receive second class treatment. The largest concentration of Tamils today is in Colombo and its suburbs. Most of them work in government offices and in private firms; many others are professionals doctors, engineers, lawyers, teachers and accountants. A few others are engaged in business. With law and order deteriorating in the North and the East, many Sri Lankan Tamils have moved over to Colombo; some of them consider the Capital as a transit point for migration abroad. Despite their vulnerability, the Colombo Tamils have nothing to gain from a separate state. In fact, in the 1994 elections most of them voted for the Peoples Alliance in the Parliamentary and Presidential elections. Similarly, a majority of them voted for the UNP candidate Ranil Wikramasinghe in the 1999 Presidential Election.

Mention should also be made of the Sri Lankan Tamil community settled abroad and its impact on the contemporary Sri Lankan scene. Sri Lankan Tamils had always been migratory. Many educated Tamils, during the British period, migrated to Malaysia, Singapore, Australia, United States and England. In fact, the earnings of these people sustained Tamil society; Jaffna was popularly referred to as the 'post office economy'. From the 1960s, due to decrease of employment opportunities, aggravated further by the blatant pro-Sinhalese recruitment policies of successive governments, a number of Sri Lankan Tamil academicians, doctors, engineers, scientists, accountants and other skilled personnel left the shores of Sri Lanka. From 1983, thousands of Sri Lankan Tamils left the island as refugees. Smarting under an acute sense of deprivation, the Sri Lankan Tamils abroad are the greatest protagonists of a Tamil Eelam. Many of them support the Tigers and provide considerable financial and propaganda support to the LTTE. According to some estimates, the monthly contribution to the LTTE from expatriate Tamils works out to one million dollars.[37] What is more, they have formed influential lobbies and have contributed in a large measure to the internationalization of the ethnic conflict.

The Indian Tamils, as Prof. Valentine Daniel points out, "are different from the Jaffna Tamils and the Sinhalese; they have also come to be different from the Tamils of the mainland."[38] whom they left 100 to 150 years ago. They are the descendants of Tamil labourers, who were brought to the island by British colonialists to provide the much-needed labour for tea, coffee, rubber and coconut plantations. They formed the bulk of the labour, that turned the malaria infested forests of Sri Lanka into smilling plantations, that sustain the Sri Lankan economy even today,

Unfortunately, after independence, the Indian Tamils were reduced to the status of merchandise, to be divided between Colombo and New Delhi, in the name of good neighbourly relations. To the ruling elite in New Delhi and Colombo, they represented an agonising and embarrassing set of statistics; for the estate management they constituted cheap, docile labour to be exploited to the hilt; for the fanatics among Sinhalese, they were easy and defenceless victims in times of conflict. By the Sirimavo-Shastri Pact of 1964 and the Sirimavo-Indira Gandhi Pact of 1974, New Delhi agreed to confer citizenship on 6,00,000 (plus their natural increase), whereas Colombo agreed to confer citizenship on 4,00,000 (plus their natural increase).

It is the tragedy of India-Sri Lanka relations that these agreements, which had a great bearing on the lives of thousands of people of Indian origin, were finalized by the two Governments without taking into consideration the feelings and views of the plantation workers. S. Thondaman, the leader of the Ceylon Workers Congress, aptly described the situation:

> We are a community of human beings,
> with soul, mind and body with personality
> and cannot be apportioned between
> countries like beasts of burden at others'
> whims and fancies only to maintain good
> neighbourly relations. Humanity cannot be
> converted to merchandise in this modern age.[39]

In his absorbing novel *Refuge,* Gopal Gandhi movingly describes the inhuman conditions in which the plantation workers of Indian origin live. When their applications for Sri Lankan citizenship were rejected, they did not know what to do. Avadai, a toothless old man, called by the fellow workers as the wise one echoed their feelings:

> We came to this land, because our own land could not sustain us... I remember how parched the earth was, how hungry we all were in our village of Avur in Pudukottai. My father said 'Come, let us go and register in the Ceylon Office'. And so we registered and came here. We came in order to be able to work, to eat...And now we have lost all links with our native land, when we have sent our roots deep into this soil like the tea bushes planted by us, we are told, we are told... that we do not belong here that we must go back to India, that if we stay on here we will have no rights. Is this fair? Is this just?.[40]

Though the Indian Tamils share common bonds of ethnicity and language with the Sri Lankan Tamils, the problems they face and the aspirations they entertain are, in many ways, different from those of their counterparts in the northern and eastern parts of the island. Unlike the Sri Lankan Tamil settlements in the Jaffna peninsula, the plantations are surrounded by Sinhalese villages, which are located in the heartland of the Sinhalese people. This stark reality has made them realize that their present and future are closely intertwinded with the Sinhalese and they must co-exit with the Sinhalese population. In other words, Tamil Eelam, if it comes through, would not lead to the political salvation of Indian Tamils.

If the problem of statelessness, hanging like a Damocles sword above the Indian Tamils, was resolved amicably, it was mainly due to the astute and dynamic leadership of Thondaman. With a judicious mix of parliamentary and extra-parliamentary struggles, he was able to extract from unwilling Sinhalese leaders the prize of citizenship for his people. But the basic question of their safety and security still remains. Though the Indian Tamils do not subscribe to the demand for Tamil Eelam and their most representative organization, the Ceylon Workers Congress (CWC), is part of the Government since 1978, the Indian Tamils are the most vulnerable in times of communal conflict. The communal violence of 1977, 1981 and 1983, clearly demonstrated the utter helplessness of these people against lumpen elements in the Sinhalese population.

Attempts made by the Tamil militant groups to co-opt plantation youth into their movements have not made much headway. Except for isolated pockets, the Indian Tamils remain aloof from Sri Lankan Tamil militants. However, in the long run, the winds of change will cast their impact on the Indian Tamils. In other words, the future of this community and the question of Sri Lankan Tamil — Indian Tamil relations will be determined by the manner in which the wider question of Sinhala- Tamil relations is settled.

Of equal importance is the changing political profile of the Muslims in Sri Lanka. They are scattered throughout the country, but concentrated in the East. The Muslim settlements can be traced back to the heyday of Arab maritime activities in the early medieval period. Confined initially to the coastal areas, they gradually spread to other parts of the country. The Muslims seek their identity on the basis of religion, not language. Most of them are traders, though in the eastern parts of the island, they also engage in agriculture and fishing. Most of them are bilingual, with equal proficiency in Sinhala and Tamil.

In the early years of independence, the leadership of the Muslim community came from the affluent trading classes. They looked to Colombo and not to Jaffna, for political inspiration. Being pragmatic, they supported the two major Sinhalese parties, the UNP and the SLFP The Muslims were against the idea of Tamil Eelam. If it came about, they would become a mini-minority within a minority. A divided country would endanger the very existence of the Muslim population. In day-to-day activities, the community hardly co-operated with the Federal Party and its successor, the TULF. In the 1977 election, the TULF fielded a few Muslim candidates, but all of them were decisively defeated. Moreover, the UNP and the SLFP were vying with one another in wooing the Muslims.

As the ethnic conflict gathered momentum, the Muslims in the East began to assert themselves. In 1980 the Sri Lanka Muslim Congress (SLMC) was formed under the leadership of M.H.M. Ashraff. The SLMC made its debut in Parliament in 1989 with four seats; in the 1994 elections, the SLMC allied with Chandrika and won seven seats. Given the slender majority of the government, the SLMC's support is crucial to Chandrika's survival.

The emergence of the SLMC and its stout opposition to the demand for Tamil Eelam led to violent clashes between the LTTE and the Muslims. The creation of an armed civil defence force, the Muslim Home Guard, further exacerbated the situation. In August 1990, the Tigers massacred 122 innocent Muslims who were offering prayers in two mosques in Kattankudy village. Two weeks later , 164 Muslims were hacked to death. In April 1992, 75 Muslims were massacred in Alinchipothana village in Pollanaruva district; six months later, nearly 250 Muslim men, women and children became victims of LTTE violence in Palliagodalla village in the same district. In October 1990, the Tigers ordered the Muslims in Jaffna district to vacate their homes. Nearly 75,000 Muslims fled, leaving behind their property, which was looted by the LTTE. The displaced Muslims have taken refuge in Muslim settlements in Puttalam, Anuradhapura and Kurunegala districts. Though the LTTE admitted that its policy towards the Muslims was a mistake, LTTE-Muslim relations continue to be tense.

An unfortunate irony of the Sri Lankan situation should be highlighted. The Sri Lankan Tamils complain and complain rightly, that they were discriminated against by successive Sinhalese-dominated governments. But how have the Tigers treated the Muslims? All parts of Sri Lanka are in varying degrees multi-ethnic, but the only mono-ethnic part in Sri Lanka are the Jaffna peninsula and the Tiger-controlled areas in the Wanni jungles. The tragedy of Sri Lanka as Neelan Thiruchelvam has pointed out:

> ...the violence of the victim soon consumed the victim and the victim also became possessed by the demons of racial bigotry and intolerance which had characterised the oppressor. These are seen in the fratricidal violence between Tamils and Muslims, in the massacres at the Kathankudy mosque, in Welikanda and Medirigiya, and in the forcible expulsion of Muslims from the Manner and Jaffna districts.[41]

War without an End

Meanwhile the savage war in Sri Lanka continues without an end. Nearly 60,000 precious lives Tamil, Muslim and Sinhala — have been lost. Over all the protracted 17 year conflict has resulted in a "reduced standard of living, reduced levels of foreign investment, fall in tourist numbers and expenditures, drastic slippages in the production of food and export crop in the north and the east, declining fish catches and the loss of two or three percentage points in GDP growth for a decade"[42].

What cannot be quantified, however, is the cost of the brutalizations of Sri Lankan Tamil society. As Rajani Thiranagama has written:

> A state of resignation envelops the community. The long shadow of the gun has not only been the source of power and glory, but also of fear and terror. In the menacing shadow play, forces complementing each other dance in each others momentum. The paralysing depression is not due to the violence and authority imposed from outside, but rather to the destructive violence emanating from within the womb of our society.[43]

Indian observers of the Sri Lankan scene are convinced that in the new millennium Sri Lanka desperately needs peace. Fresh initiatives should be undertaken to break the present deadlock. But any dialogue with the LTTE should be preceded by a Sinhala consensus so that the issues of war and peace are not subjected to the vagaries of competitive Sinhala politics. In the present context, consensus means the support of 94 per cent of the Sri Lankan population. Colombo should go farther than the present devolution proposals and new ideas like asymmetrical devolution should be explored. In the same way the merits of an international mediator should be seriously considered. It is certain that no government will extend support for the idea of a separate state of Tamil Eelam. What is more, except for the support of Sri Lankan Tamils abroad, the objective reality today is the international isolation of the LTTE. The mediator can use his good offices in finalizing an agreement; the mediator should also ensure that the agreement is implemented in right earnest.

The major impediment to peace continues to be the intransigence of Prabhakaran. His past record clearly indicates that he will use the interval of negotiations to build up his strength. According to Sri Lankan participants in earlier negotiations, the LTTE 'would drag on and on' and put forward new conditions for return to normaly. No serious talks about political settlement took place.[44] In order to pre-empt such a possibility, the LTTE should be persuaded to spell out the details of a 'viable alternative'. Sri Lanka can ill afford to embark upon another futile exercise. Let not posterity judge that another chance for enduring peace was missed by both sides. As Maya Angelou, the Black American poet, wrote few years ago: "History, despite its wrenching pain, cannot be unlived; but, if faced with courage need not be lived again."[45]

REFERENCES

1. M.A. Nuhman, "Murder", D.C. R.A. Goonetileke, Ed., *The Penguin, New Writing in Sri Lanka,* (New Delhi, 1992), pp. 239-40.
2. W. Howard Wriggins, *Ceylon: Dilemmas of a New Nation* (New Delhi, 1980), p. 232.
3. E. Valentine Daniel, *Charred Lullabies: Chapters in An Anthropology of Violence* (New Jersey, 1996), p. 3.
4. *Ibid.*, p. 207.
5. Quoted in Willaim McGovern, *Only Man is Vile—The Tragedy of Sri Lanka* (Delhi, 1992), p. XV.
6. A.C. Alles, *Insurgency, 1971 (*Colombo, 1976).
7. K.M. de Silva, *Managing Ethnic Tensions in Multi-Ethnic Societies, Sri Lanka, 1880-1985* (New York, N.Y. 1986), p. 241.
8. Jani de Silva, "Praxis, Language and Silences: The July 1987 Uprising of the JVP in Sri Lanka," Michael Roberts, Ed., *Collective Identities Revisited,* Vol. 2 (Colombo, 1998), pp. 163-98.
9. C.A. Chandraprema, Ruhuna: *A Study of the History, Society and Ideology of Southern Sri Lanka* (Nugegoda, 1989), p. 241.
10. Chandrika Kumaratunga, "Message to the Nation," *The Hindu* February 4, 1998.
11. Eric Hobsbawm, "The New Threat to History," *Pravada* (Colombo), March-April 1994, pp. 23-25.
12. S.J. Tambiah, *Sri Lanka. Ethnic Fratricide and Dismantling of Democracy* (Delhi, 1986), p.5.
13. *Ibid.*
14. *Ibid.*
15. Gananath Obeyesekere, "Ethnicity and Pluralism in Sri Lanka," *Thatched Patio* (Colombo), March-April 1994, pp. 30-35.
16. K.S. Singh, *The People of India: An Introduction* (Calcutta, 1992), p.82.
17. Bryan Pfaffenberger, "The Kataragama Pilgrimage: Hindu-Buddhist Interaction and Its Significance in Sri Lanka's Poly-ethnic Social System," *Journal of Asian Studies*, Vol. 38, February 1979, pp. 253-70.
18. Obeyesekere, n. 15.
19. R.A.L.H. Gunewardene, "The People of the Lion: Sinhala Identity

and Ideology in History and Historiography", Jonathan Spencer, Ed., *Sri Lanka: History and the Roots of Conflict* (London, 1990), p. 75.
20. Jonathan Spencer, "Popular Perceptions of Violence: A Provinicial View", John Manor, Ed., *Sri Lanka. In Change and Crisis* (London, 1984), p. 192.
21. Gananath Obeyesekere, "Sinhalese-Buddhist Identity in Ceylon," George de Vos and Lola Romanucci-Ross, Eds., *Ethnic Identities, Cultural Continuities and Change* (London, 1984), pp. 223-30.
22. Quoted in Jeyaratnam Wilson, *The Break-up of Sri Lanka: The Sinhalese—Tamil Conflict* (London, 1988), p. 44.
23. *Golden Threads* (Department of Government Printing, Colombo, 1984).
24. Sankaran Krishna, "Producing Sri Lanka: J.R. Jayewardene and Post Colonial Identity," *Alternatives* (New Delhi), Vol. 21, 1996, pp. 303-20.
25. *Ibid.*
26. *Golden Threads*, n. 23.
27. *Ibid.*
28. N 20, p. 192.
29. Paul Sieghart, *Sri Lanka: A Mounting Tragedy of Errors* (Report of the Mission to Sri Lanka in January 1984 on behalf of the International Commission of Jurists) (Colombo, 1984).
30. Valli Kanapathipillai, "The Survivor's Experience", Veena Das, Ed., *Mirrors of Violence: Riots and Survivors in South Asia* (Delhi, 1990), pp. 321-44.
31. R.R. Sivalingam, *The Anguish of a Tamil* (Mimeograph)
32. Radhika Coomaraswamy, *Ideology and the Constitution: Essays on Constitutional Jurisprudence* (Colombo, 1996).
33. *Ibid*, p. 27.
34. Regi Siriwardena, "Foreword", *Ibid.*
35. G.L. Peiris, "Towards Effective Devolution", *Sri Lanka: The Devolution Debate* (Colombo, 1996), pp. 9-10.
36. Neelan Thiruchelvam, "Ethnicity and Resource Allocation," Robert B. Goldmann and A. Jeyaratnam Wilson, eds., *From Independence to Statehood: Managing Ethnic Conflicts in Five African and Asian States* (London, 1984), p. 185.
37. Chris Smith, "South Asia's Enduring War," Robert I Rotberg, Ed., *Creating Peace in Sri Lanka:Civil War and Reconciliation* (Washington, 1999), p. 34.

38. E. Valentine Daniel, *Three Dispositions towards the Past: One Sinhala, Two Tamil* (S.S.C. Pamphlets 2) (Colombo, 1992), p. 20.
39. S. Thondaman, *Presidential Address: Ceylon Workers Congress: Twenty Seventh Session* (Nuwara Eliya, March 12-14, 1982).
40. Gopal Gandhi, *Refuge* (Delhi, 1989), p. 149.
41. Neelan Thiruchelvam, "Devolution and the Elusive Quest for Peace," Rotberg, n. 37, p. 194.
42. Smith, n. 37, p. 10.
43. Rajan Hoole and Others, *Broken Palmyrah* (Claremont, 1988), p. XI.
44. Bradman Weerakoon, "Government of Sri Lanka (President Premadasa) and LTTE Peace Negotiations," Kumar Rupesinghe, Ed., *Efforts, Failures and Lessons* (London, 1998), pp. 145-60.
45. Maya Angelou, "On the Pulse of the Morning" (Poem composed and read on the occasion of the installation of Bill Clinton as the President of the United States) *African-American Women in Literature* (Washington, n.d.), pp. 8-9.

CHAPTER 22

Maoist Terrorism in Nepal : Growth, Spread and Prospects

Parmanand

What has been the overall effect of Maoist terrorism in terms of loss of men and material in the South Asian mountain kingdom of Nepal? The Home Minister of Nepal, Govinda Raj Joshi, delivering a statement of public importance at the House of Representatives (lower and popular house of the kingdom's bicameral Parliament) on June 20, 2000, disclosed that a total of 1,366 persons, including 223 innocent citizens, 194 police personnel and 946 Maoists, had been killed and property worth Rs 180 million (160 Nepali rupees are equal to 100 Indian rupees) had been looted so far in the course of the 'Maoist People's War' since February 13, 1996.[1] This happening if anything has been unprecedented and unknown in Nepal's history.

The Home Minister added: "So far, some 217 persons have been abducted by terrorists. Of them, 21 have been killed, 113 have been released and 83 are still being held. Police have released 3,994 out of 5,565 people arrested in the course of investigations and action has been initiated against the remaining." He further said on that occasion: "As the first and foremost duty of the government is to guarantee security, extra security arrangements are under consideration."[2]

Home Minister Mr Joshi also stated : "The government has released 123 Maoist workers after the issue of talks came up in order to build an atmosphere for talks."[3]

When did it all begin? On February 22, 1996, the Home Ministry spokesman told the press: "More than 60 people have so far been arrested in connection with the terroristic activities that have taken place in Ropla, Rukum, Jajarkot, Sindhuli, Gorkha, Salyan and Sindhupalchok districts. One person has been killed and 21 persons have sustained injuries, 7 of them seriously. Those who are seriously injured are being treated at the Teaching Hospital in Kathmandu." The spokesman further said that the government was determined to put an end to such criminal and terrorist activities and provide the innocent people with a sense of security.[4]

According to local people, big mobs of armed and masked men raided houses shouting slogans and creating terror from their hideouts in forests.[5]

Indeed, February 13, 1996, is believed to be the date of the beginning of the activities by a political outfit called the Nepal Communist Party (Maoist) under the leadership of Dr Baburam Bhattarai and Comrade Prachand, alias Pushpa Kamal Dahal. On February 13, mobs of unidentified people raided police checkposts at Holari in Rolpa district, Athbiskot in Rukum district[6] and Sindhuligadhi in Sindhuli district and looted explosives and other weapons.[7] The same day, a mob of about 300 people attacked the office of Small Farmers Development Project at Chyangli in Gorkha district and set fire to documents and furniture.[8]

What was the immediate provocation for the beginning of the activities of the Nepal Communist Party (Maoist) ? On February 11, 1996, the then Prime Minister Sher Bahadur Deuba, was leaving for India for a week's state visit. There he signed the Mahakali Treaty along with his Indian counterpart. Much homework had been done for that in Kathmandu by P.V. Narasimha Rao, Prime Minister Deuba, who had tried his best to carry along leaders of various political parties on this issue. Earlier, on September 11, 1995, Sher Bahadur Deuba had been sworn-in as Nepal's Prime Minister in his capacity as the leader of the Nepali Congress. His government was a coalition of the Nepali Congress, the Rashtriya Prajatantra Party and the Nepal Sadbhavana Party. People like Baburam Bhattarai and Comrade Prachand had been opposing new treaties with India and demanding the abrogation of earlier ones. As such, the Deuba visit to India—which was obviously announced much in advance—provided them an opportunity to strike. It gave them an opportunity, *to inter alia*, criticize Indian 'expansionism' and 'hegemonism' et al.

Significantly, on February 4, 1996, Baburam Bhattarai, President of the United People's Front (UPF), led a 3-member delegation to the Simha Durban Secretariat (headquarters of His Majesty's Government) and handed over a memorandum to Prime Minister Sher Bahadur Deuba.[9] The memorandum contained 40 demands one of which was the immediate cancellation of the Tanakpur Treaty—which was signed in December 1991, between India and Nepal during the visit of the then Nepali Prime Minister, Girija Prasad Koirala, to India and pertained to bilateral cooperation on the front of water resources. Other demands included: (1) The special privileges of the King and the royal family should be abolished; and (2) A new republican Constitution prepared by the elected representatives of the people must be promulgated.[10]

The memorandum gave an ultimatum of February 17, 1996, for the fulfilment of the demands. It threatened to start a struggle in case the government failed to take any positive initiative.[11]

Relevantly, addressing a press conference in Kathmandu on February 5, 1996, Baburam Bhattarai described the Tanakpur Treaty as 'more traitorous' than the previous agreement. He said: "The Treaty has established India's monopoly over the water resources of Nepal."[12]

In a statement, Comrade Prachand, General Secretary of the Nepal Communist Party (Maoist), declared: "Betrayal of the nation's interests in the Tanakpur issue cannot be compensated only by providing some more water and electricity as charity by India. The new treaty has been signed by ignoring the question of unequal treaties and agreements between the two countries, including the 1950 Treaty, problems of trade and transit, the refugee problem, etc."[13]

According to Prachand, the treaty was "nothing but a new conspiracy designed to avert the crisis that is now facing the powers that be in both Nepal and India because of the struggle started by the Nepali people on the Tanakpur issue." He went to the extent of saying that there "is no doubt that the Indian expansionists are trying to capture the entire Mahakali river according to the neo-colonial concept of so-called equality."[14]

If the Nepali Prime Minister's India visit had provided the Maoists an opportunity to begin their terrorist activities, the Kingdom's domestic politics was no less appropriate. By February 1996, when the Maoists launched their violent and terroristic activities—the Movement for Restoration of Democracy (MRD) had become 6-year old. The Kingdom had by then witnessed two nation-wide elections—February 1991 and November 1994. People's participation, of course, increased, but political instability, corruption and administrative inefficiency were becoming more pronounced. Between February 1990 and February 1996, the Kingdom had already witnessed four Prime Ministers. The circumstances were honourable for Maoist terrorists.

What are the main aims and objectives of the Maoist terrorists in Nepal? The Maoists have been quite clear in their aims and objectives from the outset and we have seen some of their statements at the time when they launched their violent activities in February 1996. They have been rather consistent on that count.

In February 1999, Comrade Prachand, General Secretary of the Nepal Communist Party (Maoist), appealed to all leftist, progressive, patriotic and republican forces to extend cooperation to the people's war, which was aimed at the formation of a revolutionary government and boycott the so-called parliamentary elections."[15]

Baburam Bhattarai, a member of the NCP (Maoist) Politburo and President of the United People's Front Nepal, said: "The campaign to establish a republican state through the people's war has reached a new height. The reactionary state power has already been demolished in a number of base areas. Participation in the reactionary parliamentary elections in any manner is to strike a blow at the revolutionary movement."[16]

Comrade Prachand issued a statement in February 1998, throwing light on the objectives of the 'People's War'—a phrase that came to be associated with their group. The statement, *inter alia*, said: "The people's war was launched with the objective of liberating the people from feudal and imperialistic domination. Today, this war has opened up the only revolutionary alternative line. The progress made by the people's war during the past two years has put an end to confusion among the workers of revisionist forces. There is now a wave for joining the people's war."[17]

Sufficient light was thrown on the objectives of the people's war by a weekly functioning as a mouthpiece of the Nepal Communist Party (Maoist) in February 1998. It wrote: "The success of the people's war is sure because it is being carried forward through the cooperation and participation of the people. Reactionary forces must one day surrender before the people's forces. The people's war is aimed at truth, justice, equality, freedom and liberation." The paper also threw light on the fact that the people's war was giving rise to a new culture and wrote: "It is replacing the decadent capitalist art and culture by a people's art, literature and culture." It also alluded to the ethnic dimension and wrote: "In the name of community, Brahminist forces of top-ranking castes are subjecting indigenous and other communities, as well as women, to severe exploitation and oppression. The people's war is aimed against such trends. It has shown how women can be liberated from household drudgery and how ethnic communities can attain full liberation."[18]

One objective of the people's war is also stated to be to find an alternative to the 'reactionary state power.' The paper wrote: "The Maoist people's war has been able to put forward a new alternative to the reactionary state power. This alternative is based on the Marxist-Leninist-Maoist philosophy and ideology, which will completely uproot exploitation and ensure equal rights to the people."[19]

Clearly, on the ideological plane, the NCP (Maoist) has adopted a new path altogether for itself. In a country, where monarchy—in whatever form—has been the oldest institution and which to a very great extent, had been responsible for the unification of the kingdom in 1769, the slogan of republicanism would appear to be as novel as strange. But the Maoists have been consistent on that count.

A significant question that arises at this stage is: how correct it would be to call the NCP (Maoist) a terrorist organization? Terrorism has been defined as "the use or threatened use of violence on a systematic basis to achieve political objectives." True, there is no agreed comprehensive definition as to its character, motive or mode of operation, most analysts agree that "the element of fear-inducement both horizontally and vertically is crucial." Besides, ruthlessness, a disregard for established humanitarian values and an unquenchable thirst for publicity are characteristic traits.[20] On the other hand, *The Concise Oxford Dictionary*: 10th edition (1999) defines terrorist as "a person who uses violence and intimidation in the pursuit of political aims." (p. 1480)

Graham Evans and Jeffrey Newnham (1998: 530, op.cit.) mention 5 methods used by terrorists for achieving their objectives: (1) hijacking, (2) hostage-taking, (3) bombings, (4) indiscriminate shooting and (5) assassinations and mass murders. Fred Halliday is of the view that the "range of activities which the term covers has been wide, but four main forms of action tend to be included: assassination, bombings, seizures of individuals as hostages, and, more recently, the hijacking of planes."[21]

Both on the basis of the definitions mentioned above and the methods used by terrorists world over as enumerated by Evans and Newnham and Halliday, it would not be difficult to call the NCP (Maoist) a terrorist organization. Like several similar outfits in the world, they do not seem to have any objection to being called terrorists. The NCP (Maoist) appear to be using all the methods enumerated by Evans and Newnham and Halliday in varying ways and degrees.

The Maoists in Nepal have thus far functioned as an underground organization. Explaining it in 1996, Baburam Bhattarai stated: "Those of us who have gone underground have been forced to do so. We had wanted to carry forward our movement in a constitutional manner and openly. But this reactionary regime violated its own laws and unleashed a reign of terror on the leaders and workers of the UPF by labelling them as Maoists."[22] Showing his desire to come into the open, Baburam Bhattarai said: "If the reactionary forces have the courage to face us openly, we too are ready to come out in the open. We do not want to remain underground."[23] Socio-political circumstances, though, have forced the Maoists to remain underground thus far.

Gianfranco Pasquino has, on the basis of the goals of various terrorist organizations, enumerated three types of terrorism: repressive, revolutionary and secessionist.[24] Various writings, statements and actions of the NCP (Maoist) leaders, thus far would suggest that their terrorism is more repressive and revolutionary. It has not shown any predilection for secessionism thus far, for its leaders think they would be able to change the nature and character of the whole state structure. Not less significantly, the influence of NCP (Maoist) is apparently increasing throughout the kingdom and as such, they are better placed than their counterparts in various parts of the world, whose influence—no matter howsoever, deep and serious—is limited to several areas only. For instance the influence of the Liberation Tigers of Tamil Eelam (LTTE) and the Hizbul Mujahideen (HM) is limited in a particular part of the country concerned and their terrorism pertains more to secessionism.

How much has the influence of the NCP (Maoist) spread in Nepal over the years ? According to a report: "The government has taken 31 districts as Maoist-affected districts. Seventeen of them are considered to be 'affected', while 14 are 'highly affected'.[25] In all, Nepal has 75 districts. So far, the Maoists have been able to increase their influence tremendously in the districts of western Nepal, Rukum, Rolpa, Jajarkot, Gorkha, Parbat, Dolkha, Pyathun, Dang, Ramechap and Syangja are some of the most prominently influenced districts in western Nepal. News about some activities of the NCP (Maoist) has also started surfacing from various districts of the Terai (plains), which was not even thought of by many earlier.

Why did Maoist terrorism succeed in western Nepal in the beginning? David Carlton has very rightly pointed out that "one person's terrorist is another person's freedom fighter."[26] Maoist terrorism grew when extremely uneven economic development in Nepal became more visible and pronounced in the post-multiparty democracy era. The growing political consciousness of the people of western Nepal was utilized by the Maoists in that area. The United People's Front—which subsequently became a significant component of the NCP (Maoist) and which eventually dissolved itself[27] in order to "consolidate and integrate the freedom movements of indigenous and ethnic communities as well as regional groups, with that of the new people's movement"—had a strong mass base in that part of the Kingdom. The Front had, indeed, won 9 seats in the Pratinidhi Sabha in the May 1991 elections, polling 4.83 per cent of votes. The increased and increasing transparency in the media also made the western Nepalis more well aware of their socio-economic backwardness. Monarchies of various kinds in this area in the pre-1769 phase of Nepali history had also subjected its people to all kinds of exploitation. All this contributed to the overall growth of 'terrorists' or 'freedom fighters' in this area.

Surprisingly, though, the activities and influence of the Maoists could also be said to be spreading in the Terai (the plains) to some extent.

Amiya Kumar Yadav, President of the Siraha (in the Terai) District Nepali Congress Committee and a member of the Rashtriya Sabha (upper house of Parliament) told this to the present author in a personal interview. Maybe it is becoming fashionable politically, or maybe political consciousness is taking a new shape there, too.

As for the methods used by the Maoist terrorists in Nepal, we have already seen above that they are resorting to the methods enumerated by Evans and Newnham (1998) and Halliday (1993). It would, though, be in order to enumerate the following methods (the observation is based on the scanning of various literature and interactions with various people from Nepal) used by the Maoist terrorists in the mountain kingdom: confiscating allegedly forged loan documents, asking people not to pay loans, looting banks, looting individual's property, cultivating crops in various plots of lands snatched from people, collecting salaries from teachers, kidnapping people belonging to various political parties, killing leaders and workers of various political parties (largest number of them belonging to the ruling Nepali Congress), killing policemen, attacking police posts and looting arms therefrom, exploding bombs at the residences or offices of high officials, etc.

Those indulging in the people's war in Nepal, then, have been resorting to many more methods than generally enumerated in literature on terrorism. This may be due to exigencies of the new circumstances.

How seriously have the Maoists taken military training Probably, the Maoists had thought of a long-drawn war with the state and as such, they seem to have prepared themselves well from the outset. As early as January 1997, a newspaper reported: "According to Maoist sources, special training is being given to Maoist workers in the forests of some remote districts."[28] Another newspaper reported in July 1997: "According to a Police Officer, Maoist activists who were taking part in the people's war were being trained by the Muslims of Kashmir and ex-servicemen of the Indian Army. This, he said, was revealed by a Maoist activist who fled from Rukum."[29]

On the other hand, in an interview in August 1997, Inspector-General of Police Dhruba Bahadur Pradhan said: "The Maoist leaders who are engaged in a people's war with the objective of establishing a people's republic in Nepal have established very close relations with extremist organizations of India, such as the People's War Group (Communist Party of India, Marxist-Leninist) of Andhra Pradesh, the Maoist Communist Centre of Bihar and the United Liberation Front of Assam."[30]

As late as July 2000, Nepali Prime Minister Girija Prasad Koirala, before the beginning of his week-long state visit to India, said in an interview about the Maoists: "They get their money and training in India because of an open border, we cannot control them."[31]

The NCP (Maoist) formed its Central Military Commission (CMC) with the objective of operating the people's war. A press statement issued by the Party in the name of Comrade Prachand, CMC chief, in this connection said: "For a proletarian state power, an army is needed in order that ultimately classes, the state, the army and war may be abolished once for all, according to the scientific principles of dialectical and historical materialism. In Nepal, the people's war has been started with the aim of destroying the exploitative state power and the establishment of a people's republic. For this, an army is necessary under the leadership of the NCP (Maoist). This will be a people's army. Hundreds of squads of such a people's army are operating in Nepal today and fulfilling their historic responsibilities."[32]

How have the various mainstream Nepali political parties been viewing the Maoists' activities? Indeed, no mainstream political party with a negligible exception has ever expressed any support or sympathy for the *modus operandi* or the cause of the Maoists. Prime Minister Girija Prasad Koirala has been one of the most prominent targets of criticisms of the Maoists—whether as the Prime Minister of the country or as the President of the Nepali Congress. And he seems to be adopting the toughest position *vis-a-vis* them. He has gone to the extent of suggesting the use of the army to break the backbone of the Maoists. In his capacity as the President of the Nepali Congress Party, Koirala—described by the Maoists as their Enemy Number One—undertook a 5-day tour of the Maoist-affected areas of the mid-western and far western regions in February 2000. Koirala—oblivious of his personal safety and security—has been the only democratic leader to have achieved this distinction. At that time, Koirala was not the Kingdom's premier. Various sections of Nepali society and the media praised his endeavour.[33]

During his tour, he visited Liwang of Rolpa, Khalanga of Salyan, Khandchakra of Salyan, Khandchakra of Kalikot, Jumla, Dhangadhi and other places and addressed mass meetings, met leaders of various political parties and government employees in the course of which he expressed his commitment to resolve the Maoist problem and fulfil his pledge guaranteeing peace and security to the people. Most importantly, he called on the Maoists to give up violence.[34]

UML leader Bharat Mohan Adhikari said in September 1999, in clear and cogent words: "We are strongly opposed to the Maoists."[35] Significantly, the UML is the main opposition party in the Nepali Parliament.

As early as August 1997, the Rashtriya Prajatantra Party (RPP) leader and then Prime Minister, Lokendra Bahadur Chand, had described Maoists as terrorists. He said: "How else should we describe those who spread terror among the people and harm their life and property? It is in the light of such activities of the Maoists that the Terrorist and Subversive Activities (Control and Punishment) Bill is being enacted."[36] Justifying such a measure, Prime Minister Shri Chand stated: "Such a step is necessary because the judiciary orders the acquittal of Maoists who are arrested by the police. We need a law which empowers the government to keep Maoists in detention for a few days more on the orders of the judiciary itself."[37] Significantly, the Maoists have killed several leaders and workers of the Nepali Congress and the Rashtriya Prajatantra Party ever since their movement was launched.

It is only the Communist Party of Nepal (Marxist-Leninist (ML)), among the mainstream political parties—having no seat in the lower house, but having 3 seats in the upper house of parliament and having secured 6.42 per cent of votes in the last election to entitle it the status of a national party—that has showed some sympathy for the Maoists. Probably with a view, *inter alia*, to soliciting the Maoist support in the May 1999 election, ML General Secretary Bam Dev Gautam said in May 1999: "The Maoists of Nepal have undergone much sacrifice. Accordingly, I am trying to join hands with them in the task of national reconstruction. After it forms the government, the ML will hold negotiations with the Maoists and accept their legitimate demands."[38] The ML has not supported the Maoists publicity thereafter.

Even the above statement of Bam Dev Gautam would appear to be palpably and completely incongruous in the light of his statement made on May 15, 1997. In his capacity as the Deputy Prime Minister and Home Minister, Gautam had then said: "The new government has demonstrated its liberal policy by trying to solve the Maoist problem through political means. However, the Maoists have regarded this policy of the government as its weakness and continued their terrorist activities in different parts of the country. In this situation, the government will not lag behind in taking appropriate steps for maintaining peace and security....Rather, the Maoists are mercilessly killing people and terrorizing them in the remote and inaccessible areas of the country."[39]

Clearly, the statement of May 1999, thus, showed Bam Dev Gautam's political compulsion, helpless and isolation. No wonder, the ML failed to get a single seat in the May 1999 general elections.

How have the foreign governments and agencies viewed the Maoists' activities over the years? The UK and the USA have made their anger over their activities quite obvious. During his visit to Kathmandu in April 2000, British Foreign Secretary Robin Cook said in Kathmandu on April 21,: "Human Rights violations by the Maoists are real and must be condemned as they are the root of the problem. I have also discussed with the Minister the impulse of making sure that the people understood that the government is on their side, it is the Maoists who are their enemy."[40]

According to a report in February 2000, the US Embassy in Kathmandu had received information to the effect that the Maoists would intensify their activities from February 12 to 19 and that the USA had asked its citizens to remain on the alert.[41]

As early as April 1996, the US Peace Corp volunteers were recalled from Rolpa, Jajarkot and Pyuthan districts one or two weeks before the expiry of their term, while two volunteers were shifted from Jajarkot to Lamjung.[42]

A report published by the Amnesty International, London, on March 10, 1997 said: "In the course the people's war, both the Maoists and the police have committed a growing number of human rights abuses. The Maoists have killed 14 persons in Rolpa, Rukum and Sindhupalchok districts."[43] In its report in August 2000, the Amnesty International has pointed out that the Maoists have been indulging in kidnapping children below the age of 14 years to train as terrorists and pointed out that 30 such children have been kidnapped recently.[44]

His Majesty's Government, on November 30, 1999, formed a 6-member high-level committee under the convenership of ex-Prime Minister Sher Bahadur Deuba to hold discussions with the main opposition parties, other political parties and distinguished persons "on the situation ensuing from the terrorist activities being carried out for the past few years in the name of the Maoist people's war" and submit suggestions "as to how the situation can be contained." Former Speaker Ram Chandra Poudel, Nepali Congress General Secretary Sushil Koirala, Local Development Minister for Works and Transport Khum Bahadur Khadka and Home Minister Purna Bahadur Khadka were appointed members of the Committee.[45]

The Deuba Committee—appointed during the premiership of Krishna Prasad Bhattarai—started to hear the views of various mainstream political parties on the Maoist-created problems and their proposed solution immediately after its formation. On March 22, 2000, Krishna Prasad Bhattarai was replaced by Girija Prasad Koirala as the kingdom's premier and thanks to the intra-party politics of the ruling Nepali Congress, it appeared that the Deuba Committee would have no role to play. But rather surprisingly, Prime Minister Koirala asked the Deuba Committee to continue and complete its task.

The game of upstaging each other over the Maoist terrorism apparently continues in the ruling Nepali Congress, however. The Maoists had even sent the name of their representative who would talk to the Deuba Committee on their behalf. But under one pretext or the other, the talks have never been held. The game of blaming each other on the part of Prime Minister Girija Prasad Koirala and former Prime Minister Sher Bahadur Deuba—at times even publicly—continues unabated in one form or the other.

In the meanwhile, the suggestion of Prime Minister Koirala to seek the assistance of the Royal Nepalese Army to suppress the Maoists was subjected to severe and trenchant criticism both in the public and the press. The army also seems its reservations over the issue.

Amidst all this, the Maoists appear to be increasing their influence in various parts of Nepal. Apparently, administration of various districts in western Nepal has been seized by them. At many places government employees do not go to their offices.

Significantly, they have successfully prevented various elections in the areas of their influence from time to time. They have, on the other hand, held elections at several places for various tiers in the so-called Maoist state. The Maoists have, by and large, proved that they command some support among *hoi polloi* of western Nepal.

Not less significantly, demoralization is setting in the police force of the kingdom. Various policemen transferred to the Maoist-dominated areas have refused to join their duty even though disciplinary action has been taken against them. Several reports suggesting that the policemen with political connections are able to avoid postings in the Maoist-dominated areas, whereas those without connections are forced to go there risking their lives.

All this probably suggests that the problem has really assumed serious and sinister proportions and warrants immediate solution. No government can afford to politicize the issue without denting its credibility. A national consensus arrived at by various mainstream political parties, meaningful talks with the Maoist terrorists and quick economic development in the area generating people's confidence in the national government are things which could be avoided only at the peril of the legitimacy and credibility of the state apparatus and structure.

The problem has become complex and difficult and complacency of the state, if anything, has contributed to this complexity and difficulty. Any solution now would involve serious efforts by all concerned.

REFERENCES

David Carlton, 1996, "Terrorism", in Iain McLean, ed., *The Concise Oxford Dictionary of Politics*, Oxford: Oxford University Press, pp. 492-93.

Fred Halliday 1993, "Terrorism", in Joel Krieger, ed., *The Oxford Companion to Politics of the World*, London : Oxford University Press, pp. 902-04.

Graham Evans and Jeffrey Newnham, 1998, *The Penguin Dictionary of International Relations*, London: Penguin, pp. 530-31.

Parmanand, 2000, "Nepal Today-I: Problems Ahead For Koirala", *The Statesman*, New Delhi, April 3, 6.

Gianfranco Pasquino, 1989, "Terrorism", in Adam Kuper and Jessica Kuper, *eds., The Social Science Encyclopedia*, London: Routledge, pp. 851-52.

FOOTNOTES

1. See *Kantipur,* Kathmandu, June 21, 2000.
2. See *The Rising Nepal*, Kathmandu, June 21, 2000.
3. See *Kantipur*, June 21, 2000.
4. See *Rising Nepal*, February 23, 1996.
5. See *Gorkhapatra*, February 22, 1996.
6. *Ibid. February 15, 1996.*
7. *See Nepali Patra,* Kathmandu, February 16, 1996.
8. The *Rising Nepal*, February 15, 1996.
   See *Rising Nepal*, February 23, 1996.
9. See *Gorkhapatra*, February 22, 1996.
10. See *Nepal Press Digest*, Kathmandu, Vol. 40, No. 7, February 12, 1996, 52.
11. See *Janadesh* weekly, Kathmandu, February 6, 1996.
12. *Gorkhapatra*, February 6, 1996.
13. See *Janadesh*, February 6, 1996.
14. *Ibid.*
15. See *Kantipur*, February 12, 1999.
16. *Ibid.*
17. See *Janadharana* weekly, Kathmandu, February 12, 1998.
18. See *Janadesh*, February 10, 1998.
19. *Ibid.*
20. See Graham Evans and Jeffrey Newnham, 1998, *The Penguin Dictionary of International Relations*, London: Penguin, 530.
21. See Fred Halliday, 1993, "Terrorism", in Joel Krieger, ed., *The Oxford Companion to Politics of the World*, London: Oxford University Press, 902.
22. See *Janadesh*, July 16, 1996.
23. *Ibid.*
24. See Gianfranco Pasquino, 1989, "Terrorism" in Adam Kuper and Jessica Kuper, eds., *The Social Science Encyclopedia*, London: Routledge, 852.
25. See *Kantipur*, January 10, 2000.

26. See David Carlton, 1996, "Terrorism", in Iain Mclean, ed., *The Concise Oxford Dictionary of Politics*, Oxford: Oxford University Press, 492.
27. See *The Kathmandu Post*, February 15, 2000.
28. See *Nepali Patra,* January 24, 1997.
29. See *Kantipur*, July 21, 1997.
30. See *Jana Astha* weekly, Kathmandu, August 20, 1997.
31. See "Let Us Look At the Future": Nepal Prime Minister Girija Prasad Koirala, 2000, *The Asian Age,* New Delhi.
32. See *Nepali Patra,* February 13, 1998.
33. See Parmanand, 2000, "Nepal Today-I: Problems Ahead for Koirala" *The Statesman*, New Delhi, April 3, 6.
34. *Ibid.*
35. See *Kantipur*, September 18, 1999.
36. See *Kantipur*, August 15, 1997.
37. *Ibid.*
38. See *Gorkhapatra*, May 5, 1999.
39. *Ibid.*, May 16, 1997.
40. See *The Kathmandu Post,* April 22, 2000.
41. See *Kantipur,* February 13, 2000.
42. See *Gorkhapatra*, April 27, 1996.
43. See *Ibid.*, March 14, 1997.
44. *BBC* Hindi Service, August 9, 2000, 7.30 p.m.
45. See *The Rising Nepal*, December 1, 1999.

CHAPTER 23

Narco-Terrorism The Case of the Golden Cresecent

Kshitij Prabha

Narco-terrorism refers to nexus between terrorism and drug trafficking. It is a phenomenon in which terrorists and drug traffickers work together to achieve their respective goals. They are two partners in crime who make quick bucks at the cost of human suffering. While terrorists aim to capture political power, the drug barons are concerned in economy of drugs. Narco-terrorism, however, is concerned with both politics and economy of drugs. Thus, the relationship between terrorism and narcotic drugs is not limited to monetary transaction but is also concerned to its political implications.

The word narco-terrorism was used for the first time in the US when drug smugglers in Bolivia, Colombia, Peru, Nicaragua and other central American countries organized the illegal trade as profession and ran an almost parallel government. These countries produce cocaine and cannabis in huge quantity. As a matter of fact their economy is dependent on cultivation and production of cocaine and cannabis. The US besides being neighbour is the biggest market for these drugs. The growing population of drug addicts compelled the US government to respond to the situation. Its realization, however, came much later i.e., when President Reagan decided to fight against communist expansion in American countries during 1980s. The word narco-terrorism was used for the first time during this period in international politics.

Sponsoring terrorism is an expensive affair and money for killing, kidnapping and sabotage does not come through proper channels. It comes through illegal and unofficial channels. The market value of narcotic drugs is much higher than any consumer products in the world. It fetches voluminous amount of money and that too in hard cash. For instance, one kilogram of heroin from Golden Crescent that costs approximately one lakh in South Asia fetches nearly a crore in the US market. The figure varies from place to place, which further depends on law and order situation. The price for heroin originating from Golden Crescent ranges from 30 lakhs to 1 crore a kg. It is worth noting here that Pakistani heroin and the Colombian Marijuana are the most demanded narcotic drugs in the US and the European countries. The volume of money these drugs generate in the West is mind boggling. Che Guevera had realized the importance of narcotic drugs way back in 1960s. He rightly said that there could be no better source for funding terrorism than drug trafficking.[1] Terrorists have established links with drug traffickers, smugglers and underworld dons to meet the expenses involved in operation terrorism. This diabolic alliance between terrorists and drug traffickers is popularly known as nacro-terrorism.

Narcotic Drug Trafficking and Terrorism

The hypothesis that drug trafficking funds terrorist activities needs logical explanation and that logic is based on certain facts and figures. These are:

- Terrorism is the most serious threat to socio-economic and political system of India.
- Pak-sponsored terrorism in India is considerably funded by illicit drug trade run by the Pakistani Syndicates in the South West Asia.
- India is sandwiched between the two major narcotic drug-producing regions of the world—the Golden Crescent and the Golden Triangle.
- India is the only country to produce opium for medicinal purpose in the world. Indian farmers take advantage of the legal position. Several cases of embezzlement have been reported by law enforcement agencies in India. The licensed farmers in UP, Madhya Pradesh and Rajasthan get involved in illicit trade as well because it fetches more money compared to government price.
- The drug proceeds are laundered through numerous legal and illegal financial institutions and petty business enterprises.
- Politics and economy cannot be divorced from each other. There exist a symbiotic relation between the two.

- The economy and polity of narcotic producing countries are dependent on the illegal drug trade.
- Criminal elements have already ventured into the realm of political system especially in developing and underdeveloped countries.
- Narcotic drug trafficking is the most lucrative trade in the underworld operation.
- Terrorism needs huge sum of money to carry its operation. Since it is difficult to acquire that sum from official and legal sources, terrorists approach drug syndicates and underworld dons for co-operation.
- The criminal dons and drug smugglers too find the proposal attractive because it gives them an opportunity to collaborate with aspirants of political power (terrorists) and thereby access to politics in due course of time. The criminalisation of politics is the result of the same.
- The Pakistani drug syndicates run a parallel economy in connivance with the political establishment to foment trouble in India.

Narcotic drugs have been an important source of income for tribal population at the Pak-Afghan border since time immemorial. It emerged as socio-economic and political problem only during the recent past. Cultivation of poppy and cannabis was encouraged during the military dictatorship of Zia-ul-Huq to fund terrorist activities in India. Until 1978, opium production was consumed locally. It did not emerge as a lucrative trade. 'General Zias' support for cultivation of narcotic drugs gave new dimension to international drug trafficking and terrorism in India. Heroin addiction spread like epidemic in Pakistan during his martial administration. The regime, which was popular for its iron hand did not control free distribution of heroin and *hashish* in universities and colleges in Peshawar, Karachi, Lahore and Rawalpindi where these drugs were cheaply available for Rs. 15 to 60 per packet depending on purity.[2] During this time drug traffickers operated freely and became billionaires within a short span of time and organized themselves as syndicates on the same line as in Latin America. They established contacts in the law enforcement agencies, funded political parties, used economic platforms and bribed officers to maintain production and supply of narcotic drugs in the international market.

The Case of Golden Crescent

Poppy is known as the golden plant, and the countries that grow these plants are known as Golden Triangle and Golden Crescent. As gold is the costliest of all the widely used metals, poppy is the costliest of all the accessible plants in the world. The difference between the two lies in the fact that while the former is licit the latter is illicit. The 'illegal tag' is the main reason for the exorbitant market value of narcotic drugs and its demand among smugglers and underworld operators.

The South West Asia popularly known as Golden Crescent comprising Afghanistan, Pakistan, India, Bangladesh and Sri Lanka is the largest producer of illicit opium in the world. It is relevant to note that India is the only licit producer of opium in this region. Nepal, Bangladesh, Maldives and Sri Lanka do not grow opium, but small quantity of cannabis is grown in Nepal and Sri Lanka, which is locally consumed. These countries are used for trans-shipment of heroin from Afghanistan and Pakistan. The ports of Maldives and Sri Lanka and Bangladesh are frequently used for shipment of narcotic drugs. Afghanistan and NWFP of Pakistan is the biggest producer of opium in the world. According to a UN estimate, Afghanistan alone produces 4,600 of the 6000 metric tons of the world's total illicit production.[3]

In the context of Pakistan, it needs to be emphasised that local tribal norms and regulations govern tribal areas at the Pak-Afghan border i.e. NWFP. The Government of Pakistan cannot intervene in the local economy, which is heavily dependent on production of narcotic drugs and conventional small weapons. Officially, Pakistan produces 100 to 200 metric tons of opium (1996 estimate of DEA, US Dept. of Justice).[4] In practice Afghanistan and Pakistan work together in so far as business of narcotic drugs is concerned. Afghan farmers cultivate poppy and Pakistan produces the opium and heroin. It would be wrong to blacklist Afghanistan alone for the illicit narcotic drug trafficking. Pakistani law enforcement agencies are hand in glove and need to take collective responsibility for the growth of drug mafia in this region.

The Pakistan government, the ISI and the army work together in 'operation terrorism'. Pakistan has been sponsoring terrorism right from 1947 to foment trouble in India. All this costs money. A rough estimate could be something between 40 to 50 crores a month. The North East Times reports that ULFA spends nearly 4 to 6 crores a month.[5]

Since all the monetary transaction is done in cash, there is no evidence to support this argument. However, on the basis of information gathered from militants and drug traffickers it could be roughly estimated that they spend 20 to 30 crores on payment to militants alone. During personal interaction I was informed that besides weapons and logistics, the ISI pays Rs. 15 to 20 lakhs to militant leaders per month, 3 to 5 lakhs to Afghan Mujaheeds on contract basis and 15 to 20 thousands to new recruits from both sides of Kashmir. The economy of Pakistan does not allow such involvement. Apparently, the source of funding lies beyond the official exchequer, and that is the parallel drug economy.

The only easy source for generating the required volume of money is heroin produced at the Pak-Afghan borders. The US Drug Enforcement Administration (DEA) official reported to the Congress that they face tough challenges because illicit drug business is intimately linked with cross-border terrorism and arms trade.[6] Iqramul Haq, a Pakistani scholar gives a candid account of drug trade in different phases-from cultivation to market in the US.

- An acre of poppy flowers produce approximately 7 kilogram of raw opium, which the farmer sells for around Rs. 12,000 to 15,000.
- The second phase is processing of opium. The raw opium is now refined into heroin in a local factory. The heroin now sells Rs. 50,000 to 70,000 per kilogram.
- In the third phase, heroin is smuggled out of the country by couriers. In the dealer network its value goes to approximately Rs. 13,50,000.
- Finally, heroin is cut and packed into small bags for sale on the streets in the US and the European market. This now fetches Rs. 47,00,000.[7]

This again depends on the purity of heroin. The number one quality with 80 per cent purity fetches nearly one crore in the US depending on the price index of the respective cities. For instance, number four quality i.e. heroin from Pakistani wards can be cut into four or five times, mixed with inferior quality powder. It makes one kilogram extra for supply without further cost.[8]

The drug proceeds are now distributed among syndicates, the ISI, law enforcement agencies and political leaders. This money is now utilised for individual as well as collective goals. Sponsoring terrorism in India, being the collective and national agenda of Pakistan, obviously gets the lions share in the entire business deal.

The porous Indo-Pak border is vulnerable to transaction of narcotic drugs and weapons. The common boundary, common people and common economic needs, inspire Pakistan government and the ISI to use India as the main transit route for narcotic drugs. These drugs along with the consignment of weapons are sent across the border from Rajasthan, Punjab, and Jammu and Kashmir; and then to Mumbai and other port cities for trans-shipment to the west. Notwithstanding the fact that the narcotics enter India from the above mentioned bordering states of India, the main centre for business transaction is Mumbai where underworld criminals operating from Dubai controls the drug trade. For instance, Iqbal Mirchi who operates from Dubai also has units in Mumbai. Similar is the case of Salim Kurla, who was arrested by CBI at Secunderabad on 22nd January 1995, in connection with the Bombay Blast case. He was close associate of Dawood Ibrahim's brother Noora. Kurla was not merely involved in drug trafficking, but also funded for training youths in Pakistan for the serial bombing that shook Mumbai in 1993. The Pak-Afghan-Mujahideen, drug traffickers and smugglers in this region operate in concert.[9]

Conclusions

Before concluding the discussion on narco-terrorism, it is worth mentioning that until 1978 opium was consumed locally. It was not a money generating trade. Its financial viability was first discovered during military regime of General Zia-ul-Haq. He encouraged cultivation of poppy to generate fund for sponsoring terrorism in India. During his tenure, drug traffickers operated freely, organised themselves as drug syndicate and became billionaires within a short span of time. They could manage to achieve their target in coalition with political leaders and bureaucracy. General Zia's involvement in drug trafficking was revealed when the Norwegian police arrested Reza Qureshi, a Pakistani drug trafficker at Oslo's Fornebu Airport in 1984. During interrogation he revealed that General Zia was the main beneficiary of illegal drug trade. The Norwegian police disclosed three names of Pakistani nationals—Tahir Butt, Munawar Hussain and Hamid Hussain patronised by General Zia.[10] Under mounting pressure from Norwegian government these three were reluctantly arrested by the Pakistan authority one of the culprits, Hamid Hussain, the Vice-President of government owned Habib Bank, was very close to General Zia's family. He managed Zia's financial matters and used banking channels to launder drug proceeds.

Hazi Iqbal Mirza was another important Pakistani drug trafficker who had political connection. A Lahore based landlord and owner of innumerable business enterprises ran a powerful drug syndicate and exercised control over Narcotics Control Board and Police of Pakistan. He along with his partners, Sohail Butt (cousin-in-law of Nawaz Sharif) and Shaukat Ali Bhatti continued to maintain contacts with the Pakistani Premier. Both Beg and Bhatti were elected members of the Punjab Legislative Assembly on the tickets of Islamic Jahmuri Ittehad (IJl), a political party led by Hamid Gul (ex chief of ISI). The former Prime Minister, Nawaz Sharif also maintained close contact with them and helped Beg acquire denationalised industrial unit including the Muslim Commercial Bank in which Sharif is a *Benami* partner.

There is no dearth of evidence in support of Pak-sponsored narco-terrorism in India. A long list is not essential to prove this hypothesis. It is opium that feeds the cross-border terrorism in India. The nexus between the two is based on mutual benefits, which suits Pakistan's agenda in India. The ISI and other government agencies in Pakistan exploit the situation to settle standing disputes between India and Pakistan.

FOOTNOTES

1. Che Guevera, *Guerilla Warfare*, Middlesex: Penguin Books, 1961, pp.87-97
2. S K Ghose, *Traffic in Narcotic Drugs and Addiction*, New Delhi: Ashish Publishing House, 1987.
3. The UN Information Service, Press Release *AFG/107/SOC/NAR/811.* Opium Production in Afghanistan in 1999, 10th September 1999, Vienna.
4. US Dept. of Justice, National Narcotics Intelligence Consumers Committee Report, DEA, 1996.
5. *North East Times*, Jorhat, 23rd October, 1998, p. 4.
6. lqramul Haq, *Pakistan: From Hash to Heroin,* Lahore: Anoor Publishers, 1991, p.17.
7. *Ibid.* p. 14.

8 Fenton Brester, *The Trial of Triads*, London: Weidenfield and Nicolson, 1980, p. 14.

9. Nemisharan Mittal, *World Famous Drug Mafia*, New Delhi: Family Books Pvt. Ltd., 1990, p 23.

10. Iqramul Haq, *op. cit,* p. 348.

Appendix: P.N. Haksar's Vision

I have been asked to sum up the wide-ranging discussions which have taken place in this seminar spread over two days. This can be done easily enough by stating that there was an overwhelming consensus in favour of promoting regional cooperation with the countries in South Asia and, in that context, an all round improvement of relations between India and Pakistan was necessary and desirable. Some participants viewed the actual possibilities of cooperation in diverse fields in rather optimistic terms. Others had serious reservations about cooperation in matters of trade, commerce and economic development. On the crucial question of regional cooperation concerning the security of South Asian countries, there were differing perceptions of the nature of threat and the improbability of all the countries in the region sharing a common threat perception. And the difficulty was certainly the greatest when one came to consider the whole gamut of history of Indo-Pakistan relations.

Though the discussions ranged widely, and many interesting points were made, we did not quite succeed in evolving an appropriate framework of policy. I may be mistaken, but I feel that we have still a long way to go in dealing with the political, social, economic and cultural realities of our neighbouring countries especially of Pakistan. Unless we do this, our policy prescriptions would be unrealistic and we shall slide into the error of dealing with the domain of 'ought' in a manner totally unrelated to the domain of 'is' and also fail to see the processes of historical evolution.

Both within this seminar and even more outside the seminar the discussions centring around the case for regional cooperation tend to fall into the error of viewing regional cooperation as a 'thing in itself'. It is, for instance, argued that our country ought to concentrate on promoting regional cooperation and not get involved in 'globalism'. To my

This article was written by Mr. P.N. Haksar in 1984. However, the basic postulates of this article are still relevant.

mind, this juxtaposition of 'regionalism' versus 'globalism' is as false as it is spurious. I have often wondered whether the protagonists of this point of view are just naive or ignorant or led by some political motivations.

Take up any issue which might be described as regional, e.g., 'security', one instantly comes across Pakistan. We then have to take into account Pakistan's own reactions to the situation in Afghanistan which, in turn, brings us to consider the involvement of the Soviet Union in Afghanistan and that of the United States with the so-called freedom fighters from Afghanistan operating from the territory of Pakistan and Pakistan's own involvement with the United States' perception of its security interest not merely in Afghanistan, but also in the Gulf area and the Middle East. It is equally well-known that NATO, which was conceived to be a military alliance system involving western Europe, United States and Canada has, from time to time, attempted to enlarge its domain of concern beyond the frontiers of Europe. In recent years, there is a palpable American pressure on their NATO partners to involve in the Third World countries. There is a similar pressure exerted on Japan to broaden its security concerns to include Asia and the Pacific basin.

Travelling beyond the security concerns to matters concerning economic sphere, it is contended that the South Asian region can insulate itself from the effects of economic vicissitudes of Europe and America? I do not wish to go on elaborating the absurdities of the critics who say that India should, as it were, cure itself of the disease of 'globalism' and concentrate its attention on South Asian regional development.

I hope, I have said enough to caution our academics, diplomats and policy makers from pursuing the valid aim of promoting regional cooperation in an ostrich-like manner failing to take into account the fact that the world of today needs to be dealt with as an integral whole.

Any person sensitive to the discipline of facts would instantly recognise that in the world in which we live, nothing can remain confined to your immediate concerns as these concerns are often found rooted somewhere else. This arises from the very nature of the world in which we live today. This was obviously not the situation in medieval times or even in the world the 18th, 19th and early 20th centuries.

To understand the specific nature of our time, one has to acquire some sensitiveness to history and historical processes. 1 was deeply disturbed when one very distinguished participant In the seminar expressed contempt for history. It alarmed me. It is completely unreal to discuss problems of foreign policy, even if these problems are confined to our own region without any historical perception or historical understanding. In the course of my years in foreign service, I discovered to my horror that problems were often posed and discussed even without asking oneself the question: How did it come about? Why did it happen?

In the inter-dependent and inter-penetrating world of today, things are different from what they were in the earlier periods of history. Even if we go no farther than the situation obtaining before the First World War, one would find that things then were rather simple. Issues of peace and war were decided in a small corner of this world situated in western Europe and Great Britain. Others hardly mattered. Just about hundred years ago, in 1884, a few European powers divided up Africa sitting in Berlin. Financial transactions, loans, raising of capital resources were all done in Europe. The United States of America hardly made any impact on the dynamics of international affairs. I would go so far as to say that right up to the middle of the World War II, the American factor, while important economic terms, was politically, a minor one until Japan dragged United States into the vortex of war by attacking Pearl Harbour. The USA was no doubt busy building its informal empire in the Caribbean basin and in the central and south America. This was done through 'open door policy' and the Monroe doctrine.

Let us have a brief look at the world of today. If one measures power in economic and financial terms and sees its division between the United States and the Soviet Union, one might expect them to reach a worldwide political understanding so that one would have, once again, division of the world into corresponding sphere of dominance and influence. Indeed, the arrangements arrived at the Congress in Vienna provided a basis for maintenance of peace in Europe for nearly 100 years between 1812 to 1914, despite minor breaches of it in South Africa and in Crimea. But today, with all the power which the United States possesses, it is unable to impose even on central and south America an acceptable system of political, social and economic order. And if one critically studies the tensions in the relations between the United States and western Europe on economic as well as security issues, one becomes conscious of the emerging contradictions both in perception and in terms of interests.

I hope I have succeeded in burying forever the notion that we can work out our destiny in isolation hiding ourselves within the cacoon called South Asian regional cooperation. However, our difficulties do not end even when we recognise the entire complex of interrelationships in the world of today. This is reflected in the kind of studies produced in our country on problems of foreign policy. We resort to shortcuts. One of the shortcuts is to reduce the United States of America to a single word called 'superpower'. We do the same also to the Soviet Union. Both are certainly superpowers. But that is not saying a great deal about them. And this certainly does not absolve us from studying in depth each country and discovering for ourselves the whole gamut of motivations governing the foreign policy of each. One cannot get out of this difficulty by talking about superpowers, their confrontations and the need for the non-aligned countries to place themselves in a position of equidistance from each. This might be a good exercise for those who wish to preserve their innocence as a nun does in entering a Convent of Jesus Christ. But if one wishes to deal with the real world, one has to grapple with it in trying to understand it. Unless this is understood and grasped, we shall constantly be masquerading as so-called realists when we are actually being simply fanciful.

A few years ago, some of our very distinguished foreign service officers flattered themselves on being realists by saying that the two Zias, namely, one in Bangladesh and the other in Pakistan, were our best bets. Frankly, I have never quite understood what they meant by this. If the argument was that Zia-ul-Haq, and Zia-ur-Rahman were in power in the countries concerned and that we had to deal with them, it is obvious enough. I do believe that it cannot be and must not be the aim of the foreign policy of India to be an instrument in changing regimes in our neighbouring countries. At individual levels, we may have our sympathies and antipathies towards a given political system. We are certainly entitled to have such views. But the task of changing governments must rest squarely with the people of the countries concerned. That is why I have always felt disconcerted by the tendency of Pakistan or India to act as the protector of minorities in the other countries. That is why 1 wholly agree with Prem Shankar Jha when he urged that the time had come for an explicit recognition of the logic of the formation of 'sovereign states' in our subcontinent.

Having said this, we are not absolved from the necessity of understanding the motivations, the compulsions, the inner dynamics of political, social, economic and historical processes working in Pakistan, Bangladesh or Nepal. Only in the measure when we do this, we shall have a realistic and viable policy.

Listening to the debates and discussions we have had, I get the impression that we have not yet come round to mastering and understanding the dynamics of, let us say, Pakistan. We do not have detailed knowledge of their power structure; the relationship of that power structure to the economic structure; the distribution of economic, political and military power between the various regions of Pakistan; the historical reasons for the direct involvement of the United States with Pakistan since 1954 at least or with China. Unless we unravel all these things, we cannot have a meaningful policy for promoting cooperation between our two countries. Similar set of questions would arise in relation to Bangladesh and Nepal. And since Sri Lanka is very much part of the proposed South Asian regional co-operation, we cannot overlook the evolution of internal politics within Sri Lanka and the fact that President Jayewardene has openly sought comfort and support from the United States and Britain and restricted India's role to that of being merely a spokesman for the Tamils or a mediator on their behalf.

Some of our trade delegations who have visited Pakistan have been rather naive in entertaining expectations of a large turnover of trade and this naivette has been articulated even in this seminar. Any meaningful cooperation in the area of commerce, trade and economic development would require a deeper understanding of how the structure of Pakistan's economy has grown during the last three decades or more. It is, in my view, not enough to declaim against the role of multinationals in Pakistan. One has concretely to study the entire structure of economy and the limitations which that structure imposes upon expectations of economic and trade relations, between our two countries.

In the course of negotiating the Shimla Agreement, and in the subsequent negotiations, both with Bangladesh and Pakistan, there emerged in my mind a structure of durable peace in our subcontinent. While I had no great illusion about the durability of Bhutto regime, the Shimla Agreement was in the nature of an investment in the future and was, in my view at any rate, an attempt to make an impact upon the wide mass of people of Pakistan that India, in a moment of victory, would act as a long-term friend of the people of Pakistan and not as an enemy. However, it is still incumbent on our part as the largest country in the subcontinent to think seriously and in depth about building up, step by step cooperation between India, Pakistan and Bangladesh. This can only be done if we study concretely the natural endowments of the respective countries, the demographic problems, river water resources, including those of Nepal, and work out a development strategy which would help to articulate our respective natural endowment, and our natural complementalities. It would be necessary for us to articulate the conceptual framework of security where none of the countries concerned, e.g. Pakistan, Bangladesh, Nepal and India, subserve the security interest of the big powers, and that we should consistently work together and raise voices against the armaments, race, against the inequities of international economic order and cooperate with one another not merely in economic field, but in the fields of science, technology, culture, travel and tourism. In my view, for what it is worth, we have not even begun to do our homework on these lines. Unless we do so, our negotiations become ad hoc and unconnected with a viable vision of a structure of durable peace and cooperation between the countries of the subcontinent.

President Zia-ul-Haq's peace offensive would have been more credible if one had an assurance that it did not stem from the situation now obtaining on the western frontiers of Pakistan. It would have been more credible if Pakistan had shown concern for the subcontinental security and not play a subsidiary role to America's strategic world view which is so visibly in operation in the Arab world, the countries in the Gulf and in the Indian Ocean. So far as I am concerned, I have no difficulty in saying that I would be prepared to sign a 'No-war Pact' or a 'Non-aggression Treaty' with Pakistan. However, this would not delude me or lull me into thinking that unless the worldview of the present power structure of Pakistan changes dramatically, such treaties would be of no particular use.

In the course of our discussions, a great deal was said about Pakistan's nuclear probability. I have little doubt that they are developing such capabilities. The logic of development of these capabilities will produce, in time, nuclear weapons. In such an event, no government in India could fail to respond to Pakistan's nuclear threat in the military field. Either we allow matters to drift and let the difficulties persist or we talk to Pakistan with all the seriousness and earnestness at our command to ensure that our respective programmes of peaceful nuclear, development remain so, guaranteed to be peaceful. Here again, we should get a firm evidence that there is no third party involvement, conniving at Pakistan's ambition to become a nuclear power.

Finally, I should like to address myself to the plea made here about supporting the movement for restoration of democracy in Pakistan. As I said earlier, this plea is not addressed to our government. The government must remain strictly uninvolved. But as citizens of free, democratic republic of India, we cannot but have our sympathies. And our sympathies certainly are with the people of Pakistan and Bangladesh who are struggling to free themselves from the shackles of military dictatorships and come into their own. It is my view that the interplay of democratic forces in our respective countries are a better guarantee for cooperation and peace.

In conclusion, may I articulate one of my major obsessions. The credibility of India's foreign policy *vis-a-vis* Bangladesh, Pakistan and Nepal will be greater. We must in our country set better examples on two extremely crucial matters. The first is to ensure a passionate and consistent adherence to the cardinal principle of our statehood, namely secularism. I do not have the time at my disposal now to elaborate this theme. However, I should like to state my conclusion. India today, as a state, is getting increasingly eroded by non-secular and pseudo-religious approaches, thought structures and practices. The second point is about the efficiency and the effectiveness with which our federal system functions. India should present itself as an example of how we have successfully woven together our diversities of language, religion, culture, ethnicity, etc., into a harmoniously functioning unity of our state system. We have to seriously ponder over the question of secularism and the question of our federal polity.

Index